CHANGING ON THE JOB

CHANGING ON THE JOB

*Developing Leaders for
a Complex World*

JENNIFER GARVEY BERGER

STANFORD BUSINESS BOOKS

An Imprint of Stanford University Press
Stanford, California

Stanford University Press
Stanford, California

Special discounts for bulk quantities of Stanford Business Books are available to corporations, professional associations, and other organizations. For details and discount information, contact the special sales department of Stanford University Press. Tel: (650) 736-1782, Fax: (650) 736-1784

Printed in the United States of America on acid-free, archival-quality paper

Library of Congress Cataloging-in-Publication Data

Berger, Jennifer Garvey, 1970- author.
    Changing on the job : developing leaders for a complex world / Jennifer Garvey Berger.
        pages cm
    Includes bibliographical references and index.
    ISBN 978-0-8047-7823-7 (cloth : alk. paper)
    1. Leadership—Psychological aspects.   2. Career development—Psychological aspects.
3. Adulthood—Psychological aspects.   I. Title.
HD57.7.B4695 2011
658.4′092—dc23
                                                                        2011032255

Typeset by Newgen in 10/13.5 Minion

For Jeff Gorrell, my dean at George Mason University, and Robyn Baker, my director at the New Zealand Council for Educational Research. You are the best leaders I ever had, and you contributed to this book not only with your unflagging support and thoughtful suggestions, but also by creating learning-work spaces where I could change on the job.

CONTENTS

LIST OF ILLUSTRATIONS

TABLES

FIGURE

EXHIBITS

ACKNOWLEDGMENTS

Sometimes books are themselves spaces of learning and development for their authors, and this was clearly true for me. This book started as a series of key ideas in my office in Washington, D.C., expanded over a glass of red wine in the Blue Mountains of Australia, and was finished in my writing shed in the garden of my house in Paekakariki, New Zealand. This book has lived on three laptops in three houses in two countries; it has seen my son Aidan learn to read and my daughter Naomi head to high school. It took so long to write that my original editor fell in love, had a baby, left the press, and then—most horrifying—that press actually went out of business before the book was done. This book and I have lived and grown together.

Like any other growth, the development of these ideas unfolded in the good company of teachers, friends, colleagues, and clients (many of whom share multiple designations). I am indebted to those giants on whose shoulders I gently stand. Robert Kegan has been my professor, my doctoral advisor, and my mentor; the better I know him, the more I admire his deep compassion, profound intellect, and contagious sense of humor. Susanne Cook-Greuter has impressed me with both the spaciousness of her theory and the depth of her humility—a rare combination. David Rooke and Bill Torbert are my guides in how to bring adult developmental ideas into real practice. Marcia Baxter-Magolda is a model of longitudinal developmental research I can't hope to match but from which I can happily learn. Joan Wofford and Barry Jentz have shown me in practice what psychologically spacious thinking and teaching really looks like. Bill Joiner and Steve Josephs, whom I've never met, have inspired me to think beyond the conventional, and to see the ways that I have not reached far enough in my belief about what is possible. If my work helps anyone as much as these writers and thinkers have helped me, it will be a great achievement, indeed.

I am grateful to those people with whom I worked at various points while the book was underway: my partners at Kenning Associates, my colleagues at

George Mason University and the New Zealand Council for Educational Research. Of those folks, it was Ally Bull, Carolyn Coughlin, Daryl Ogden, Jane Gilbert, Mark Addleson, Mark Ledden, Mark Hicks, Michael Milano, Neil Stroul, and Robyn Baker who provided the most feedback and helped shape these words. Your thoughts are so woven through with mine by now that I could hardly untangle them. I love the tapestry we've woven together in work and play.

Those folks to whom I've taught the Subject–Object Interview have also been a source of both feedback on the words I've written and also stories and support for the words that were not yet written. I am grateful to all of my students in my classes in Cambridge, Massachusetts; at the Oxford-Brookes University in England; and at the University of Sydney in Australia. Particularly strong voices and lasting friendships are with Jane Gray, Janet Smith, John Derry, Mark Leach, and Patsy Dodd. The University of Sydney, in launching a major research study into the developmental outcomes of coaching, brought me into a community of coaches and scholars who have enriched my thinking and my practice; I wish there were space here to name every person whose thoughts touched mine (but I have to name Alan Snow and Sean O'Connor for help and support in so many ways). I'm grateful to Paul Atkins, Michael Cavanaugh, and Tony Grant for leading the University of Sydney study, and Anna Booy, Gordon Spence, Ingrid Studholme, Jane Cox, Kate Wisdom, and Nickolas Yu (the Growth Edge Group) for testing these ideas, pushing around my thinking, expanding my practice, and modeling the most extraordinary form of a learning community. Your questions and thoughts and stories are with me always, and I'm grateful that our three-day workshop has extended into new possibilities for learning and laughing and working together. Special thanks to Jim Hammerman, Carolyn Coughlin, and Keith Johnston who have all co-taught SOI workshops for coaches or researchers with me in one country or another; I learn as much from your questions as from your answers, but it is your friendship I value most of all.

This book could never have been written without my clients who have so generously shared with me their stories, their challenges, and their thinking. In leadership development programs, coaching engagements, developmental interviews, and collaborative engagements, my clients have always given me insight into their worlds and their particular challenges. I would like to especially thank Al Morrison, Angela Geerts, Bill Hodgetts, Felicity Lawrence, Sally DeWitt, and everyone in the DOC and LINZ leadership development programs. I have been honored by your thinking and moved by your commitment. Most of what I know I have learned from you.

And then there is the set of people without whom I could not have kept up with this project and would not have seen it finished. Derek vanBever, who came to a workshop I was teaching at the Center for Public Leadership while he was studying at Harvard, made the most generous and out-of-the-blue commitment to introduce me to his editor, Michael O'Malley. Mike held my book for a time, provided fantastic feedback and an introduction to Margo Beth Crouppen at Stanford University Press, where my book finally found a happy home. Margo was a safe port in a stormy sea, and she renewed my love for a book I had spent too much time with. She is the reason you hold this volume in your hands. Libby Binstead, a participant in one of my Subject–Object Interview workshops in Sydney, sent her recipe for a kind of thin biscotti, which fueled the last several chapters of the book (if you think I'm kidding, you don't know me—and I've included the recipe in Appendix B for those of you who need fuel to get through the reading of it!). And, because a woman can't live on cookies alone (although she might try), Rob Katona and Melissa Garber were often my partners in the kitchen, cooking up delightful food and even delicious friendships.

Jim and Jamie Garvey never stopped believing that this book would finally make it into print, just as they have never stopped believing in me more generally. Thank you for listening to all the chapters of this saga! Catherine Fitzgerald, who was the first editor on the coaching book we published together, was an unflagging support and role model for me, in part because she's an astonishing coach and thinker and in part because she's my mom. Keith Johnston, who introduced me to the magnificent country I now call home, has taught me a lot about systems and thinking and leadership and just a little about cricket, and he shows me the most beautiful paths to walk—whether on a trail through the mountains or in a tricky theoretical passage. Who knew when you first suggested a chapter combining organizational theory with adult development theory that I'd make you write it with me—and create leadership development programs with me to test the ideas out?

And, cliché as it is, my family is the foundation on which everything else rests. My kids—Naomi and Aidan—are a source of inspiration, joy, and constant learning. I have watched them grow and develop like crazy over the course of this book, and I have been awed and amazed by the insight, intelligence, and humor with which they stay steady on the shifting sands of childhood (made perhaps a little shiftier by a move from Washington, D.C., to New Zealand when they were 5 and 9). And it is not in any way metaphorical to say that my partner Michael makes everything possible. Who knew that there was a man in the world so willing to pick up my responsibilities when I got carried away by work or writing, to comment on a draft when shoved under his nose at bedtime, or to take my laptop out of my hands and coax me out on the beach with the dogs when I had been festering with the manuscript just a little too long. Finding you when I was 17 was a miracle. Keeping you all these years was on purpose. I would tell you that I'm back now, but I had this idea for my next book . . .

CHANGING ON THE JOB

INTRODUCTION

We are collectively lost in the wilderness, and we don't always notice that we're lost. The difficulties of the present era have included environmental, social, and technological change on a scale that would have been inconceivable even 50 years ago. The way organizations and leaders navigate this time will not only matter in the bottom line for their organizations but might well change the course of life on our planet. We need to marshal together our collective work in order to make changes on a bigger scale—and more intentionally—than we ever have before in the history of the human race. This is a pretty serious demand on us, and it's not likely one that we're up to—at least not today. We hope it's one we could be up to if we worked hard enough. But how would we work hard enough to meet these demands? And what would we be actually doing in the first place?

Several thousands of years ago, it is likely that your ancestors—whoever they might have been—had clear systems and rituals that would support their movement from one stage in their lives to another. Some of these systems and rituals would have been potentially dangerous, others more communal and supportive. In any case, if you had lived back then, you'd have known from the time you were a small child what path you might follow, and you'd have had a guide to where you might hope to arrive one day, when you were older and wiser and seemed to have the respect of all around you. It wasn't always a pretty map, or a kind one, but there were markers that would let you anticipate what might be next for you.

Today, we have all different kinds of maps. You can google my address and see a satellite picture of the roof. You can walk into an HR department and see the salary steps and performance bands you might expect to progress through. You can go to a foreign city and plug an address into your GPS and have a woman with a soothing English accent (or North American, or Australian, if those make you more confident) tell you which direction to turn and how long until your final destination.

With all of our mapping, though, we've lost what our ancestors probably had thousands of years ago—the sense of how we'll progress through our lives. There's no Google Maps that shows the interconnections of our ideas and relationships from 6,000 feet. There's no GPS that will help you successfully recalculate your direction after you make a wrong turn in your 40s. And there's no articulated path that I've ever seen in any HR department that shows you which paths to take and which hills to climb if you are to really walk into your leadership potential and show up as a leader in a different and more helpful way. With all of our technology and all of our maps, we still aren't sure how to think or talk or feel or live our way through the incredibly difficult terrain of our present or the winding maze of conflicting possibilities and challenges of our futures.

This book is meant to help with all that.

It turns out that even in our modern world, there is some pattern and predictability to our growing as adults; that there is, in fact, a map of modern adult lives that might be useful in helping you understand and navigate the difficult passages and transitions of your life—and support others in their lives as well. This support might not only save you some of the pain and anxiety of getting lost, but also it might help more of us work together to push farther along our own pathway, so that we can collectively think up totally new ways of solving the problems that our current solutions seem to only exacerbate.

This book is written for people who are interested in understanding the shape and features of adult growth so they can either support their own growth and development or support the growth and development of others (or, most likely, both). This support matters deeply, because so much evidence suggests that we are expecting adults to be able to think and act in ways that they cannot yet do—and we don't always know how to support them to be able to grow the new capacities they need. As you read this book, you'll likely be thinking about yourself and your development, and you'll be thinking about the people you work with and the ways you might support them.

I've written the book in three parts to help different types of readers. Part One, Growing Complexity, is for those of you who want to get your head around adult development theory itself—how it works, how it's measured, how we might change over time. Chapter 1 gives a broad overview of the theory and why you might find it useful. Chapter 2 gives a more in-depth look at the theory with lots of case examples for those of you who want to really understand the building blocks of adult development and what the different forms of mind might look like in the organizational world. Chapter 3 is a quick introduction to measurement: to what questions you might ask yourself or others, and how you might begin to listen carefully and make a hypothesis about the development of those around you. Together, these chapters offer a deep—but I'm hoping fun—look at some of the most powerful theories about the way we make sense of the world (and about the ways the world sometimes doesn't make sense to us).

In Part Two, Helping Others Grow, we turn to what we can actually do to support the growth of people in organizations—or what we can do to support people who might not be interested in growing at this time. These chapters will be differently useful to you, depending on how you support the growth of others—and you'll notice that each chapter deals with ever-larger groups and systems. Chapter 4 looks at the intersection between adult development and coaching, useful for coaches, organizational consultants, and anyone who works with others one-on-one. Chapter 5 is for larger group interventions—professional development programs, workshops, and the like. Chapter 6 is at a higher level still—offering the building blocks for professional development of any kind which helps people grow and learn. Each of these approaches is geared specifically toward those who support the growth and development of people in organizations: leadership coaches, organizational developers, leadership experts, HR professionals, consultants. If you're a leader, you'll read these different sections with that purpose in mind, and with your (and my) full knowledge that the best leaders often act as coaches, intentionally developing the organization, and generally caring about the growth of humans as they care about the growth of their core business.

Part Three, Changing on the Job, takes the possibility of changing on the job directly into the work we do each day, and imagines a world where our work lives were themselves a core and thoughtful part of our development. While Part Two looked at those interventions that happen occasionally during our work lives (e.g., coaching or development programs), Part Three goes right into the workday itself. I'm a big believer in interventions like coaching and other learning and development experiences (indeed, I make my living by offering them), but if we are really going to change the world, we're going to have to set our sights on changing— at least a little—of what we do at work every day, not just on special occasions. Chapter 7, which I've written with Keith Johnston, looks at the increasing need for leaders to handle complexity and ambiguity, and it offers supports to help them do that. Chapter 8 offers practical ideas for how to begin weaving all these ideas into your own work life.

In every case, I've tried to help you both understand these ideas about what growth and development look like and how to support them, and also how you might construct new ways of thinking about the tools you use and the ways you help yourself and others grow. The field of adult development is itself quite young, and you and I are right now creating the future for how these ideas may be used. So while this book looks finally (and blissfully) finished, it is really just the beginning of a conversation we can be in together about how we can support ourselves and others to grow and to do our part to help save a world in trouble. If each of us were to believe in the core idea that our workplaces could become the central space for the cultivation of the wisdom our planet needs to survive, we could create powerful new possibilities for what our working lives would look and feel like into the future. These new possibilities could help us grow what is in greatest demand on this planet—not oil or steel or gold, but the capacity of human beings to create more-compassionate, thoughtful, healthy spaces for one another and for all of the creatures with whom we share this fragile planet. I welcome you into the conversation, and I look forward to hearing about the discoveries you'll make along the way.

PART ONE   GROWING COMPLEXITY

1 MAKING SENSE

See if this sounds familiar.

A senior vice president (SVP) in a small corporation called me for some help.[1] Her division had just reorganized, and one of the units in it had been newly created to help with some issues that had plagued the division for years. While this new unit was trying to get its focus and its vision, there was increasing conflict in the whole division. The reorganization had pulled some people off of the work they had been doing, and everyone was feeling pinched and irritable. The SVP noticed that conflict was springing up all over, and that the lines of communication, which had never been stellar, were disintegrating. She worried that unless they began to really understand one another and learn how to deal with their disagreements, new silos would spring up that were worse than the ones the reorganization was designed to dismantle. She thought some kind of retreat would be just what the group needed, including a few days of the basics: listening skills, Myers-Briggs, and so forth, to get into a better space with each other. We decided on a joint focus of, on the one hand, trying to understand and make sense of this new structure now that it was in place; and, on the other hand, building skills around listening to one another and dealing well with the inevitable conflict. We picked a date, the client found a venue, and I bought airplane tickets.

The first day of the retreat was fantastic. The group was much less divided than I had feared, and they were eager to learn new skills and tools. It wasn't until the end of the first day that I picked up on the murmurs about two of the members of the group—both in the newly organized unit. By the end of the morning session on the second day, I had begun to pay attention to those two fellows, and it was clear that they hated one another. In clipped, polite-in-front-of-the-outsider tones, they interacted tersely, each of them looking like he might swat at the other given any provocation. How had I missed this on day one? Because I thought the problem was *between* units inside this division, not *inside* a single unit, I had designed the first day to mix the units up; this was a team-building retreat, after all. It was only as we began to unpack strategy that the units got together, and I saw what the SVP had seen. Now the level of anxiety in the room was high. Other groups of people were warily watching the two at the heart of the conflict, and the easy banter of the day before was gone. I took my client outside the meeting room at a break time, and asked her to describe these two guys. "They hate each other," she said. "That's another thing that's going on here."

It turned out that one of the fellows was a supervisor of the other, and the supervisor (Jacob) thought the subordinate (Perry) was out of line. Jacob thought Perry was a maverick, breaking rules and not following the chain of command. Perry thought Jacob was an idiot, following the policy manual like the Bible and ignoring the common sense that he saw. They were both under advisement that this was unacceptable behavior, and Jacob had written up a behavior plan which Perry was to sign by the end of the retreat, or be fired. It was at this point, in the warm California sunshine, that I realized that this whole retreat—with the whole division off site for two days—was to deal, in great measure, with the ripple effect on the culture and on the work when two of its members were openly hostile to one another. This piece about these co-workers who hated each other was not peripheral; it was a key part of the system of negative feelings that the department was facing. And they didn't just have different opinions about things or need additional skills to get them up to speed on their work; it was possible that these two fellows had totally different ways of being in the world—and no way to make sense of one another. I knew that without attention in the direction of this conflict, the whole retreat was partial and not likely to be very useful, like giving a decongestant to someone who has avian flu. Faced with this knowledge mostly too late to do any good, I shuffled some things around, recreated some exercises, and finished the retreat with both a clearer idea of the problem and far less clear idea of the solution.

Perry and Jacob were smart, interesting men with long and successful track records. They each got along well with most of the others in the organization. They had similar backgrounds, educations, and personality types. So what was the problem? Somehow each of them violated core ideas and values of the other. They talked past one another and each felt deeply misunderstood. Yet when I asked their boss what the problem was, she could hardly put it into words. "They just clash," she told me.

It is the subtlety that makes human interactions so difficult—and so rich. And the more time you have to spend with different sorts of people, the more difficult it is. With some skills or tasks, it is simple to see what people can do and how they understand the world. When the task is clear, well-defined, and easy to evaluate, a person's competence is clear—and so is the need for additional training or support. When the task is complex and unbounded, and the evaluation difficult or impossible to connect easily, it is much harder to determine competence. Even once we determine it (e.g., not great people skills), we do not quite know what to do next. Do we offer training? Coaching? Team building? Helping to build the complex skill sets needed in the modern business world is significantly more difficult than it once seemed.

In addition to skills or behaviors we can learn, there are also the reflexes we were born with. When you touch a hot pan, you pull your hand away without thinking about it. This is a helpful reflex and saves you from real pain. If you had to think about the heat and weigh your choices (shall I put this hot pan down and risk my new countertops?), no matter how fast you processed the variety of choices, none of them would be fast enough to save you from a burn. This is a gift from your unconscious mind that protects you from harm. Other reflexes, however, are much less helpful. If every time a manager asks you a question you feel she is questioning your competence and you become defensive, that reflex is likely to get you burned instead of protecting you. And yet changing it is as hard as holding on to a hot pot—and feels, to some part of you, just as stupid. Lots of our ancient reflexes—fight versus flight, for example—that served us on the savanna hurt us now. Our inner wiring is still better suited to the tribal world than the corporate one.

So, in a world where our reflexes are increasingly misleading, and the skills we need are increasingly complex and multifaceted, how can we manage ourselves better? And if we need more-sophisticated leaders throughout our organizations and our world, how can we help organizations actually cultivate leadership and complexity?

UNDERSTANDING THE DIFFERENCES THAT YOU CAN SEE—AND THE DIFFERENCES THAT YOU CANNOT

Anyone who has ever worked inside an organization will tell you that different people make decisions, deal with conflict, and understand their relationships with colleagues quite differently. They have different strengths and weaknesses, different kinds of skills, and different backgrounds and personalities. In this book, I explore another component of difference: people's capacities to make sense of the complex world in which they find themselves and the way those capacities grow and change over time. While we do not often consider the growth of people's *minds* in the same way we consider the growth of their *skills*, both kinds of growth have a vital part to play in a person's success and effectiveness.

Although people have long recognized that as children grow, their ability to make sense of the world in a complex way grows, the idea that adults have minds (and not just skills) that are growing and developing over time is relatively new. It is easy to see these different worldviews in children. For example, when a three-year-old in the bathtub sees the water go down the drain, she makes a fairly straightforward connection between the water that disappears and her body and toys that seem in imminent danger. A kind grown-up who tries to soothe her by explaining that water and people are different will likely have no luck. At this stage in her life, the child does not have the *capacity* to see the difference between the water that disappears and the toys that are too large to wash away; crying, she begs to be removed from the tub and she struggles to save all of her precious things as she escapes. Several months later, the same child—with something of a different mind now—calmly and playfully watches the last bit of water disappear, poking it with her toys as it goes. The water has not changed at all, but her ability to make fine distinctions has grown more complex; she now has a different form of understanding the world, a greater level of what I call "self-complexity."

Self-complexity refers to these qualitatively different ways of understanding the complex world around us—an idea I'll talk about here as "forms of mind" and others talk about as "order of mind"[2] or "action logics."[3] These terms all describe the changing capacity of humans to cope with complexity, multiple perspectives, and abstraction. And the key news is that this pattern—being able to make sense of greater and greater levels of complexity—continues throughout the lifespan, long after we can handle the magical properties of bathwater.

In adults, self-complexity is not marked by anything so obvious as fear of washing down the drain. Instead, as adults grow and change over time, their ability to deal with the many pressures of their lives changes in important but subtle ways. Leaders with different forms of mind will have different capacities to take the perspectives of others, to be self-directed, to generate and modify systems, to manage conflicts, and to deal with paradox. We do not have to go very far to find ourselves in the middle of complexity and ambiguity; we face complex, unclear situations over and over each day. Here is a quick example of one such unexpected dilemma:

You go to make an appointment to meet with your manager, Monique. While you're scheduling, Monique's executive assistant makes reference to the fact that Monique has a meeting the next day with one of your direct reports, Jonathan, and that Jonathan scheduled the meeting. Monique is relatively new to this division, but she long ago finished the meet-and-greet meetings with everyone in your area. Now, mostly she deals with you on projects from your unit, but on several occasions over the last several months, you have felt blindsided by Monique's tendency to deal directly with your direct reports on her favorite projects, making decisions you only find out about later. You pride yourself on being approachable and easily accessible to your employees. How might you respond to this new information?

Think for a minute about how you would deal with this situation. Would you confront Monique? Jonathan? What would you say? What is the real problem here? What might you be most worried about?

Here is how three different people might deal with this same situation. As you read, think about their perspectives—what does each of them see as the problem? What are they each worried about? Which one most shares your thoughts and concerns?

DIRECTOR 1

You scheduled your meeting quickly, and then walked away to think the situation through. You had never had a situation quite like this and you didn't really know how to deal with it. For a minute you wished that you had never found out about the stupid appointment in the first place. It would be better just not to know, because now you were angry at Jonathan for going over your head and breaking all of the appropriate chain-of-command rules. And you were irritated with Monique, too, who shouldn't encourage this kind of inappropriate behavior in her employees. What could this meeting be about, anyway? Your anger quickly turned to concern—what if Jonathan was going to Monique to complain about *you*? You began wracking your brain to see what you had done that might get you in trouble. Maybe it was something that came up when you were working on that outside project last month. You knew that you were not supposed to take on these consulting assignments, but this one looked fairly easy and the money was good. You didn't understand why you shouldn't do other work on your own time, anyway—it was a stupid rule. And how could Jonathan have found out about that in the first place? Maybe what you would do was get to Jonathan and talk to him kind of casually and find out what he wanted to talk about with Monique. Yes, that was the thing to do, talk to Jonathan and see what the whole thing was about, and then see if you could stop the meeting before it happened. Maybe you would remind him of all those times last fall when he had left early to go to his daughter's soccer games. That kind of reminder had worked well in the past. And it wasn't about blackmail at all; rather, your point was that if you didn't work together against the higher-ups, your lives would be overtaken by stupid rules and regulations. Now you felt glad that you had found out about the appointment because now you would be able to fix it before things got too far out of hand.

DIRECTOR 2

You scheduled your meeting quickly, and then walked away to think the situation through. You had never faced a situation like this because your previous manager had been so well-aligned with the appropriate ways communication was supposed to happen. This new manager was either stupid or wrong-headed to be breaking out of these roles, and it made your head spin sometimes. If all of the reporting chain was up for grabs, how do you even understand your role as a supervisor? Were you supposed to take this as Monique's hope that *you* would start meeting with the direct reports of your own direct reports? Perhaps that was the message you were being given, but you wished Monique would give the message with more clarity—you weren't a mind reader, even if you tried to be. You never had to scramble this way with your previous manager; you two were on the same page, and there was never any confusion over roles. For a minute, you felt a little unsteady. If you didn't know your role as a leader, how could you do your job? And if you couldn't do your job, how could you contribute to your family? What would your friends say? This felt like a terrible mess, and you didn't know how you could begin to fix it. There weren't any guidelines for this in any leadership book you had ever read, and now that your former manager had been replaced, you didn't know whom you might go to for advice.

DIRECTOR 3

You scheduled your meeting quickly, and then walked away to think the situation through. You had never had a situation quite like this, but you had been in other interpersonally difficult situations before, even a couple that involved some confusion over organizational roles, and you never enjoyed them. For a minute you wished that you had never found out about the stupid appointment in the first place. It would be so much easier to just go about your business and not worry about the meeting between Monique and Jonathan. But now that you knew, you would have to confront the issue because it pointed toward important philosophical differences in both your manager and your subordinates. You wondered briefly what Monique and Jonathan might talk about together. There were some things that might merit a meeting between the two of them (where Jonathan was bringing a grievance you had ignored, for example, or where they were planning a surprise party for you, you thought, smiling ironically), and if this were one of those meetings you could happily ignore it until directed otherwise. But those scenarios didn't ring particularly true to you. The fact was that ignoring the chain of command was something of a pattern for Monique, and it was beginning to be a destructive pattern. You had noticed new tensions among your employees lately, had noticed the subtle ways they were competing for Monique's time and attention, and you knew that it was hurting both morale and productivity. You decided that you needed to talk to Monique to figure out what her goals were for these meetings. She clearly had different visions of what was expected up and down the chain of command, and maybe if you understood one another more explicitly, you could find styles that were best for the whole team.

Perhaps you did not find yourself in any of these people, or perhaps there were bits of your reactions in one or two of them. In any case, these three leaders face the same problem, but they think about it and act on it in different ways. Director 1 took what she felt was a novel situation (because nothing exactly like it had happened before) and immediately began to worry about the impact this situation might have on *her*. Her perspective was narrow and focused—on this time, on the particular consequences to her. Director 2 was confused about what his reaction *should* be. He tried to understand the subtext in the situation so he could figure out what was expected of him and what his role might be. Director 3, while not having had exactly this experience before, was able to get a more broad perspective and see the ways that this experience was similar to other interpersonally complex experiences she had had. Similarly, she had a bigger perspective about why such behavior (which she remembered as a pattern) was problematic. While this problem affected her, her own stake in it was not her primary concern. Instead, she worried about a larger issue—about the morale and productivity of her entire unit.

There may be many differences between these leaders that create the various ways they have handled the situation. They may have different kinds of leadership training, different amounts of experience, different styles of leadership. When I ask others about the variations between the thoughts and actions of these three managers, they point to many possible differences, but they almost all conclude that Director 3 just seems more "grown-up" than Director 1, and more "secure" than Director 2. It is that sense of "grown-up" and what it means to be "secure" that are explored by theories of adult development. Instead of making claims about the skill or effectiveness of any of these leaders, I focus on the possibility that these are not simply leaders with different *styles,* but rather that they are leaders with different *current capacities* for self-complexity.[4] Using the lens of self-complexity, we may decide that perhaps Director 1 is not selfish or self-centered or short-sighted, and that Director 2 is not insecure or lacking assertiveness (all of which are enduring personality or character flaws). Perhaps Director 1 and Director 2 do not yet have the *capacity* to take the same perspective as Director 3. No amount of leadership training or other forms of intervention will teach them to quickly understand what is going on, just as the three-year-old could not be taught about the bathwater. Like the three-year-old—like all of us—Directors 1 and 2 need to *develop* this understanding over time. Similarly, Director 3 likely could not point to the particular training or event that led her to take the perspective of her whole unit. She probably cannot remember a time when she was unable to take on such a complex perspective. She is likely to assume that everyone else sees the world her way, and when she talks to her manager and direct reports, she may have a hard time believing in the legitimacy of their perspectives—especially if those perspectives feel more simplistic than hers.

If, then, there are differences that are difficult to understand and recognize, and if those differences lead to profound distinctions in the way each of us sees the world, what can we do about it? One helpful option is to learn something about the patterns of adult development—and learn how to recognize them and use them to create workplaces more conducive to growth. Adult development theory may help us articulate more of what we mean by "grown-up," because it describes the qualitatively different worlds of meaning people grow to have over time. It also describes their current capacities—those things people can and cannot do or think about. These theories are more than simple descriptive tools, though. Developmental theories chart a path that each person might take to develop more-complex forms of mind. Additionally, these theories also help us examine the *match* between a person's form of mind at any given time and the form of mind that may be required by a particular task. Because of the great difference in roles and organizational environments, each person's situation may require more or less capacity for complexity. The match between capacity for self-complexity and environment is a key factor in a person's ability to be successful. In fact, while the form of mind tends to grow over time, such growth is only important in relationship to the demands made upon each individual. Developmental models seem to suggest that higher is *necessarily* better, but I'd like us to hold that idea with a little more subtlety. Having a greater capacity for self-complexity is important—even vital—in some leadership situations. In situations where the tasks are clear and not filled with complexity, though, it is possible that there would not be any advantage to having a greater level of self-complexity. Again, it is the *interaction* between the demands made on the leader and the leader's capacity for self-complexity that matters the most. It is also true that having high levels of self-complexity does not guarantee success, any more than greater height guarantees more points on a basketball court. Having the capacity to deal with complexity does not necessarily mean that a leader is a careful observer, has good interpersonal skills, or even that the leader exercises good judgment in general. It does mean that the leader has the capacity to see more nuance and deal with paradox and ambiguity—and the capacity to be agile and responsive. My hope for us all here is to lose a simple higher = better sense of development and instead work to construct workplaces where we can recognize—and help develop—the complexity necessary to do the work well.

CONSTRUCTIVE–DEVELOPMENTAL THEORIES OF ADULT DEVELOPMENT

Early theories of adult development were most often connected to age or phase of life; they described the various life stages as related to age or key task (e.g., finding a career) and described the different perspectives, hopes, and goals a person might have at these different ages or phases (e.g., early 30s as a time to settle into young family life).[5] In contrast, *constructive–developmental* theories are centered on the particular meaning-making of each individual rather than on age or phase of life.[6] They are *constructive* because they are concerned with the way each person creates her world by living it (rather than believing, as some theories do, that the world is outside us and there is some kind of objective truth to be discovered). They are *developmental* because they are concerned with the way that construction changes over time to become more complex and multifaceted. Unlike the age/phase theories, constructive–developmental theories do not assume that years lived or life stages completed necessarily mean anything developmental at all. There are a wide variety of constructive–developmental theories—all with broad similarities in their orientation to development, and all describing similar trajectories. While this book is informed by the many theories of adult development, the theory upon which this book is primarily based is Robert Kegan's theory of adult development. Most of the names I use for the forms of mind also come from Kegan.

Constructive–developmental theories tend to focus on development in specific ways. They look at issues of authority, responsibility, ability to tolerate complexity and ambiguity. The easiest way to understand them is as they relate to perspective-taking and relationship to their own responsibility. As people develop, they become more able to understand and take into account the perspectives of others while, at the same time, becoming more aware of their own responsibility for their emotions and life events. As people develop, the *content* of their ideas may not necessarily change (e.g., someone might retain a belief he developed in his MBA program that a good leader maintains open lines of communication with his direct reports), but the *way* they understand these ideas is likely to change (e.g., what "open communication" means may be revised and expanded).

As an example, think for a minute about what leadership books want you to be able to do. One of my favorite leadership books—Ron Heifetz's *Leadership without easy answers*—asks leaders to "get on the balcony" and away from the action on the dance floor.[7] This is a helpful piece of advice, because it reminds leaders to step outside the particularities of their situation in order to see the whole picture. What Heifetz does not tell you, though, is that there are a variety of different "balconies" depending on your form of mind. Developmental theories describe different balconies which each offer a different perspective. How far you can get above the dance floor depends on your current form of mind. Is your perspective changed by how high you go in the balconies? Certainly. Is your decision making *necessarily* changed or your allegiances or beliefs *necessarily* different? Absolutely not. While your higher perspective may allow you to see a bigger picture that ultimately changes your mind about something, the new perspective might also confirm—or even intensify—your commitment to some person, theory, or decision.

A key feature of development that is different from going to a club and looking down at the dancers on the floor is that your image of what "the story" is expands as your vision expands. When you go to a club, no matter how far away you are from the dance floor, the main action is way down there—you just get farther away from it as you go up. But when your form of mind grows, you discover that what you once thought was the main action was simply a tiny portion of what was going on; now the club is much larger and has far more interesting characters. You might get a perspective on the band, on the line cooks in the kitchen, on the conversation the owners are having about whether to raise drink prices again. You might also gain a perspective on your own reactions as you look down at the dance floor—and be able to think about which buttons are being pushed by which people and what you might do about that.

Developmental theory describes the ability of people to gain these new perspectives—and what it takes to be able to move from one balcony to the next one. In this way, it is a useful lens through which to look at the world. Every theory has its limits, though. Constructive–developmental theories focus on complexity and perspective-taking; thus they do *not* focus on many other aspects that make humans interesting and unique—nor do they focus on group or system interactions (although there is much to be learned about groups and systems from paying attention to the meaning-making of individuals). These theories do not claim that perspective-taking is the most important part of an individual; they just attempt to understand (and sometimes measure) this one facet of human experience.

What does any of this have to do with changing on the job? Nearly everything. Developing professionals in the workplace requires, to a greater or a lesser degree, actual *development*. As you think about supporting another human being at work, it is vital that you understand just what you mean by *support*. Are you guilty of that supremely human error of assuming that others operate from the same form of mind as you do? Are you designing training, support, systems of rewards and sanctions that might work for someone like you? How might you think more broadly about your constituents—or perhaps think more specifically about a particular person you have never understood? An understanding of adult developmental differences allows us to both reach the diversity of groups more thoughtfully (as we create programs and systems) and also reach the uniqueness of a single human being more carefully (as we listen in ways we may not have listened before and hear nuances that may have been inaudible to us previously). In the next section, I describe the rhythm of development and sketch out the four most common forms mind of adulthood (longer descriptions, implications and strategies are in the subsequent chapters).

FORMS AND TRANSFORMATION

From our earliest days, each of us has been engaged in an ongoing journey to learn and to grow. These two human forces are often connected, but they are not the same. Learning can be about acquiring a new skill or knowledge base. If I master PowerPoint in order to put together a slide show for a client, I have learned something. I have new information in my head. But have I really *grown*? From a developmental perspective, real growth requires some qualitative shift, not just in knowledge, but in perspective or way of thinking. Growing is when the *form* of our understanding changes; we often call this "transformation." Learning might be about increasing our stores of knowledge in the form of our thinking that already exists (in-form-ation), but growing means we need to actually change the form itself (trans-form-ation).[8] Each moment of our development, then, is a potentially temporary form of mind that, with the right support, can become more expansive. As we grow, the previous form is overtaken by the new form, leaving traces of the less-mature form behind like rings in a tree trunk.

The rhythm of this movement is about increasing our ability to see more complexity in the world. When we are young, we have very simple ways of understanding the world (the earliest form of mind mostly just makes the distinction between "caregiver" and "not-caregiver"). We grow to see and understand more and more fine gradations in the world, and as we do this, we begin to question assumptions we had made before (perhaps there are differences between those beings formerly considered to be "not-caregiver"). Theorists for centuries have named the distinction between *subject* (that which you cannot yet see because you are fused with it) and *object* (that which you can see and make decisions about because you have gained more distance from it). As elements of understanding move from subject (hidden) to object (seen), our worldview becomes more complex, and constructive–developmental theorists would say we have developed. This can happen when we discover a choice where we once saw only one option, when we discover multiple perspectives where we once only saw through a single lens. Each small shift from subject to object increases our scope, but enough incremental changes collectively add up to qualitatively different ways of seeing the world, to transformation, the creation of different forms of mind.

These forms of mind generally fall into identifiable, qualitatively different ways of making sense of the world in adulthood (as well as many identifiable in-between places where a person will have parts of one form of mind and parts of another).[9] In Table 1.1, I offer a quick sketch of the four central forms of mind of adults by looking at perspective-taking and authority. Then I offer quick descriptions of each of the forms of mind of adulthood.

The self-sovereign form of mind. This form of mind in adults is marked by the combination of a sense of self-centeredness and a focus on what *I* want (much like our visions of spoiled imperial youth). More common in teenagers and young adults, the self-sovereign mind is nonetheless sometimes seen in adults in their 40s, 50s, and beyond. At this form of mind, people discover that they have beliefs and feelings that remain constant over time (e.g., I love chocolate but hate mashed potatoes; I'm great at ice skating). This insight lets them know that other people have opinions and beliefs that remain constant, too. Their concrete understandings let them know that a rule yesterday is probably a rule today. Their orientation is to figure out how to get past the rule if it is in their way. While they are aware that others have feelings and desires, true empathy is not possible for them yet because the distance between their minds and other minds is great. Mostly other people's interests are important only if they affect the interests of the self-sovereign person. When annoying rules are not broken, it is because of a fear of being caught; when friends do not lie to each other even when they're tempted to do so, it is because of a fear of retaliation. Children—and adults—at this form of mind are self-centered in the most literal, least judgmental meaning of that word. Because they cannot yet take the perspective of others, the thinking and feeling of those around them is generally mysterious. This means that they often see others as helpers or barriers on the road to their desires. Authority lies outside them

TABLE 1.1 Comparison of orientation to authority and perspective-taking across the adult forms of mind

Form of mind	Perspective-taking	Authority
Self-sovereign	The only perspective a person can automatically take while in the self-sovereign form of mind is his own. He may experience all other perspectives as mysterious, and can only get make a guess at them from what he sees.	Authority is found in rules and regulations. When two external authorities disagree, it can be frustrating but not internally problematic.
Socialized	Looking through the socialized form of mind, a person can take—and become embedded in—the perspectives of other people/theories/organizations/religions. When she sees the world, she sees it *through* these other perspectives, judging right and wrong, good and bad, from the perspectives of others.	Authority is in an internalized value/principle/role which comes from outside herself. When those important values/principles/roles conflict (as when her religion disagrees with an important value from her partner), she feels an internal tearing, as though parts of herself were pitted against one another.
Self-authored	Seeing the world through the self-authored form of mind means a person can take multiple perspectives while maintaining his own. He can understand the views and opinions of others and often uses those views or opinions to strengthen his own argument or set of principles.	Authority is found in the self. The self-authored system determines the individual's rules and regulations for himself. When others disagree, it can be inconvenient or unpleasant, but is not internally wrenching. (When one internal value disagrees with another, however, that can cause an internal tearing.)
Self-transforming	With a self-transforming mind, a person sees and understands the perspectives of others and uses those perspectives to continuously transform her own system, becoming more expansive and more inclusive. She does not use the perspectives of others to fine-tune her own argument or principles as she did when she was self-authoring; rather, she puts the entire system at risk for change with each interaction with others.	Authority is fluid and shared, and is not located in any particular person or job. Rather, authority comes from the combination of the situation and the people in the situation. A new situation (or different players) may cause a shift in where authority is located.

and is marked by both the formal authority of a title and also power over them in some way. Because of this, those with the self-sovereign form of mind appreciate (and obey) rules because of the direct consequences of the rules. They are unlikely to be motivated by mysteriously abstract factors like loyalty or a commitment to the relationship.

Of the three people earlier who faced the same difficult situation between their manager and their direct reports, Director 1 saw the world through the self-sovereign form of mind. Notice that her focus in this situation is on herself—what is the impact on me, what can I do to change any negative consequences, and so forth. Director 1 does not stop to wonder about the perspective of her manager or direct report in any way other than to worry about herself. This is because she cannot yet take the perspectives of anyone but herself. The feelings and actions of her colleagues are mysterious to her; she does not yet realize that they are interesting characters in a larger play. In the club as she understands it (right from the middle of a crowded dance floor), people are mostly visible only if they are dancing with her. Director 1 is the only star character; the others play bit parts in her quest to get her own way. She is not selfish or self-centered (although she may appear so to those with a larger perspective than hers); she is simply stuck in the middle of her own story, and she has no perspective from which to view the rest of the action. She is doing the best she can with the view she has now.

While there are likely to be few people with this form of mind in the leadership ranks of an organization, studies have shown that as many as 13 percent of adults see the world through this form of mind—or who are growing to (but not yet arrived at) the socialized mind. This means that especially the younger and less well-educated members of an organization have the potential to have this form of mind. Those with this mind can be very frustrating to colleagues and managers who have moved beyond it, and those colleagues can wrongly assume developmentally related capacities are stable personality flaws.[10]

The socialized form of mind. As a person's worldview increases in complexity, he leaves behind his image of himself as the center of the world and takes inside him the opinions and perspectives of others; he comes to see the world through the ideas and theories of other people. Sometimes this transition begins in adolescence, but it can happen at any point throughout adulthood. If this increasing perspective-taking continues, eventually he will grow to have a socialized form of mind. He will become a full member of whatever society he belongs to, and someone who takes on the rules of that society as *the right way* to be in the world. With a socialized mind, the formerly imperial self-sovereign mind is enlarged to include other perspectives and understand authority in a new way. It is at this stage that people can begin to become devoted to something larger than themselves and become loyal to—and embedded in—some larger system, theory, or relationship. This larger system, however, is not for me to make decisions about, believes a person with a socialized worldview. Rather, having internalized the importance of the authority of others, the person with the socialized mind no longer believes in his own authority. As he grows to take on this new perspective, he sees through that new perspective, becoming fused with it. Those with a socialized mind internalize the feelings and ideas of others and are guided by those people or institutions (such as a synagogue, a political party, or a particular organization) that are most important to them. They are able to think abstractly, be self-reflective about their actions and the actions of others, and are devoted to something greater than their own needs.

The major limitation of this form of mind is that, when there is a conflict between important others (or between a single important other—like a spouse, and an institution—like a political party), those at the socialized mind feel torn in two and cannot find a way to make a decision. There is no sense of what *I* want outside of others' expectations or societal roles. This is generally admirable in teenagers, but in adults it can often seem like a personality flaw. A developmental perspective, however, shows us that this is an achievement rather than a flaw. For a person to arrive at this form of mind requires leaving the solitary confinement of his own mind and welcoming new members into his perspective and decision-making process. Like an executive looking for guidance beyond himself, he has created an internal Board of Directors to help him see the world and make decisions. This metaphorical Board may be made up of important theories, relationships, or ideas. Problems can arise, though, because someone at the socialized mind is not yet the chairperson of this internal Board, leaving room for disagreements or power struggles among Board members.

Director 2 currently sees the world from the socialized form of mind. Comfortable with his responsibilities for others, comfortable with abstract theories of leadership and complex organization charts of reporting systems, he is stymied by the interaction between his direct report and his manager. The theories and relationships in which he is embedded—and which have served him well before—are not helpful to this situation. In the absence of helpful guides, he clings to any message he might find, and assumes that there must be some directive in his manager's actions. As he searches for the messages that must be hidden between the lines, he feels off-center and confused. He sees enough of the dance floor to guess at a larger subtext and to notice abstract patterns, but he cannot gain enough distance from the voices of others to hear his own voice.

The socialized mind—and the midzone between the socialized and the self-authored mind—is the most common form of mind for adults; perhaps as many as 46 percent of adults currently have a socialized mind (or are on the journey from the socialized to the self-authored mind). Because of this, it is likely that many of your colleagues (and maybe even you) see the world from this form of mind. The modern organizational world, however, often assumes that most people have a perspective that is beyond socialized, and so many organizational structures and programs are "over the heads" of the majority of adults.

The self-authored form of mind. In a modern, global world, those with a socialized form of mind are likely to begin, eventually, to bump up against conflicting ideas and perspectives that are incomprehensible to their form of mind. When this happens, they need to find some mediating force to help them decide among the different—and reasonable—options. To continue an earlier metaphor, as their Board of Directors begins to disagree (or not keep up with the times), they need some way to break the tie or add new information. They need, in short, a Chair of the Board to mediate among the different ideas, relationships, and theories that formed in these internal Boards. When finally they themselves become the Chair of their own internal Boards, they have developed a new form of mind.

The opinions and desires of others which they internalized, and to which they were subject when they were making meaning with a socialized mind, are now object to them. They are able to examine those various rule systems and opinions and are able to mediate among them. Those with self-authored minds have an internal set of rules and regulations—a self-governing system—that they use to make their decisions or reconcile conflicts. Unlike those who make meaning with a self-sovereign mind, those who are self-authored feel empathy for others, and take the wishes and opinions of others into consideration when making decisions. Unlike those with a socialized mind, though, those with a self-authored mind do not feel torn apart by the conflicts of those around them because they have their own system with which to make decisions. These are the people we read about in the business literature who "own" their work, who are self-guided, self-motivated, and self-evaluative.

Director 3, above, understood the leadership challenge through her self-authored form of mind. She is not enmeshed in either her own sense of the risks to herself (she ironically wonders if her direct report might be bringing a grievance, but she does not feel concerned about it) and is not puzzled as she tries to unpack her manager's odd sense of organizational communication. Instead, she weighs the situation against her own values and experience, and creates (authors) her own response. She has enough distance to recognize and hear, simultaneously, the perspectives of others and her own self-authoring voice. Instead of viewing the dance as a member of the audience, she now understands that she creates the dance by her actions, and she choreographs it while she watches.

The self-authored form of mind is common in organizations, especially in leadership roles (although so is the socialized form of mind, so it is important to never assume that the leader with whom you are dealing is necessarily self-authoring). About 41 percent of adults see the world through this form of mind, or, much more rarely, in the midzone between the self-authoring and the self-transforming form of mind.

The self-transforming form of mind. As I describe above, when someone with a socialized mind questions the infallibility of her external guides, she begins to develop the internal guide that is the hallmark of the self-authored form of mind. Similarly, when someone with a self-authored mind begins to question the infallibility of his internally driven self-authoring system, he begins to take steps toward becoming self-transforming. This move toward the self-transforming form of mind is almost never been seen before midlife, and even then it is seen rarely. Still, because the world today may make demands on leaders for capacities beyond the self-authoring mind, the self-transforming mind is an important one to begin to understand.

Those at this form of mind are tuned in to all the various constituencies around them. They see multiple layers of every issue and can hold even very different perspectives simultaneously. Instead of viewing others as people with separate and different inner systems, those making meaning with a self-transforming form of mind see across inner systems to look at the similarities that are hidden inside what used to look like differences. These people are less likely to see the world in terms of dichotomies or polarities. They are more likely to believe that what we often think of as black and white are just various shades of gray whose differences are made more visible by the lighter or darker colors around them. Unlike those making meaning with a self-authored form of mind, those who are self-transforming are likely to be less ideological, less easy to pin down about a particular opinion or idea. This is because those with a self-transforming mind are more oriented to the *process* of leadership than to any single product or outcome.

So what would someone with a self-transforming mind make of the leadership challenge described earlier in this chapter? First of all, the challenge itself is likely described incorrectly for it to be the thinking of someone who is self-transforming; he is unlikely to feel "blindsided" at all. Instead, he is likely to feel the central pulls of curiosity and open-mindedness. Take Justin as an example.

He knew that he would have to bring up this pattern at his next meeting with Monique, but he did not feel worried or concerned about that. Remembering a time when he would have cared very much about vertical reporting line, Justin smiled at his former self. These days, he appreciated Monique's interest in his direct reports, and felt good about a place with open doors regardless of reporting structure. Indeed, he had found that lately people from all over the organization were seeking him out for his thoughts and perspectives on a variety of things—or for him to ask them questions to help them get clear. Still, Justin would need to talk with Monique about it, because Justin knew that many of his direct reports were uncomfortable with the ambiguity of who should talk to whom about which projects. It was even changing the culture of the team, and there were both good and bad parts to that change. Some people liked more clarity about such things, and that perspective should be as valuable as Justin's own. In fact, he carried that perspective inside himself even as he moved away from his attachment to it. Justin welcomed the chance to stretch his own thinking in conversation with Monique, Jonathan, and others.

The self-transforming form of mind is by far the least common: Less than 1 percent of the population understands the world in this way. With the aging of the baby boomers, however, and the medical innovations—at least in the developed world—that keep people healthy and sharp into increasing old age, it is likely that there will be more and more people who see the world with at least the beginnings of a self-transforming mind. As this happens, organizations will have to reconceptualize important parts of senior roles and responsibilities if they want to take advantage of the great riches of this, the most complex perspective yet described.

SO WHAT?

The most important question to ask of any theory is "so what?" If there are these differences, what does that mean for me and my work? The answer to this from my perspective is: Everything. Whether you think about it or not, your own form of mind shapes your world and influences everything you see or think about. And every time you speak to another person, think about another person, or want something from another person, that person's form of mind becomes important to you whether you like it or not. So why is it that this theory is not common knowledge? Because it is complicated, and mostly it has been useful only to people with the time and energy to study it in academic circles. This is changing, though. In this book I build on work being done by practitioners who are trying to make adult developmental theories useful to adults in organizations.[11]

ETHICS

If you have hung in with me to this point, chances are good that you have some willingness to try on this adult developmental thing (a willingness which, among other things, bodes well for your own development; more on this later). You might even be beginning to think that this developmental idea might be useful in your work in some powerful ways. Let me say a couple of things about that here, and look for me to add to the list of moral and ethical issues as the book progresses.

Perhaps the two most serious pieces of criticism lobbed at developmental theories are (1) that they are necessarily judgmental and (2) that they privilege some things over others. These concerns are important because they are true. Developmental theories *are* hierarchical, and they do have the internal belief that as you move along your developmental path, you have more of some things than you had before (and, necessarily, more of some things than others who are not yet as far as you). Developmental theories do also privilege some things; constructive–developmental theories privilege ability to take multiple perspectives and see many shades of gray.

I believe that while these critiques are true, they are not inherently problematic. We all have judgments inside us about other people in our lives. Developmental theories do not create such judgments; they shape them and offer a framework for making good decisions about them. The difference between "I'm frustrated with Peter because he can't ever make up his mind for himself" and "I'm frustrated about what to do with Peter because he hasn't yet developed the capacity to make up his mind for himself" is enormous. While both sentences point to the same issue, the second sentence—aided by a developmental perspective—points to a time in the future when Peter might be able to do that which he cannot yet do, and also hints that there may be some practical ideas to support him before he gets there. Similarly, we all make decisions about more and less (we may have colleagues who are "super smart" or "incredibly high on emotional intelligence" or "really in need of people skills"). Development is just another way of categorizing our judgments, so that we can test them and decide whether they're worth holding on to—and worth helping our clients work on.

Developmental theories, like all theories, are tools. Good theories (like the one this book uses) are particularly useful tools. Any tool can be used for good or used for harm. Because the theory described in this book is a particularly potent one, and because it deals with something most people do not even begin to think about, those who understand it have a distinct advantage. Understanding developmental theory gives you the advantage of tailoring interventions more carefully to the individuals involved, of opening opportunities, of giving people a chance to grow into a job instead of assuming that someone does not have "leadership potential." But it is also true that knowing about the meaning-making systems of others allows people to create more useful propaganda, better-targeted manipulation. Also, since many people have a higher-is-better orientation, using developmental models is far more risky than talking about someone's personality style.

By the time you finish this book, you may have yet another ethical problem on your hands, so consider this fair warning. You may walk away with not only an understanding of these developmental differences but also a desire to support people to grow. It is in fact my hope that you do acquire both of those things on our journey together. This leads us into even more complex ethical territory, though. Growing is difficult work, and it brings losses along with the gains (as we lose who we once were in order to become who we will be next). You may find that you suddenly have a long list of people you think could use a little push to get back onto the developmental highway. Or you might want to do as I suggest throughout and try to make our workplaces more supportive of people's growth.

It's one thing to try and grow when you have your eyes open about what you're doing and what the risks are. It's another thing to support others to grow when you're not sure they know what they're in for. And yet at the same time, it doesn't seem like a very helpful idea to withhold developmental possibilities and supports from people for fear that they won't like where they end up. You see the quandary. I've dealt with this by offering developmental supports and at the same time creating ways for collectives to work together to bring their highest capacities to the team. Ultimately, my hope would be that as we understood the journey of our lives and what was possible for us, we would be able to make good choices that help us live into our full potential, remembering that not every child who has an ear for music and long fingers that can span two octaves on a piano actually wants to be a concert pianist.

This all means that we will plunge ahead carefully, noticing the powerful things we can learn and the important things we cannot learn as we peer through this lens. If together we can be both open to these ideas and also skeptical, together we can shape this theory into a set of new and potentially transformative set of ideas and practices to support everyone who wants to change and grow on the job.

2 DIVING DEEPER

You are in an endless line, waiting to pass through security to get to your airplane. You've been inching forward, transferring your briefcase from hand to hand, shuffling to hold your book and coat and lunch. Finally, you get to the table and begin to load your things into bins to go through the X-ray machine. You chat with the people in front of you and behind you as you all take off coats and shoes and belts. Then, just as you lift your final bag toward the conveyer belt, a man three people behind you steps forward and begins putting his bags and trays on the belt in front of you. You watch, open-mouthed, as he finishes with his bags and then saunters through the metal detector. You shuffle through, watch your first bag come off the conveyer belt and then his, and finally, after he is long gone, your last. You are stuck between amusement and irritation, and you know that if you had been afraid of missing your plane, you would have felt rage.

People do selfish, thoughtless things every day. They do kind and generous things every day. Sometimes they do not even notice the difference. The question about the rude traveler above and all the other people whom you brush against isn't so much, "Why did you do that?" (although that might be a good question, too) but rather, "How did you make sense of your actions there?" The rude traveler does not think of himself as The Rude Traveler. He thinks of himself as the harried traveler, the frustrated-with-the-person-in-front-of-me-with-too-much-stuff traveler, the almost-missing-my-plane traveler. Or maybe he was lost in thought and did not notice that he had skipped ahead in line. Or maybe he was a flight attendant and used to skipping to the front of the line and forgetting that he was not in his uniform that day. In any case, your staying lost in *your* experience of him will never open up a profitable place for learning and change. In order to be a good help on someone's journey toward transformation, you need to understand the world as *he* sees the world, not as *you* see him.

In this chapter, we will dive more deeply into the four forms of mind of adulthood, and we will spend some time seeing how each of these forms of mind sees

TABLE 2.1   Strengths, blind spots, and central areas of growth for the self-sovereign form of mind

Key strengths	Key blind spots	Central areas of growth
When a straightforward job is important, the person with a self-sovereign form of mind is in her element. She is great when there are clear images of right and wrong, good and bad, that can be reinforced through external rules and rewards. She sees a direct connection between external rewards and external results—for this person, linking salary to productivity is likely to be a key incentive.	She is unable to take on the perspectives of other people or be influenced by abstractions. She does not have an orientation to her own inner psychological world—or anyone else's—and so isn't able to understand the subtleties of human interaction. She lives in a world with only two choices for every decision—us and them, right and wrong, what I want and what others want. She is likely to follow the rules of the organization to the extent that following such rules is in her own best interests rather than because of abstract concepts such as loyalty or duty.	The central issue for growth in the move from the self-sovereign to the socialized mind is for her to learn to understand—and internalize—the perspectives of others. This happens gradually as she begins to understand the connections between herself and others, and begins to want to affiliate with those others she considers most important.

the world. Because constructive–developmental theory deals with something most people rarely consider, each of these longer descriptions offers several different ways of helping you enter into the different forms of mind. To help you track a complex journey, the strengths, blind spots, and central areas of growth for each form of mind are summarized in each of Tables 2.1 through 2.4. As you read, think about the people in your life, and think about yourself.

SELF-SOVEREIGN FORM OF MIND

Anna was a supervisor for a clothing manufacturing company. She had dropped out of school when she was 16 to work on this shop floor herself, and now, at 41, was managing 20 shop-floor workers. Married with three children, Anna thought she was doing pretty well in the world—she had worked up through the ranks, her people listened to her and did what she said, she rarely got in trouble with the higher-ups, and she was making an excellent salary. Understanding the world through her self-sovereign form of mind, Anna knew that her job was to follow the rules and keep her people in line. As long as she didn't rock the boat, the higher-ups would leave her alone and she could do her own thing with her people. She had an understanding with those who worked under her; they knew that this was a world of give and take, of you-scratch-my-back-and-I'll-scratch-yours. As a manager, Anna knew that she could cut her people some slack and that they'd return the favor, but she also knew that she needed to use her power to keep folks in line. She was enormously frustrated with her managers who sometimes asked her to do something outside her job responsibility "for the sake of the team." She felt great about this company and had worked here her whole adult life, but her job was her job—she knew it well, and if they wanted something done outside the parameters of the job, they'd better pay her outside the parameters of her job. Anna had the largest possible number of supervisees in a line position, and she knew that if she was going to get promoted, it would be off the shop floor and into a cubicle somewhere. Without direct connection to the people who were making the products, Anna figured she'd be unhappy. She didn't know what the higher-ups did, and she didn't much care as long as they stayed out of her way. Anna was happy staying right where she was.

Self-Sovereign Description

The person who sees the world through the self-sovereign form of mind may be curious about the perspectives of other people, but she cannot make sense of those perspectives by herself. She can try to imagine what others might feel, but that imagining is most interesting when she finds that she will benefit from thinking it through; she does not naturally or easily think about the inner workings of other people.

She does not think about her own inner workings, either. When asked to describe herself, she is likely to offer a list of things she likes or does not like, or things she is good at or not. She does not orient toward thinking in abstractions about herself. Looking out from a self-sovereign mind, the world seems teeming with confusion that needs to be cut through with black-and-white decisions. Perhaps the most confusing piece of all is the way other people make sense of the world and claim to see shades of gray that the self-sovereign mind does not see. At this form of mind, she can see that others claim to see a complex world, but she has no access to it herself. There are clear answers to everything as far as she is concerned; she can get frustrated when someone brings up "complex social problems" like abortion or assisted suicide. She and someone else making sense from the self-sovereign form of mind might disagree about what the obvious answer was to these problems, but they would both agree that the problems do not actually seem so complex and that politicians and others spin words around the problems just to confuse people.

Her way of seeing the world can prove wildly frustrating to colleagues who see a more-complex picture. They may find her "shallow" or "self-centered"; sometimes people with a self-sovereign form of mind are described as "obnoxious" or even sometimes "stupid" (although people at any form of mind might be obnoxious or stupid, shallow or self-centered). None of these things is necessarily true. An adult with a self-sovereign form of mind is "over her head" in almost every venue of adult life. She is unlikely to be fully accepted in society, because she hasn't fully "socialized" or taken society into herself. This can result in her willingness to engage in a variety of self-serving behaviors, some of which can be unpleasant. Disproportionate numbers of people in prison see the world from this perspective. It is these people who steal from the rich because they would like to be rich themselves.[1]

Sometimes we punish people simply for having this view of the world. Some years ago, I worked with the leader of the justice system in a district of a European country. As she learned about this theory, she became increasingly upset about the work in the courts, which, at that time, required certain changes in thinking as it required changes in behavior. She mentioned a common problem in the family court system: Young single mothers were leaving their young children at home alone while the mothers went to their jobs. The neighbors would complain, the family service organizations were brought in, and a hearing would be set to decide whether the children could return to their mother's house. In these cases, judges wanted two things from the mother: They wanted her to change her *actions* (and never leave young children alone again) and they also wanted her to change her *mind* (and understand that leaving children alone was a horrible thing to do). In some cases, this worked. But in many cases, the young mothers agreed to change their behaviors ("And you can check up on me whenever you want!" they would say), but they would not change their mind about their actions.

A typical case would have the judge asking the mother something like, "Do you see that what you did was wrong?"

The young woman might answer, "I didn't know it was against the law."

"But do you see that whether it is against the law or not, it is a dangerous and terrible thing to do to leave your young child alone?" the judge would ask again.

"It doesn't matter what I think, because you're telling me not to do it or you'll take my kids away."

As the judges pushed for some evidence of genuine regret and learning, they became more disturbed. The logic of the self-sovereign mother was clear: "I needed to work to support the children, I couldn't find someone to watch the children, so I left them alone so that I could go to work." The clear, cause-and-effect logic of this, uncomplicated by the feelings or the risk to the children, upset the judges. In many cases, they decided that the mother, even if she did stop the behavior, was unfit to be a mother, not necessarily because they thought she would break this specific rule again but because they didn't trust mothers who *thought* this way.

As I teach about this to groups all over the world, I get a wide range of responses about these young mothers. Some people think the judges are unfair; others say, "But the judges were right—those women can't be trusted to take care of children if they don't understand what's wrong about what they did!" The point here—and often the point in organizations with employees who have a self-sovereign form of mind—is that we generally make laws and rules about *behavior* and then we become outraged and frustrated by what someone *believes*, or the way she makes sense of the world. You can legislate all kinds of behaviors (and of course, that is mostly what our legal system does), but you cannot legislate what or how someone must believe. And yet our beliefs, some of which are made possible by our form of mind, are the roots from which all actions grow. I do not pretend to have answers to all of these problems, but I think it is important for us to be asking good questions.

In the case above, if the "higher-ups" want Anna to *do* different things in her work, they just need to tell her and be sure that those new things fit inside the hours and the structure of the rules about her day. If they want her to *see* the company in new ways, be more loyal, be operating for the good of the team, then they will have to help Anna grow to meet those demands. It may, in fact, be possible that Anna needs to have a different set of beliefs about the company for her to be most effective; it is certainly true that in the complex and confusing world of parenting—especially when that parenting is taking place outside the cultures of extended family support that have helped parents for hundreds of generations—a more-nuanced perspective would be far more helpful. But it might be, in both of these cases, that this person, with the support of her environment and the structures around her, can do the job at hand while developing the capacities to do it without those supports. In any case, looking at these examples through a developmental lens helps us remember that nothing is ever really simple (an insight that would frustrate those with a self-sovereign mind!).

It's hard to be promoted into managerial responsibilities with this form of mind, so it is likely that the greatest concentration of this perspective will be found in the lowest rungs of the organization (in entry-level administrative positions, among the maintenance crew, or on the shop floor) in those who have had the least access to educational and other privileges that tend to promote development. This is not to suggest that these positions are likely to be *correlated* with a self-sovereign mind or that anyone should ever assume that a housekeeper sees the world from this perspective. It is merely to say that the responsibilities of a more entry-level position leave more room for those with this form of mind than the responsibilities of a manager. And, because this form of mind is more generally associated with adolescence and very early adulthood, it is likely (although not guaranteed) that a 30-year-old who seems to have some self-sovereign ways of seeing the world is most likely in the midzone, on her way toward a socialized form of mind.

Self-Sovereign/Socialized Midzone

The transition between the self-sovereign and the socialized forms of mind is characterized by a growth in awareness of outside theories and perspectives—and a growth in ability to act from inside those perspectives and theories. Gradually, the world begins to become too complex to handle with the simple right/wrong of the self-sovereign mind, and people grow to identify with larger groups or ideas that can hold and explain some of the complexity. A person with a self-sovereign mind begins to move toward affiliation and expertise (even if the affiliation is with an antiestablishment or antisocial group, and even if the expertise is a theory or person who proclaims the futility of expertise). As the person with a self-sovereign mind becomes more willing and able to adopt the perspective of another and subordinate his own interests to the interests of the group, he begins to develop a socialized mind—not to replace the earlier mind, but to encompass it and gain perspective on it. At that time, when the socialized mind is *almost* fully developed, he has something of an allergy to anything that might threaten to pull him back to the self-sovereign mind. He is likely to be passionately clear about the perspective/community/theory in which he has become embedded, and he may be especially frustrated with or angry about anyone who sees the world differently.

SOCIALIZED FORM OF MIND

Charlie was a retired Army officer in his early 50s who was hired to direct the IT division of a financial services company. From his first days on the job, some of Charlie's direct reports joked that they could not walk into a room without feeling like they should salute before asking their question. Although Charlie was not an expert in the field of technology, the VP who hired him was impressed with his leadership style and felt that he could improve a division that many considered sloppy and without a good work ethic. Charlie agreed with this assessment, explaining that he felt he could lead any troops to victory, and whether that was in a peacekeeping mission or in a mission to keep the computers up and running did not matter much to him. Entering the division filled with ideas about what needed to happen, Charlie implemented a strict series of work-order changes and clear work-flow design procedures. Some of the employees complained vehemently about these changes, but Charlie persevered; he had told the people who had hired him that this would be a tough transition for some of the staff and that he would cut all the deadwood he could. And Charlie seemed to be right; soon those who remained were following the new regulations, and the mess seemed to settle down, and the internal customers were marveling at how well IT was performing.

More than a year into Charlie's tenure, however, frustrations began to mount. Those who had been grateful to Charlie for his ability to get the IT support to fix a printer or install the right phone lines began to forget the difficulties of IT in the pre-Charlie days. Now they reminisced about the good-old days of IT when you could request a software program without filling out six different forms, and where an out-of-date laptop was replaced without hassle. And while other companies seemed to be moving forward and using technology to create a more knowledge-driven workplace, it seemed that Charlie treated technology as a simple tool like a pencil and not as new way to think about doing business. More and more people became frustrated with what they sensed was Charlie's lack of vision; it seemed he only wanted to implement mandates from his superiors and did not want to create new ways to influence the technology needs of the organization. Charlie ignored all such criticism, explaining that his manager consistently told him he was doing a good job. "And if your commanding officer says you're doing it right," Charlie said, "you're doing it right and you don't change it!"

TABLE 2.2   Strengths, blind spots, and central areas of growth for the socialized form of mind

Key strengths	Key blind spots	Central areas of growth
With the socialized form of mind, a person's strength is his ability to take on others' expectations for good performance. He can be reflective about the issues involved and perhaps name and value the perspectives of others. He is loyal to the idea, group, or organization with whom he identifies—so loyal that he subordinates his own interests to the interests of that group.	A person with a socialized form of mind lacks the ability to untangle divergent perspectives or resolve conflicting viewpoints; he cannot mediate between the perspectives of important others. Similarly, he cannot yet mediate between his own internal competing identifications, so that when his role as Good Son conflicts with his role as Good Employee, he is likely to feel stuck and unable to find an appropriate course of action.	As he moves toward the self-authored form of mind, he will benefit from opportunities to move away from external theories or rules of leadership and to reflect on overarching principles and values that can help him resolve the conflicting perspectives of others. He will grow to see that no one theory, group, or organization is infallible, and he will develop a more individual and nuanced set of beliefs and loyalties.

Roxana had trained as a management consultant at a prestigious graduate school. At the top of her class, Roxana was recruited right out of graduate school by a leading consulting firm and immediately became highly focused on her journey toward partner. Two years into her work as a consultant, Roxana used her wealth of knowledge of business systems and training techniques—as well as her tireless drive to know everything about the field in which she was operating—and contributed to some highly praised changes in the morale and effectiveness of several newly merged divisions in a large merger initiative her firm was running. Although she was doing well in the firm, a key mentor told her that her rise to the top might be aided by some time on the other side of the desk—as someone who was a manager inside an organization and not just a consultant on the outside. When the head of HR at the client organization let Roxana know that a position at her level was opening up in another division, she jumped at the chance, and got the job with ease.

Her new job—like her consulting—involved helping to merge disparate units into a single division. She got the position and moved into the job with the skill and competence that had marked her work as a consultant, and her direct reports were thrilled with their new manager. Several months later, however, the morale of the department began to decline as those in her division tired of what they thought was the party line from her previous consulting firm. While they had appreciated her clear dedication and obvious knowledge about management theories, they began to find her inflexible and not easily adaptable when situations arose that did not exactly fit within the boundaries of her theories. It felt to them that if an issue had not appeared in one of her graduate school cases, Roxana believed it could not exist. And while Roxana had been so effective in helping other managers shape their own mission statements and create a common vision for their departments, she had much more difficulty implementing these ideas for herself. She followed the plan from her previous consulting life and conferred with all of the players in the newly combined division, but found prioritizing the many different opinions and values enormously difficult. When even her own management team had widely divergent opinions, Roxana was ready to throw up her hands and name the task impossible. How was she supposed to craft a vision out of the mush of multiple opinions? Her employees sensed her confusion, and the division became more scattered instead of more coherent.

Socialized Description

These leaders have little in common on the surface. Their ages, experiences, and leadership styles are extraordinarily different. It is likely that you have some key hypotheses about what is wrong with these situations and how you think they could be fixed. You might see problems of personality, fit with past work experience, or team leadership, and you might already have formulated some sense of what you would suggest to these folks if you had a chance. I suggest that as valid as any other hypothesis might be, one other piece to pay attention to is the form of mind held by these leaders. While their direct reports might not recognize it at first if they discussed their managers over coffee one morning, these leaders experience their worlds in remarkably similar ways, as they see through the socialized form of mind. The socialized mind is common throughout adulthood and in people of all ages and at all places on the organizational chart.

Someone who sees the world through a socialized form of mind is far better able to deal with abstraction than he was when he saw the world through a self-sovereign mind. No longer locked in his own perspective, he can gain some distance from himself in order to see a bigger picture (as he steps up to the balcony to see much more of the play than was possible when he was on the floor with his self-sovereign view). In so doing, he has learned to take the perspectives of others—to walk a mile in their shoes. But this new and vital part of his development comes with some costs. Now that he has internalized the perspectives of others, he has become *fused* with those perspectives; and, in order to make this developmental step possible, his own internal perspective has been temporarily lost in the process.

When people first hear about developmental theories, they tend to recognize many things from their lives and experience. But this question about "losing" the inner voice often feels troubling. Where does this voice go? Where is the self? What happens to the *you* inside you when you make meaning from the socialized form of mind? And when do you get you back?

Someone with a socialized mind does not feel as though she has lost her self. She is being the very biggest, most complicated self she knows how to be, and that self is created by the incredibly complex network of cultural, relational, ideological external pieces. It feels—rightly so—as though she is bigger than she once was, that she contains far more than she once did. Before she grew to this point, she was locked in her own self-sovereign mind with only glimpses of other perspectives and points of view. She did not yet see the connections between things that are, to other people, extraordinarily well-connected (like, I know it's important for me to do a good job, but I don't understand why it is good for me, personally, that my whole team is successful). When she first glimpsed the connections between things and began to see the shades of gray that allow her to make better choices, she was delighted but also overwhelmed. How was she ever going to function, to make decisions, to figure things out? She looked for guidance in the theories, cultures, and relationships around her, and some of what she found helped her make good decisions. She came to trust some theories/cultures/relationships, and she internalized them. They were the buffer between her growing sense of the complexity of the world and her panic that she did not yet know what to do with that complexity. She did not lose her self in this process; her self got larger and more complex as she was able to take in the ideas and perspectives of others.

Do we tend to honor this growth in adults, though? Do we say, "Hey, look at how exciting it is that this person is growing and can take on these new perspectives and ideas until she grows her own capacity to make sense of the complexity of the world!" No. Someone who seems overreliant on the perspectives and opinions of other people, theories, or cultures can be called a "yes man" (if he relies on his boss), a Stepford wife (if she seems too intent on the images of perfection from media and popular culture), or a militant (if he happens to be embedded in the teachings of a militant religion or group).

Let's look at what people might say about the two leaders whose stories began this section. Remember that those with a socialized mind can see many of the complexities of the world but cannot yet *do* anything about those complexities. Therefore, they adopt rules, guidelines, and perspectives that come from trusted others. What they cannot do yet, however, is write their own rules, guidelines, and perspectives. They do not know that people who are not "experts" (as the socialized-mind person defines "expert") could ever do such a thing. Even some sophisticated, thoughtful senior executives with whom I have worked consider someone else to be the expert. "We have a company policy that helps us make that decision," they will tell me. And if the policy does not help with the decision, they either model it on the policy or consult about the decision with someone whom they consider to have a higher level of authority.

This leadership style is sufficient in situations where the tasks are clear and well-defined, and where the hierarchy is obvious enough that a leader who does not know what to do in an unexpected situation can simply turn to someone with more authority who will have the right answers. In the first of the two examples above, Charlie found that his work in the military was a good enough fit with his new position so that he could make direct transfers. The upper-level managers in his agency were clear enough about what they wanted him to do so that he could carry out their orders in ways that felt familiar to his background and well within his capacity. His problems began when client groups (in this case, the internal customer) wanted more from him. They were not satisfied that he was following the rules of the game; they wanted him to rewrite the game, invent a new thing. Charlie did not have the technical expertise to find a sophisticated new guidebook (on using IT to create new forms of corporate community and new wisdom sharing), so he relied on his own manager, who was happy getting the technology in working order and not pushing Charlie to create a vision (which, in fact, Charlie could not yet author).

Roxana, who also saw the world through her socialized form of mind, was less fortunate. While her consulting firm and graduate school classes had let her see leadership as a kind of exact science, the complex and organic world of day-to-day organizational life proved to be something of a mystery. Unable to create her own vision for what the mission of the newly combined division should be, Roxana looked for clarity all around her. Finding none, Roxana was lost in the fog. While her theories and her experience were solid, they could only guide her so far down the path of the day-to-day complexities of leadership. Her socialized form of mind left her unable to travel the rest of the path alone.

Notice that while we all spend some part of our lives, like Roxana and Charlie, embedded in the perspectives and ideas of important other relationships/theories/cultures, the particular cultures in which we find ourselves embedded vary wildly. Here is where the specifics of an individual's context make such a big difference. While perhaps we are, by our upbringing or psychology, predisposed to some kinds of cultures over others, much of the move from the self-sovereign to the socialized form of mind is a process of internalizing perspectives to which you have access. You cannot be embedded in any culture to which you have had no exposure. Teenagers who feel rebellious may find a nonconformist culture in which to find some solution to the complexity they cannot yet handle. In the absence an actual of a nonconformist culture with other people, they may seek one out in movies, on the Internet, or elsewhere. Those who go to college may find themselves embedded in the jock culture, the science-major culture, the fraternity culture. Those who head straight into the world of work may find themselves embedded in the organizational culture. In each of these cases, those who are socialized internalize and become made up by the key principles, theories, and rules of that culture.

Now the person with the socialized mind follows the rules because he believes in them and wants to belong, not because he is worried about the concrete consequences to himself. Note that this rule-following does not guarantee that he will be what you might think of as law-abiding or moral. Now that he is of a socialized mind, he is a full member of a group, and if that group finds illegal or destructive behavior acceptable or desirable, he is likely to engage in illegal or destructive behavior. And someone who with a socialized mind might not *sound* as though he is going along with the crowd, either. Indeed, he can sound very internally driven.

It's just that when he is pushed, he might explain that he knows it is best to make his own decisions, because that is what a trusted advisor or theory tells him is best.

Those who see the world through a socialized form of mind can have a complex, psychological understanding, and can describe some pieces of their internal dialogue in ways that they could not when they had more of a self-sovereign mind. Instead of simply lashing out in anger or fear, as those who see the world from the self-sovereign mind often do, the person with the socialized mind can name the anger and fear as the cause for the lashing out that she might do. This causal connection is tied very tightly, though. When the socialized person says, "You made me so angry," she really believes that you did something which *internally created* a feeling of anger inside her; she cannot imagine that she had any control over that experience herself (by noticing that you did something, after which she created a reaction in herself called "angry"). She feels her strings pulled by other people, and thus gives responsibility to other people for the actions that stem from that pulling. She can name her emotions (something those who are self-sovereign cannot always do) and even subtle shades of them (knowing the difference between frustration and anger, for example) but cannot control her emotions or use her own perspective on them to moderate those emotions. She might even describe herself as a person given to anger or impatience ("That's just the way I am!"), because major swaths of our personality feel out of our control when we see the world from this form of mind.

It is likely true that for tens of thousands of years, this form of mind was appropriate for nearly all the people in any given society. When people lived in extended families in homogeneous villages, and took on the same roles that their parents had had before them, there was less complexity to manage, and there were elders who could handle the managing. In today's complex, global world, there are far fewer reliable guides—and there are far more people wanting to claim to be guides (self-help book authors, talk show hosts, religious and political leaders, and so forth). There is no more "party line" to which all those leaders agree, and there is no clarity about which ones are more right than others. Because of this, Kegan[2] claims that we are "in over our heads" if we operate from a socialized perspective.

Perhaps one of the most powerful illustrations of the over-our-heads quality of being socialized in the modern world comes not from a work context but from a personal one. Rita, an unmarried graduate student in her mid-20s, discovered that she was pregnant. The father of the unborn child was her live-in boyfriend of more than a year. He was delighted about the news of the baby, and he urged Rita to marry him—something they had been talking about already—and begin their family at this time. Rita's mother, Susan, on the other hand, had a very different perspective. Susan had married young and given up her career aspirations on behalf of starting a family, and she felt that loss in her own life deeply. Susan counseled her daughter to terminate this pregnancy so that she could be in control of her destiny, finish graduate school, and begin a family on her own timetable. Rita, loving and trusting both of these voices, had no way of knowing which direction to choose. She talked to each of them again and again, writing down the things they said and agonizing over the difference. When asked about how she would finally come to a decision, she was at a loss. Pushed to name some way out of this quandary—which was tearing her apart and causing her to be unable to eat or sleep or concentrate on her classes—she said that the only recourse she could imagine was to "flip a coin." Rita, with a socialized mind, is not to be faulted for this perspective. Her life became more complex than she could handle at this stage of development, and the intense pressure on her to grow would not speed her growth quickly enough to work her way out of this most wrenching decision.

The Socialized/Self-Authoring Midzone

So what does the path from the socialized mind to the self-authored mind look like? The path begins, as Rita's may, when the socialized perspective is not large enough to make sense of her surroundings. She may find herself torn between two different people whose opinions she values, or between different external theories or cultural pulls. At other times, her journey toward a self-authored mind may begin (somewhat appropriately) with someone she trusts (again, this can be a person or a theory or a management book—or Oprah or other figure from popular culture) who tells her that it is time for her to start making up her own mind, time to start listening to the voice inside herself. In either case, the beginning of the journey is simply a noticing, a bumping up against differences between her own voice and that of other people.

In the socialized/self-authored midzone, things may get increasingly uncomfortable as her perspective shifts. As she becomes more aware of her own voice, she notices the very real rift—psychologically at least—that develops between her and those people/theories/cultures in which she has been embedded. She feels less in tune with them and spends more time questioning them. She begins to worry about becoming "selfish" and putting her own needs first. At times, this space in the socialized/self-authored midzone may feel disconnected from those important people/ideas/theories that were once so central to her identity.

You can imagine that this might cause some real conflict in those relationships, too. While some teachers/managers/partners/parents are delighted to see the bigger perspective that emerges during the move to a more self-authored mind, others (especially those who have been developmentally outpaced) are dismayed. As conflict becomes more palatable to the person with the emerging self-authored perspective, he may be more likely to question the actions of others, or to raise questions or concerns about particular ideas that his former self never questioned. He does this to be sure that he understands the full impact of whatever he is deciding (with his new perspective); but those questions can, at times, seem a challenge to others in his life, especially those relationships or cultures in which he has been embedded unquestioningly to this point.

Finally, on the brink of the self-authored form of mind, as less and less of the socialized surround pulls at her, she often becomes almost allergic to the socialized form of mind. A boss who has nearly finished her own transition to self-authored may have no patience for the socialized mind in one of her direct reports; a man who senses his partner's socialized form of mind may become easily exasperated. Developmentally, those on the brink of becoming fully self-authored know (at some level) that they do not yet have the capacity to effortlessly sustain the self-authored mind; it is always something of a struggle. To avoid that struggle in themselves, they typically try avoid those with a socialized mind (which, as I have pointed out, is a futile effort, since there is such a large percentage of people with a socialized mind in the adult population). When the person with a nearly solid self-authored mind necessarily bumps up against these people, she is likely to feel unusually irritated or frustrated with the interactions, projecting her fear of falling back onto the socialized mind before her, and finding herself out of sorts or unnecessarily critical in the socialized person's company. Soon enough, though, she finds herself able to hold on to the self-authored form of mind with relative ease.

THE SELF-AUTHORED FORM OF MIND

The self-authored form of mind looks most familiar to us, as what adults are *supposed* to look like. People with a self-authored mind are those who own their own work, make their own decisions, and mediate among different perspectives with relative ease. While someone with a socialized mind who is embedded in a particularly robust surround might look as though she "owns her own work," that image comes from the circular direction of someone else telling her to own her own work. Those with self-authored minds, by contrast, do not need (and often do not welcome) people to tell them how to make sense of their world.[3]

TABLE 2.3   Strengths, blind spots, and central areas of growth for the self-authored form of mind

Key strengths	Key blind spots	Growing edges
Those with a self-authored mind are likely to have a clear sense of personal mission that can be extended to the organizational realm. Similarly, they have the ability to hold on to many different perspectives and make an informed decision that takes competing perspectives into account but is driven by their own sense of mission or values.	People with a self-authored mind can have an attachment to their own mission that can become inflexible. This person may also have trouble dealing with the most complex situations, such as cross-cultural or cross-functional leadership, or any tasks that require her to examine and genuinely question her own system of values or principles.	This person will benefit from seeing the way her own personal theories and practices of leadership are limited and expanding her images to include other—even competing— theories and practices.

Samantha, who saw the world through her self-authored form of mind, was a middle manager in a small financial services company. She was hired by a manager she thought was wonderful, and he and Samantha collaborated very well. They didn't always agree—as she often said, she saw things her way and he saw things his way—but they always worked through their differences in ways that arrived at the best outcomes. After a company reorganization, though, Samantha acquired a manager whom she found overly rule-bound. Instead of encouraging her to have different opinions and work through the differences together as she had done in her previous position, Samantha's new manager, with a socialized mind, wanted them to think alike from the very beginning and seemed frustrated if her opinion was different from his. He seemed to think that if she were thinking about things in the right way (i.e., his way), then she would come to the same conclusions he had.

Samantha's employees mostly valued her enormously; they thought she had a coherent vision for the group and that she could keep track of the day-to-day details it took to implement that vision. Part of that vision was about letting her employees have lots of control over their own work—as long as they were contributing to the overall shared mission of the division. Some of her employees, though, seemed at sea when Samantha asked them to think of her as a resource and not as a boss. "But you *are* our boss!" they told her. "How can we be sure we're on the right track if you won't tell us how you want us to do things?" Samantha tried to reassure them by explaining that she trusted them to find their own particular paths toward the end goal they all shared, but some of them continued to want her input in ways Samantha thought were too dependent to her. Samantha, who didn't remember the time when she needed such help herself, became frustrated with what she saw as a needy personality trait rather than a temporary form of mind.

Self-Authored Description

While the self-authored form of mind is stereotypically associated with adults in general (which is, of course, ironic in that the majority of adults have not yet become fully self-authored), there is still much to be learned from developmental theory about their strengths and weaknesses—and about how to help them grow. The person with a self-authored mind has grown from the socialized mind by weaving together a philosophy or a vision of who she is—what her work is, what her values are, what her strongest principles are. No longer does she look outside herself to know what the right way is. Instead, she turns inward, running everything through her internal judgment system.

Those with a self-authored mind may be upset when important others disagree, but the disagreement is unlikely to be devastating or tearing for them. Rather, it is when two important internal values conflict that this person will feel torn and have a hard time making a decision. That is because, for someone with a self-authored mind, the internal values and principles are the same as the person himself; he is made up of those values, and any time he is torn between them, he is torn between parts of himself. Similarly, if he does not enact his principles (whether those principles are ones we might think of as socially beneficial like environmental awareness or socially damaging like a belief in the supremacy of one race over another), he believes he is not being fully himself.

While people at almost every form of mind tend to believe that others do (or should) see the world with the same form of mind that they do, for people with a self-authored form of mind, these judgments can take on a different force. Self-authored people are likely to see their own form of mind as the way adults *should* be, and are likely to think of other ways of being as immature or shallow. Thus, their judgment of other forms of mind can be negative, and they can attribute the lack of self-authorship in others as a kind of moral or intellectual deficiency (which is why it is so helpful for them to understand the rhythm and trajectory of adult development). Notice that while they may have strong negative reactions against other frames of mind, they may or may not have strong reactions against any particular *idea* someone else might have. Some self-authored people impose their judgments on others; some try to remain open. With a self-authored mind, you can not only author your own values and opinions, but also you can author your stance on holding judgments in general.

Those with a self-authored form of mind are sometimes on a relatively constant self-improvement plan. They believe that if they work hard enough, they can come to develop a self-authored system that can handle all complexity and deal with every situation. They may tweak their own system according to new data from other people or situations, and they may make changes in how they choose to enact their ideals—or even which ideals they might choose to enact. They also have a different perspective on their emotions than they did when they had more of a socialized mind, and this means that they can see and reflect upon their emotions and notice that they themselves create their own reactions to other people. Instead of thinking, "When she does that, it makes me so angry," they are more likely to think, "I wonder what it is about me that makes me react in this angry way to her when she does that." Because of this new distance from their emotions, they are less likely to get caught up in them. However, they are more likely to believe that they should be able to overcome their emotions (and that other people should be able to do this as well).[4]

In the case study above, you see one of the largest frustrations that self-authored people suffer in organizational life: when their manager sees the world from an earlier form of mind. This can create an untenable situation for the self-authored person (unless the manager offers some appreciation for the self-authored perspective, and quite a long leash). Samantha found that the same form of mind that brought her so much success and happiness under her previous manager gave her the most trouble with her current manager. Because she could not be in the world the way he wanted her to be (and she did not want to be in the world in this way, and potentially even had some contempt for this way of being), she found her work situation more and more distasteful. Similarly, she was unaware that the mismatch she was experiencing with her manager was the same one she was experiencing as a leader, only in reverse. With the certainty that others could "step up to the plate" and be more self-authored if they really tried to (after all, she had done it), Samantha did not recognize the unrealistic pressure she was putting on her direct reports—nor did she have a way to think about supporting them to be able to do what she most wanted. While Samantha's self-authored mind was a good fit with the overall organizational context, the particulars of the job meant that she found herself frustrated and constrained.

THE SELF-TRANSFORMING FORM OF MIND[5]

Many adults do not live their way into the previously described fully self-authored mind, and far fewer enter the space beyond the self-authored mind. For those who do, though, the path toward the self-transforming form of mind can have a different feel than earlier transformations. This is because it is rarely the context of their lives that pushes people to develop beyond the self-authored form of mind, as it is in the other transitions. Most theorists believe that modern society makes demands for the self-authored mind (or perhaps in the midzone between the socialized and the self-authored minds). In any case, there are few organizational or family contexts that push people beyond the self-authored mind and toward the self-transforming mind. Rather, the beginning of this path is marked by some sense that the self-authored system will actually never be sufficient to handle the complexities of life, the largest philosophical questions about personal purpose, mortality, and the meaning of life. In almost every case, this realization comes at midlife or beyond, when people are evaluating their past and making decisions about what might be possible for them in the future. As they come to understand that their current path is a tiny part of what the fullness of life offers—and that they will never develop a self-authored system large enough to grasp the fullness of life—they begin to reevaluate the direction of their lives, stop working on the self-improvement plan that has them perfecting their self-authored system, and begin to look across systems at what unites us as humans, or as members of a fragile planet.

TABLE 2.4   Strengths, blind spots, and central areas of growth for the self-transforming form of mind

Key strengths	Key blind spots	Areas of growth
The greatest strength of the person with a self-transforming form of mind is his ability to see connections everywhere. He is able to look at an issue from multiple sides and see the ways that the different perspectives overlap.	Because we do not yet know of a form of mind beyond the self-transforming, it is hard to know what his particular developmental blind spots might be (this doesn't mean that he doesn't have any—just that we haven't discovered them yet). What is clear, however, is that because this form of mind is so rare, these people have few peers who make meaning in similar ways. It also may be difficult for those who see the world through other forms of mind to fully understand this person's perspective, so his ideas may feel overwhelming, confusing, or just wrong.	Those at this form of mind are constantly working to grow, to question their own assumptions, to understand and cope with greater and greater amounts of complexity. Because of this, the world is a constant source of growth.

This transition can come with a loss, especially the loss of the single-minded dedication and the potential for (or hope for) certainty that they once had when they were of a more self-authored mind. This feeling can be frightening to executives who have been single-mindedly working toward goals they firmly believed in. They talk with fear about the loss of the "fire in the belly" they once had, and sometimes they can begin a quest for the job or project that will rekindle this fire. At this stage, people can become off-center as leaders, feeling that their previous strengths are lost to them, or that to make use of those old strengths would be inauthentic in some way. This transitional period, which can be marked by other life changes like the aging and death of friends and family and an increasing sense of mortality and the fleeting nature of life, is about holding on to the beauty of life along with the ugliness of it, the ways we are connected and disconnected, the strength of a vision and the knowledge that there could be 10 or 20 or 200 visions that would also accomplish wonderful things (and, conversely, that their cherished vision could be used to create harm).

José, an executive VP at an oil company, was widely respected for his intelligence, his ability to manage people effectively, and his clear vision about what he wanted the world to be like. Throughout the years, he had felt his vision becoming clearer and had worked to find staff members who could share and add to that vision. A few years ago, though, José had begun to notice what seemed to him to be his own inability to believe in his single-minded goals any longer. He found that instead of advocating strongly for a single position, he began to see the validity in all the positions around the table. And it wasn't just that his convictions were weakening; instead, it was as though the distinctions between his goals and other peoples' goals had dissolved; even when their goals were quite different, he had a progressively harder time knowing which one he believed in most strongly. He found himself questioning his assumptions about the way the world worked, noticing what assumptions others were making, and understanding the ways those assumptions shaped their ideas about right and wrong. As he noticed these connections, he began reshaping—and believing less in—his own assumptions.

As he developed, people began to be drawn to him in different ways. Instead of having only his direct reports come to him to tell them what to do, people all over the organization seemed to be coming to him for guidance or help in other ways—to get his perspective on an issue, to have him help them see where others were coming from. José really liked the new ways he and his colleagues were interacting, and he found himself less tied to organizational structures and opinions than ever before. He was also finding that he was less troubled by the daily irritations that used to bother him. Now when he felt irritated, he looked to himself to see where the problem lay, and he found that he was becoming more and more interested in the various reactions—even negative ones—which he found himself having. Even his negative reactions seemed a sign of his interest and vitality, and he began to appreciate his quick angry response (because he still had the temper that had troubled him throughout his career) as a sign that there was some important assumption or value being challenged.

Still, with all that was good in his position and all the increased interaction with colleagues throughout the organization, José was finding himself more lonely than he had felt before. While he was able to offer help to colleagues throughout the organization, he found that there were few people in whom he could really confide. While he constantly tried to unearth and question his own assumptions and the assumptions of others, there wasn't anyone who helped him do that work. A bigger issue, though, was that José was noticing a major change in the boundaries around the persona he'd bring to work and the different persona that he thought of as his home-self. He was feeling like those boundaries—which he once fought hard to create and maintain—were detrimental to his work in some way. It felt as though he was only bringing part of himself to his job, and that meant he couldn't really be with his work in the way he'd most like to. He felt as if his whole sense of the work world was shifting and he was not sure what was going to take the place of his old images. Now, when at the top of his career, José couldn't find a place for himself anywhere. Sometimes he felt really sad about that, but sometimes it felt very exciting. It was amazingly liberating to be able to escape from the world he used to know and to forge his own path to a new place.

It may be that the self-transforming mind is the gift that lets people deal with the inevitable pain and sadness of the second half of life, as parents and other cherished people get sick and die, and your own body breaks down, as you come to terms with the fact that there is no hope that you will accomplish all of your goals (or, if you have accomplished all of them, the realization can come that your goals were too small and now it feels too late to pick up the largest hopes again). This is a gift because the person with a self-transforming mind sits with each of these painful occurrences and, *at the same time*, comes to have a new vision for and appreciation for the joys of life. With a fully self-transforming mind, people see connections everywhere. Distinctions between people and ideas that seemed so clear when seen through the self-authored mind become much more fluid and interconnected. Differences, rather than being fiercely held up as separate, are now placed on a relational scale, so that the distinctions themselves become less important than understanding and valuing the scale.[6]

While the self-transforming mind might be a gift to some people at a stage where joyfully accepting the full realities of life and death helps moderate the potential pain that lies before them, it is also a gift to any organizations lucky enough to have some of these people in their ranks. What do people who have fully developed the self-transforming mind actually contribute to organizations? I don't know, because my experience often has been that as people approach this form of mind, they find organizations too constraining—and they leave.[7] It is my strong opinion, though, that as organizations become more powerful and more global, and as the threats to our planet become far too large for any group or organization to manage, we will require people with self-transforming minds to be in leadership positions. Such leaders can look beyond their own reputation and their own needs—even their own need to see their vision realized—and hold on to a more connected, global sense of the world.[8]

Self-transforming leaders, like José above, give up on hoping to create the One Best Way to accomplish their goals; instead, they begin to focus on the many goals to be accomplished and the larger picture that moves beyond a single goal. Such leaders will be able to look to both shareholder value and also quality of life issues, will hold on to the seeming paradoxes of maximizing profits and also protecting workers and the environment, and will enlarge the scope of leadership beyond the having and creating of a powerful vision. What we see from José is not uncommon, though. The transition past the self-authored mind is a transition beyond the current paradigm of leadership, a transition beyond the current understanding of most organizations. To be able to hold on to these leaders and use their strengths, organizations need to develop new ways of thinking about leadership, new ways of thinking about the contributions of their increasingly aging (and perhaps increasingly developing) baby boomer population.

As the world becomes more complex, the complexity of the self-transforming mind is going to be pivotal inside organizations. Given the tiny percentage of the population that has even begun to develop beyond the self-authored mind, it is unlikely that any organization will have many people at this form of mind, and organizations need these leaders more than ever. It may be that people at a self-transforming form of mind need to have positions of some power in organizations (and governments) if we are to find solutions to the currently intractable problems of poverty, hatred, and environmental ruin. Most of us have heard the famous Albert Einstein quote: "The significant problems we face cannot be solved at the same level of thinking we were at when we created them." Although Einstein didn't know about adult developmental theories, he could have been talking about the growth toward the self-transforming mind.

SO WHAT?

So if you have a deeper sense of the different ways people make sense of the world, and if you have begun to get a feel for the rhythms of that motion, and if you have even begun to believe that the match between current organizational context and developmental form of mind is important to consider, what do you do next? You turn your mind to your own context—and maybe yourself—and you think about how to understand the sensemaking of those around you. The next chapter will help with that.

3 FINDING THE GROWTH EDGE

By this point in the book, you are likely beginning to ask yourself personal questions: With what form of mind does my boss see the world? My partner? How about me? In this chapter, you'll get a glimpse of the techniques researchers and theorists use to measure form of mind, and (if you want) you will begin to turn this lens on yourself and also on those with whom you closely interact. If you would like to focus more on particular interventions instead of on the subtleties of figuring out how you and others make sense of the world, feel free to skip this chapter and move right into the more obviously practical chapters in the next two parts.

A reminder here. This theory is not a bigger-is-better theory. It is a bigger-is-bigger theory, and the difference between these perspectives is important. More-sophisticated forms of mind bring a variety of benefits, and they also bring losses. What counts most is the fit between what your life requires and what you are able to do. For example, people who are trained to fight fires are not necessarily better than other people, but there's no denying that they have capacities that most of us don't have. They have a set of knowledge and skill and a way of thinking about the world and the risks within it that non-firefighting people like me simply can't match. This difference doesn't matter much at the grocery store or in an office. If you have to fight a fire, however, it can mean the difference between life and death.[1] The context of the demand is what makes the major difference here.

Development is like that, too. If the context of your life doesn't call for sophisticated development, there is likely no advantage to having a sophisticated form of mind. Under some circumstances, having a bigger perspective is more useful; in some cases, having a bigger perspective might slow you down, might overcomplicate your life, might disturb precious relationships. Yet, if your context does require sophisticated sensemaking, one way to support that requirement is to have a map of the current terrain of your sensemaking and some support to help you move to a place that is a better fit with the demands of your life. This talk of fires and contexts is just to remind you that before you begin to use the developmental yardstick to measure people around you—and yourself—you need to have the right mindset. Developmental theory is about "bigness" of perspective. If your aim is to show that you are very developmentally complex (and others perhaps are less complex), this exercise is not likely to be helpful. If your aim is to get a new perspective on who you are and what your actual limits are, you might have some powerful insights.

There are a variety of measurements used to assess self-complexity. By far my favorite is the Subject–Object Interview (SOI), the measure of Robert Kegan's theory of adult development.[2] I like the SOI because it does more than just give a developmental "score" in the most expedient way possible. It offers a window into someone's meaning-making system: a window that an outsider can see into—and also that the interviewee herself can peer into to gain a new level of self-knowledge.

I have been using the SOI—and teaching others to use it—for the last decade. In that time, I have come to realize that there is a beauty and a coherence to every person's story, and that neither the beauty nor the coherence have to do with how "big" someone's perspective is. Asking questions to understand someone's sense-making has helped me become a better listener, a more thoughtful questioner, and a more compassionate person. I have learned that when I listen to someone else with thoughtfulness and care—not in order to convince, to teach, or to change that person, but simply in order to understand how that person makes sense of the world—both I and my relationships are changed.

In this chapter, I lay out some of the basic techniques and mindsets that you need in order to begin to make sense of someone's form of mind. To actually conduct the interview from which these techniques and mindsets emerge requires months of study, practice, and conversation. If you would like to use an interview as a measure of development, and also as an intervention to help someone craft a developmental plan, you will need either more training or to bring in an expert to do it for you.[3] For most readers, however, the techniques in this book will be enough to help you get a general sense of the way you yourself make sense of the world, and to help you listen and ask questions in ways that help you open up to new insights and new possibilities for others. Better still, beginning to experiment with the mindset and techniques in this chapter will open up new possibilities for you both in your everyday conversations and also when knowing more about someone's meaning-making would be most helpful.

There are at least four related skills you need to have in order to begin to understand your own form of mind—or that of anyone else. You have to:

1) Be able to tell the difference between the *structure* of someone's form of mind as opposed to the *content* of his conversation;

2) Ask questions in such a way that helps someone (you or someone else) bump up against the edges of his understanding;

3) Listen actively and carefully, being sure that you are not attaching *your* meaning to the words of the other person but are instead listening to what that other person means;

4) Keep an open mind about the various hypotheses you might draw from the information that is unfolding in front of you.

STRUCTURE VERSUS CONTENT

In nearly every human interaction, we tend to listen at the level of *story*. Who did what to whom? What happened next? Did the butler really do it? This adult developmental theory is about *meaning*, not about story, which is one reason it is so hard to grasp. You need to move through the story in order to get to the meaning that underlies the story, as if the story itself is the clothing that the form of mind wears. You can see the outlines of the meaning through the clothing of the story, but carefully examining the story itself will not help you get to its underlying structure. It would be like going to the doctor because you feared you had broken your leg, and having her put the fabric of your pants under a microscope. For this reason, asking questions to get underneath the story is so useful in helping understand another person's form of mind—and also, often, helping that person understand himself better. Not just any questions will do, though; you need questions that probe for meaning and a mindset to listen to the meaning you're hearing.

MOVE YOUR QUESTIONS TO THE EDGE

To begin to understand the shape of the world as someone else sees it, you have to ask questions that require him to reach toward the edge of his understanding. You're looking for the biggest perspective he is able to take, so you have to help him move into his biggest possible self. To do that, you have to ask questions that are slightly different than the questions we generally ask in everyday conversations. Because you are not really interested in story, you are mostly ignoring the what-happened-next conversation. You will find that these conversations have a different flavor and feel. Interviewees tend to experience the conversation itself as incredibly helpful to them, because they think in new ways about an old problem. This means that these questioning techniques are helpful in other contexts. Even when you may not be particularly interested in the form of mind of the person with whom you are talking, the conversation will likely move *his* understanding to a new place (and he will think you are a genius!).

BE REALLY CURIOUS

Everyone knows how vital listening is, and there are any number of books to read or workshops to attend that are designed to help you become a better listener—I teach some of these myself. If you are going to try to have any idea about how someone else makes sense of the world, though, no matter how good you are at listening, you will have to get better. Perhaps the most important thing you can learn to do in this regard is simply let go of any sense you have that you might actually *understand* what the person is saying. The normal shorthand that makes conversations feel easy and possible ("Ah, I see! You don't even have to finish that thought!") gets in the way of our actually seeing the subtle and all-important differences in the way people actually mean what they say. So listening in this circumstance involves a different mental and conversational muscle—the muscle that says "I *don't* see" or, perhaps even better, "I see so many ways you might have meant that sentence and I'd like to ask what was true for you." This may strike you as being a little bit *dis*connecting, but my experience is different. If you can listen well to the person with whom you are speaking (even if that person is yourself), your not-seeing will come across as powerful curiosity rather than disconnection or dimwittedness.

JUDGE SLOWLY

It is important in these conversations to be able to make good judgments. It is even more important to *suspend* your judgments until you actually have the weight of evidence to make them. It is all well and good to hear a couple of sentences and make guesses about some part of a person with whom you are talking. In fact, it is almost impossible *not* to make judgments about someone else. As you carry on a conversation, you are consciously or unconsciously taking in information about the person's age, gender, race, nationality, culture, and other characteristics, and often making assumptions about less visible things like social class, level of education, even the connection between the person's tone of voice and emotional state. Most of the judgments we make about another person happen without our even knowing they are there. Meaning-making, however, is a complex and hidden piece of each of us, and to see it in someone else you have to bring your judgments to a conscious, thoughtful, and slow place. A couple of sentences—or even many unprobed sentences—will not get you enough information to make informed judgments. So part of the skill of understanding the way someone else sees the world is to slow the judging pace and pay close attention to the other person.

SEEK STRUCTURE

Now, with an open, curious mindset in place, it is time to look for the structure of someone's form of mind and figure out what kind of questions move us away from content/story and move us toward structure. Before we look at a case together and get the mindset of the interviewer, it might be helpful for you to get in the mind of the interviewee.

Every hint of structure begins with a story. If you would like to play around and probe your own meaning-making system, now would be a good time to pause and think about something important that is going on for you. Consider: Have you had a recent success? A recent feeling of anger? Recent trouble making a decision because you were torn between two alternative perspectives (either inside yourself or outside yourself)? Take a few minutes and write a paragraph or so about that story (really, writing it down is profoundly better than just pausing for a minute and getting the story in your head—go do it). Stories about strong emotions or about decision making are often the most fruitful areas in which to explore someone's form of mind. While it is likely true that you can find someone's form of mind inside any story, asking probing questions about taking a blouse to the dry cleaner is unlikely to be particularly interesting for either of you. Stories with some emotional weight are more likely to offer clear insights into structure.

I'll begin here with a story we can all look at together to help the process make more sense. Here is the story in the words of the speaker, Aaron:

> I've been with Conglom Corp 6 years now, and I've had success that has been beyond anything I might have anticipated. I don't know whether it's good fortune, or luck, or what, but now, at 36, I find myself the youngest VP in the company, making plenty of money and mostly having a really good time. I guess the thing I've been torn about lately, though, is the idea about whether I should keep climbing the career ladder as fast as I have been. I know Kathie (my SVP) thinks I need to make some changes in order to stay on the fast track, and I know she's probably right, but I'm just not sure that I care about staying on the fast track any longer. It might be fun to slip into the slow lane for the next few years, enjoy the job I have without worrying about the next job, and spend more time with my wife and our two little kids. Kathie thinks I'm getting soft, though, and she's getting more vocal in her disappointment about my work, even though I don't think I'm doing anything really differently; I'm just not as hungry as I once was.

This story does not show us Aaron's form of mind. Rather, it offers us openings that we might go down if we were in a conversation with him about this place.

You might want to engage with Aaron at the story level now, asking, "What does Kathie want you to do differently? What did she say to you about it?" Or you might want to give him advice: "I think you should keep climbing because once you slow down, people will start to look at you funny. That happened to my cousin John and he's been stuck at the same level for 30 years now . . ." Note that the first couple of questions are about content and the offering of advice is based on you making quick judgments. I am going to ask you to slow down and not take either of those options; rather, imagine a way to ask Aaron questions that will help you understand the key pieces of his form of mind.

In the section that follows, we will walk through the steps of questioning to uncover a form of mind. I urge you to stop and consider the questions you might ask Aaron as the conversation continues. Then we will turn this lens back onto your story, and you can ask yourself these questions, too. First, a summary of the next section, as shown in Table 3.1.

TABLE 3.1   Steps for uncovering forms of mind

What do you do?	*Why is this a help?*
Step 1: Look for key issues: responsibility, conflict, perspective-taking, and assumptions about the world.	Each of these issues is likely a place where someone has the energy and interest to push her understanding to its edges. These issues are also the stories where structure is most apparent.
Step 2: Narrowing the choices.	Every time you begin to ask questions to help you understand someone's form of mind, you should keep an open mind and assume that this person could be self-sovereign, self-transforming, or anywhere in between. After a few questions, though, you will likely have enough data to begin to eliminate certain forms of mind and test for others.
Step 3: Moving to the edge: most, least, best, worst.	Because the forms of mind are cumulative, each person who is self-authored also has some piece of her that is socialized and some piece that is self-sovereign. This means that unless you help her move to the *edge* of her understanding, you cannot know whether the socialized part you are seeing represents her greatest level of complexity.
Step 4: Ask the same question in a new way to go deeper.	People tend to answer questions believing that they are being asked for more story. Generally it is the second or third of the moving-to-the-edge kind of question that actually moves away from story and into the meaning-making space.

Step 1: Look for Key Issues: Responsibility, Conflict, Perspective-Taking, and Assumptions About the World

For our purposes in determining Aaron's form of mind, we do not care what happened in the story (this would be like examining the fabric of the clothes rather than the hurt leg). Our central concern is about how Aaron understood the story and what sense he made of it. This is the structure of the story instead of the content. To find the structure, you have to know why someone made the choices he did, what was at risk for him in this particular situation, how he was seeing and making sense of the world at that time. For us to get a sense of Aaron's form of mind, we need to first look at the fertile avenues for finding structure inside the content. The first part of the process is simply to search inside the story for key markers of development: issues of responsibility, conflict, and perspective-taking. You can look for what central assumptions are at work. Go back and look at Aaron's story and ask yourself:

- What does Aaron take responsibility for? What does he not?
- What are the central conflicts in the story?
- Whose perspective can he take? Whose perspective is he stuck inside?
- What assumptions about the world shape his view?

Responsibility. Aaron's story is a story of change ("I'm just not as hungry as I once was") and his feelings about that change. You can look inside the story about change to see what he sees as his responsibility (and inside his sphere of control) and what he sees outside. It's clear at least on the surface that Aaron takes responsibility for deciding whether to speed up or slow down—which he names as the thing he is trying to decide about. It is less clear about whether he thinks it is his responsibility to create the knowledge about whether slowing down is the right thing or not. To understand someone's form of mind, you have to figure out both what they believe they can take responsibility for and also what they believe they cannot. Even when someone believes that doing the right thing is within her control, she may not know yet that deciding *what the right thing is* also inside her control. This distinction would let us know whether, perhaps, she were more self-authored (and could decide what the right thing was) or more socialized (and could only decide whether or not to do the externally developed "right thing"). In this first snippet, we don't have the information needed to decide what Aaron believes, but now we do have an idea about what kind of question we might ask next.

Central conflicts. In most meaty stories, you find conflict right away (that's what makes them meaty). Aaron mentions what are potentially two different kinds of conflicts: one with himself and one with Kathie, his boss. In his internal conflict, Aaron is deciding whether to climb the ladder as fast as he has thus far and trying to judge what he really wants from life. In the external conflict, Aaron talks about the disagreement he is having with Kathie ("She's getting more vocal in her disappointment"). The way people make sense of their conflicts tells you a lot about the structure of their thinking—especially internal conflicts. At the earliest stages, people may experience internal conflict but they tend to notice and name it in an external way. For example, a child who really wants a cookie that isn't allowed will sometimes hit a parent or a friend when the internal conflict gets too severe. A self-sovereign teenager who is in conflict about two choices might name the conflict as outside with the world—as though it is unfair or unkind for one friend to have a birthday party at the same time another one has invited him to go camping. The experience of internal conflict gets more and more familiar as people develop— and people get more and more comfortable naming the internal conflict as their own. With a socialized form of mind, a person might believe that this internal conflict is impossibly hard—and thus search for ways to make sense of which way to believe. With a more self-authored mind, a person is likelier to understand the way the internal conflict represents two principles or values she might have and thus see that the solution to the internal conflict is inside herself. Those with self-transforming minds are likely to see nearly every conflict as both internal and also external—that conflict comes from having a set of opinions about things in the world that someone else doesn't share. It isn't yet clear how Aaron makes sense of his internal conflict. This, too, is another fertile ground for questioning.

Perspective-taking. Aaron seems able to understand Kathie's perspective and hold it as reasonable. He names his own perspective as well. One key question is about what happens to the perspective Aaron names as his own when faced with the very different perspective Kathie holds. If someone is more socialized, it is possible that his own perspective will crumble away in the face of the seemingly more robust perspective of someone who appears to be an expert or have more authority on such matters. If someone is more self-authored, both perspectives can cohabitate in the same space, even if they contradict on another. It isn't yet clear from these first few lines whether Aaron can hold to his own perspective in the face of Kathie's perspective.

Assumptions about the world. Our worlds are defined by those things we think of as dichotomies. You can unpack some of Aaron's central assumptions about the world by seeing what things he places as opposites. Aaron names slowing down as opposed to being successful—he cannot imagine doing both. Neither does he yet talk about the possibility of spending time with his family *and also* continuing to climb the career ladder. Someone with a self-transforming mind will name almost no dichotomies—all just a range of grays (about life/work balance they might say, "I want to find a way to both spend more time with my family and also be successful in my work life, which means making different sets of choices about how I want to spend my time and what kind of position I might want to hold"). Those with self-authored or socialized minds are likely to have different sets of dichotomies—with the socialized mind offering more dichotomies than the self-authored mind. Looking for the pieces people name as dichotomous can sometimes help you figure out what next question to ask.[4]

You'll notice that one paragraph from Aaron has led us to wonder for several pages. This is one of the reasons that thinking about this sort of conversation requires such a slowing down. After a single paragraph, we have dozens of possible questions to ask—none of them about the story itself. We can, though, make some initial judgments about Aaron's sensemaking, as long as we hold those judgments lightly as possible hypotheses. The only important reason to pay attention to how Aaron's initial story can give us hints at his form of mind is because those hints can lead us to ask more questions. For example, Aaron does not seem motivated solely by his own self-interest, as he might if he were coming from a self-sovereign mind. Someone coming from that form of mind would be much more focused on himself and what was in it for him. Aaron seems concerned about the feelings of his wife and of Kathie—and has an orientation to something as abstract and psychological as "hungry." His concern for others and his psychological examination points away from the self-sovereign mind.

There are questions about his boundaries for understanding his responsibility for the decision to speed up or slow down—he seems to know that he can control those issues (which points to a more self-authored form of mind), but it's not clear whether he believes his opinion about this is justifiably his or whether he should take his main cues from other people (like Kathie). If he believes other people should make their opinions known, and that he will weigh their opinions and then make his own decision, that would be a more self-authored perspective. If he believes that other people need to make their opinions known and he needs to weigh them against one another and decide which person has the most authority (without any real interaction with his own perspective and values), that would be a more socialized perspective. Anything in between would be in the socialized/self-authored midzone. To get a sense of this distinction, you could ask questions about how he makes sense of the decision to speed up or slow down, asking things like· *What would be the hardest thing for you about slowing down?* Notice that you are not interested in his action steps for slowing down or what he thinks the results might be. You're interested in how he makes sense of the slowing down. This is a tricky distinction.

There are other paths to follow, too. You could focus on one of the conflicts. For example, it might be that Aaron is in conflict about slowing down because Kathy's opinions of him *create* his own opinions of him; if she says he's not doing a good job, than it must be true. This would look more socialized. It may be that Aaron is in conflict about this because he has two different values—one about succeeding in work, and the other about having a great family life—and he has discovered that he can't handle both of those values at the same time. That might be closer to a self-authored perspective, where the values are generated from inside (and still might compete with one another). As someone who was trying to make sense of Aaron, you would have to come up with a question that might test this distinction: You would try to figure out whether he was made up of Kathy's opinion of him or whether he could hold his perspective and Kathie's perspective as different. Think now about what question you might ask.

Okay, how about something like this:

> "When Kathy tells you that she thinks that you're losing your drive, does that change or shape the way you think about your drive in some way?"

Aaron responds:

> Well yeah, now that you mention it, it does. I mean, I don't feel like I'm losing anything by slowing down, but when she says it, I can totally see what she thinks, and then I start to worry about what that means for me. It's really important for me to feel good about how I'm doing in the world. Also, I know that lots of the way I see myself has to do with my sense of how good I am at my job—you know, the fact that I've been a star, kind of. And I'm not proud of that, and I know that I probably shouldn't have so much wrapped up in the title on my business cards, but I notice that I really mind it whenever I hear that another VP has just gotten an "S" in front of his title. My wife tells me not to get so worried about it. She says that I just need to remember that I'm the youngest one in the company at this level, and that I must be doing a really good job. It helps me to have her say that, and I can remember that she's right, and at the same time whenever Kathie tells me that she thinks I'm not hungry enough, it makes me feel like I've peaked at 36 and that it's all downhill from here.

Step 2: Narrowing the Choices

Now that you have more information, you can analyze it for new clues about Aaron's form of mind. Here, a useful set of things to look for is: What it is about his success that Aaron holds inside himself (in a more self-authored way) and what he holds as a kind of package from the outside (in a more socialized way)? For example, Aaron says that his sense of himself comes from inside his own opinion ("It's really important for me to feel good about how I'm doing in the world."). This sounds like it could be self-authoring. If he mentioned internally created ways he knew how he was doing "in the world," that would add evidence to a hypothesis that he is self-authored. He might have talked about his goals and whether he was meeting them, about some internal standard he had set for himself and the way he measured against that standard.

He does not do that, though. The examples he actually offers are all external (e.g., that he's "a star" and the title on his business cards), which might point more in the socialized direction.

At the same time, he mentions his discomfort about the way his sense of himself is made up externally ("I'm not proud of that, and I know that I probably shouldn't have so much wrapped up in the title on my business cards."). This is a hint that Aaron may have a perspective on his socialized mind. This shows that he also has some self-authored perspective, because you cannot see—and critique—your current form of mind until you begin to grow toward the next one.

Another clue is that Aaron specifically tells how he is mostly made up by himself at work. He says, "I know that lots of the way I see myself has to do with my sense of how good I am at my job." This is also worth testing, because our relationship to how we make sense of ourselves is also developmentally constructed. Someone who takes his whole sense of identity from one context in his life is potentially less far along on the developmental path than someone who takes cues from multiple contexts in his life. This is worth questioning about if you are looking for a way to make distinctions.

As you've probably seen, asking just one or two questions is not enough to uncover meaning-making; you have to probe deeply and create a variety of hypotheses about what that probing means. You have to ask questions that will lead to the place where the other person struggles to make sense—even to himself. This is how you know that you have gotten to the edge of his form of mind.

What we've seen in Aaron is that there might be a self-authored mind and also a socializing one together—maybe a midzone. Or he may be giving us information that is confusing, but if we understood it, that would eliminate most of one of those forms of mind, leaving us to believe he has either a self-authored form of mind or a socialized one. If the question is about the mix—how much of one and how much of the other—you must ask Aaron a question that specifically tests for that mix—some question about whether he ever has a different opinion than that of the authority to whom he looks. Then the next test is to see whether those different opinions are created *by him* (in a self-authored way) or whether they are adopted from *someone else* (in a socialized way, where he has multiple relationships in which he is embedded). If he puts his perspective alongside Kathie's (and holds his internal, possibly self-authored voice alongside an external voice), that means something different than if he puts Kathie's perspective alongside his wife's (and focuses only on two external voices), for example. What questions might you ask to get at this distinction?

For the purposes of simplicity, let's take:

> "Are there times when you think Kathie is really wrong about this? How do you come to have that opinion?"

Aaron responds:

> Yeah, sure, I guess that's why I'm torn. I mean sometimes it just seems to me that she's missing a big chunk of the world in her insistence at working all the time. She never had kids and doesn't understand how important it is for kids to have both parents around. At the same time, I've never been at her level in the company before, and she knows a lot about what it takes to get there, so sometimes I think she must be right because she has all that experience, and sometimes I think she must be wrong because she's not a parent. And then I feel stuck. I feel like I should be able to do this on my own without trusting her opinion so much. In fact, that's one of the things that makes her frustrated about me—that I listen to her too much and don't stand on my own enough. But she's the boss, after all, of a lot of people—including me—and she knows way more than me how to maintain a successful career over time.

Step 3: Moving to the Edge: Most, Least, Best, Worst

If you work hard to help someone name a piece of a conflict, he will inevitably get to a place where his arguments and language seem unresolved; that is what it means to be in a conflict, after all. In this case, Aaron is floundering inside a world of circular logic. He sees that both parenting and work are important to him, and he can only really believe the opinions of people who have done both. Because he has people in his life who have done one or the other, he cannot fully trust them to make a balancing decision that is most helpful. So he is both attached to their perspectives and also sees how partial they are. This might be a common experience—you can imagine that anyone at any form of mind might wish for people who have had similar contexts as a help to making a decision. If you look at the structure of his need for similarity, though, it's not a particularly complex or nuanced view. It's not just that someone needs to have been a parent and a worker, but it's that someone needs to have been in an organization at *exactly the same level* as Kathie. This suggests that Aaron isn't able to build the connections that transfer from one piece of knowledge to the next. This inability to transfer from one context to the next is more common at the socialized form of mind than the self-authored. To play the alternate-hypothesis-generating game, though, it could well be that Aaron understands something really important about the fundamental differences in the complexity of the tasks between being at his level and being at Kathie's, and that his reluctance to trust someone who hasn't had that experience is more about his deep and complex understanding of her work than his lack of ability to generalize.

Aaron also names a second stuck place. He relies on Kathie's opinion, and both he and she believe that he should be relying on himself more. He cannot rely on himself totally, though, because he trusts her experience and her role in the company so much. This also feels more likely to be socialized rather than self-authored, but again, we need to understand exactly what he means by it.

When you find the conversation at a stuck place, your first impulse may be to back off and not probe any more—that's what most people naturally do. If you really want to understand someone's meaning-making, though, it is a wonderful idea to ask a question that pushes just a little further. These questions are boundary-testing questions, and they ask the person to prioritize. What is the *best* outcome? What was the *worst* thing about that? What is *most* at risk for you here?

Such boundary-pushing questions are the key to testing for the structure of someone's sensemaking. When we see a place someone is stuck, it is a place where she cannot make meaning and thus is at the edge of the world she knows and understands and the world she cannot know or understand yet—her growing edge. When you ask questions of Aaron in this place, you are trying to see whether his answer to a deeper question will go in a socialized direction (external) or a self-authored direction (more internally focused). You know that Kathie's voice is of central importance, so you probe for what is on the other pole—will this be another external voice, or will it be more Aaron who is in conflict with Kathie? You ask:

"If you were to ignore Kathie's perspective, what would be your biggest fear about what might happen?"

Aaron responds:

That's a great question. Hmm. What would I be afraid of? I guess it would just be that she could be right and I would be stuck in my career and I'd get a reputation as one of those, you know, those kind of clock-watching guys that are just waiting to retire. And, you know, when I'd walk down the hall everyone would just be thinking that I was the one who might have made it big but didn't.

Step 4: Ask the Same Question in a New Way to Go Deeper

Here we see the fear that is at the bottom of Aaron's dilemma—that he might get a reputation for being stuck. This fear—about how others perceive him—is good evidence for a socialized form of mind; nearly everyone is concerned with the way others see them, but if your *worst* fear is about reputation, it is probably a pointer that the voices of others are louder in your head than your own voice. Still, the only way to be confident in this—and to eliminate any possibility that Aaron also has some part of him that is self-authored—is to do an important, if counterintuitive, thing: Ask the same question (in a slightly different way) twice.

In this case, you would mirror back to him a little of what you heard, and then ask again:

> "So it sounds like the very worst part for you would be that you'd get the reputation for being a clock-watcher—or a high-potential guy who didn't go anywhere. I can think of all kinds of reasons that would be really hard and scary. I wonder if you could tell me what about that reputation piece would be the most scary for you?"

Aaron responds:

> I guess it's just that . . . Well, now that you ask it that way, it makes me . . . Well, I know how I feel about those guys who are clock-watchers, and I know how everyone talks about those guys, and the way they look at them and . . . I guess I just never want anyone to think of me that way. But it's more than that, too, because it's not just the way *they* think about me—it's also the way *I* would think about me. I mean, I couldn't really look in the mirror if I thought I was just marking time. I guess I would start to believe that all those mean—or just pitying—things people would be saying, well, they'd really be true, wouldn't they?

Here we have moved to the heart of the issue—which circles around questions about other people and how other people's opinions create Aaron's sense of himself. There may be hints here of Aaron's own self-authored voice emerging, but it would be a big help to someone working with Aaron to understand the overwhelming power in the voices of other people. What Aaron has said in a clear and compelling way is that if other people held an opinion of him, he would come to hold that opinion as well, and that he would not know how to get away from that space. Knowing that Aaron makes sense more with a socialized form of mind than a self-authoring one, and knowing that he is working on developing the self-authored space but is not there yet, could be a big help to those who work with Aaron.

Without knowledge about Aaron's current form of mind and the idea that it was a temporary stop along a continuum, a manager, coach—even a partner—could otherwise be frustrated with Aaron's seeming inability to come to a decision for himself. It can be hard to remember, especially with those who are successful, knowledgeable, and have broad spans of control, but the socialized mind is alive and well in the executive ranks, and assuming otherwise will only lead you to frustration and unhappiness.

If it is true that Aaron is making sense of the world toward the beginning of the transitional journey between the socialized and the self-authored minds, there are any number of ways to better support him—as a colleague, as a manager, or as a coach.

For example, if his boss Kathie knew that her expectation for the *way* Aaron made sense of the world was unrealistic for him at this time, she might find it easier to focus on the quality of Aaron's work rather than her wishes for a new way he might make sense of his work. Similarly, if a coach saw Aaron's own frustration about his sensemaking and wanted to help promote the development of a more self-authored mind, she could point out to Aaron the times when his self-authored voice was strongest, and talk to him about the benefits—and losses—of strengthening that voice. There are lots more ideas in following chapters about how to put this knowledge to helpful use.

TURNING THE SPOTLIGHT ON YOURSELF

While it's helpful thinking about the way important others in your life make sense of the world, it may be most helpful to think about yourself. It's hard getting a feel for the structure of another person's form of mind, and it can be harder still to look at your own. Still, having a sense of how you experience a conflict, a tough decision, or a joyful event can give you both a sense of compassion for where you are now and a sense of possibility for where you might be next.

Asking Yourself the Right Questions—And Listening to the Answers

For now, let's return to your own story and think about how you make sense of the world. Before we dove into Aaron's sensemaking, I suggested that you might write down a paragraph or two that told the story of something going on in your life which has emotional weight or about which you are still undecided.

Since this is you that you're thinking about, not somebody else, there are ways that the probing process is easier—and ways that it is more difficult. It is easier in that you do not have to phrase questions carefully or make an effort to reach out and show your own listening (you do not have to worry about seeming too nosy when you are asking yourself questions!). At the same time, you may find it difficult to gain enough distance from your own story to simultaneously tell it and analyze it. It is worth noting here that evidence shows that we tend to overestimate our own capacities and underestimate the capacities of others (which is why almost everyone thinks they are better than average!). Giving yourself a hard and honest look isn't the easiest thing in the world.

What remains the same throughout is the need to be nonjudgmental but discerning as you try to listen with real curiosity to your own sensemaking. The good news is that the more you practice this kind of self-examination, the better you will become—and the better you'll understand your own form of mind, which will lead to the hastening of your own development.[5]

Here is the easiest method. Take a story and think about whether it is a mostly positive story (of a great success, for example) or a mostly negative one (of anger or loss). Or it may be that your key emotion is ambivalence (if you're trying to make a decision, for example). Match your emotional valence, and ask yourself one of the questions found in Table 3.2.

Ask yourself the appropriate question and see what answer you might have for yourself. This answer may surprise you, but more likely it will feel obvious, like you've already had this conversation before.

Situation: I'm feeling frustrated in my job but can't decide whether it's really bad enough to leave.

Emotional valence: Ambivalent

TABLE 3.2   Questions for different emotional valences

Emotional valence	Question to ask yourself
Positive	• What is the best thing for you about this? • What is the thing you're most pleased about?
Negative	• What is the hardest part of this for you? • What are you most worried about/afraid of?
Ambivalent	• What is the most important part of this decision for you? • What would be the worst thing about making the wrong decision here?

First question (selected from the chart above): What would be the worst thing about making the wrong decision here?

First answer: If I make the wrong decision, I might be getting my career off course in a way I'll later regret.

It is unlikely that you have reached any new insight or found any structure in this first question. Do not make any hypotheses yet (or give up on the process!). Think about your answer to the previous question and ask the same question again.

First answer (from above): If I make the wrong decision, I might be getting my career off-course in a way I'll later regret.

Second question: What would be the worst thing about getting my career off-course?

Second answer: The worst thing about getting my career off-course would be the sense that I had veered off the right path somehow and had screwed up rather than reaching my full potential.

It is possible that now you have begun to push your own thinking a little harder, and that you are now finding yourself in new territory. It is also possible, of course, that you are still on familiar ground. In any case, it is unlikely that you have gotten beneath the clothing of your form of mind to the structure. The next question, though, is likely to push you a little more toward the edge of your understanding (even though you are just asking the same question over and over).

Second answer (from above): The worst thing about getting my career off-course would be the sense that I had veered off the right path somehow and had screwed up rather than reaching my full potential.

Third question: What would be the worst thing about screwing up and not reaching my full potential?

Third answer: The worst thing would be that I really live out my values through my work, and if I had misjudged this situation somehow, it would mean that I was less able to make a difference in the way that I thought I should, and that would mean that I had, in some way, been a failure, and not contributed to the world as much as I should have.

Okay, this fictional person has likely now come a place where she is learning new things about the stakes in her decision and why it is so difficult for her to make it. She also has possibly come to some structural understanding about how she is making sense in the world. She can look at her answers and notice the absence of any external force as she thinks about what is most difficult. She can see that her wishes are not the concrete and me-specific answers of the self-sovereign mind, nor are they focused on getting the answer from some external person, theory, or idea. Rather, her answers look at least self-authoring. If she wants to be really honest with herself, she will probe more deeply into the absence of external guideposts and look to see whether it was her form of mind—or her knowledge of this theory—that kept the mention of other people out of her answers.

Once you have asked yourself the question from the chart three times, you have a choice. You can either ask it a fourth time, or you can start to look inside the answer to the third question and ask yourself more-targeted questions about each of the forms of mind. You can ask yourself questions like those in Table 3.3.

As you ask these questions about the third answer to your story, you're likely to recognize some things about yourself. You will most likely to find that you are at an in-between place, and, if you're about average statistically, you'll likely find that the questions in both the socialized mind and the self-authored mind pull at you

TABLE 3.3   Questions you ask to test particular forms of mind

Form of mind you're testing	Questions you can ask yourself about your third answer
Self-sovereign	How much do I focus on the benefits to and impact on myself without taking other people into account? Can I imagine what others might be thinking or feeling about this situation, even when those others are quite different from me or they might believe I'm wrong?
Socialized	How much of my answer is about how I think others will perceive me or what I think others will think I should do? How much do the opinions of others shape my opinions of myself? How much am I searching for The Right Answer or attempting to judge myself against some external standards instead of creating the answers and the standards for myself? Who do I think I might be if others were disappointed in me or if I did not follow the rules or guidance of theories or role-images that were centrally important for me?
Self-authored	How much of my answer is driven by my own sense of what I think is best in the world, regardless of how others might see me or react? How much am I equating *who I am* with my own ideology as it is lived out? Who do I think I might be if I did not live up to my own standards? What would that mean for how I know or understand myself?
Self-transforming	How much of the entire picture am I seeing here versus how much of my own perspective I am locked inside? When I try to look at my situation from multiple angles, how easy is it? Do I sense the positive inside the negative and the negative inside the positive in my story? Am I finding it hard to see my life as straightforward, to see things as particularly good or particularly bad, but rather simply the way that life is for me and thus is interesting and rich?

the most. You may find yourself confused about exactly which is most prominent for you if you are torn between two of these, and that confusion is likely to be generative rather than unpleasant. Having even the most basic sense about where you are in your development can offer any number of benefits to you.

Benefits of Knowing Your Own Mind

Once you have an idea about your own form of mind, you can begin to ask yourself new questions, form new understandings, and decide about how you want to make decisions about your own development. You can recognize patterns in your form of mind and the way you are pulled in one direction or another about particular things, and you can begin to change those patterns which don't contribute to your success and happiness.

In the next chapters, you'll see how knowing about adult development will help you help others, but as a reminder—this will also help *you*. The benefits of knowing your own mind are much like the benefits of knowing the form of mind of those around you. You can:

- Be more realistic with your expectations
- Understand your limitations
- Understand what pushes your buttons and why
- Design ways that you might develop if you so choose
- Design ways of thinking about what supports you might need while you are developing the capacity to take on greater levels of self-complexity

In any case, paying attention to the structure of peoples' thinking opens you up to new possibilities for supporting and challenging yourself and those around you. In Part Two, we'll look at different ways that adult development theory can support you and others to change on the job.

PART TWO HELPING OTHERS GROW

4 GROWTH EDGE COACHING

Steve, a well-regarded leadership coach, had three meetings set up with potential clients one Friday in November. He knew such auditions were necessary for getting a good match, but he had mixed feelings about them. On one hand, he enjoyed meeting new people and found their stories endlessly interesting. Even though he had been coaching for nearly a decade, he still loved the intricacies of the client stories, and the many variations on a handful of common coaching themes. On the other hand, he still disliked the feeling of the audition and the waiting to learn whether he had been chosen. Sometimes his gut feel coming out of these initial meetings was right on target, but other times he found the client decision-making process to be random. Because he liked these meetings so little—and because they were so important—he had developed a clear and consistent strategy over the years in order to be sure that, whether he was selected or not, he had shown the client who he really was and how he really coached.

Generally, his plan was to find out why the potential client had called him in the first place. Then he'd ask questions in his usual style and explain his philosophy of coaching while probing into his potential client's images of what coaching might be about for him or her. While the meetings had this standard form from his end, each was a unique event because of the potential client's ideas and perspectives. Steve's part, though, went something like this:

> I believe that each person has a story about what is going on for them at work. We are each the hero of own story, and there are forces and people who are either a help or a hindrance to our getting what we want. It just so happens that as we live these stories we are calling on some of the ancient myths and seeing ourselves as either a "hero in victory" or a "hero in defeat." These have powerful implications for what actions we take and how we interpret the events around us.

After laying this groundwork, Steve explained how transforming the story from hero-in-defeat to hero-in-victory could reduce stress and greatly increase the possibility for success. Steve was confident about this because he had coached hundreds of leaders in this way, and he had seen a high percentage of them turn around their stories and become more successful and effective—and a whole lot more happy.

At the end of this particular early-November day, Steve felt good about his performance but still unclear about which of these meetings would end up in a client engagement. Gone were the days when he would agonize over his words, replaying the tapes in his head and looking for areas of improvement. He knew that he'd done a fair job of presenting his ideas, and he also knew that his opinions about how it had gone might bear little relationship to the outcome. Agonizing about it would net him little, whereas heading off into nature would net him lots. He took advantage of unusually beautiful weather to go hiking with his daughter. (Steve had gotten the role of father many years ago, without much of an audition, and his daughter usually looked on him as a hero-in-victory.)[1]

The potential clients, on the other hand, *were* mulling over their decisions.

Soo Jin had emerged from the meeting with Steve impressed and curious. She wanted to step back and reflect over the weekend, but she was pretty sure he was the coach for her. His naming of the potential patterns in her own storytelling was immediately helpful—it rang true to her and was a novel and useful framing. She could see how thinking about her own story in these ways might lead her to new insights and new options for action. Soo Jin also noted that Steve's take on her issues was spot-on. After going back over her notes from the other two coaches she had interviewed, Soo Jin was crystal clear. Steve was the coach for her.

Shannon, however, was less certain. She had really liked Steve and found his questions interesting and challenging in a way that was different from the two other coaches she had met. She had been expecting to find someone who would offer her guidance, though, and Steve was explicit that his role was not as advisor but as questioner. His talk of stories, too, had left her mostly cold. It seemed only marginally helpful to identify what story you were living. Steve seemed to believe that identifying the story would make it easier to change things somehow, but Shannon seriously doubted that. How could knowing your that your story was, say, of a hero-in-defeat, ever be anything other than, well, *defeating*? She found herself hoping he would tell her that she was more of the hero-in-victory—or maybe it might be better not to know at all, really. Still, his questions made her think and that seemed really good. Maybe she'd ask around and find out how others made decisions about their coaches.

Lien had tried to keep her feelings to herself—a skill she had learned was useful when dealing with people you didn't like. Still, she was shocked, frankly, that this guy could even call himself a coach. He was supposed to be helpful to her and help her deal with the difficult people all over her division, but instead he wasted half their time talking about stories. Lien wasn't interested in *stories*; she was interested in *reality*. She wanted a coach to be helpful in the real world and not talk about fairytales. Steve would be the fifth coach she had turned down in the two weeks since HR had insisted she get a coach in the first place. If HR kept sending her terrible coaches, though, it was their own fault that she kept sending them back!

Our form of mind plays a role in each of our impressions and decisions, which of course means that giving thought to a client's form of mind can improve a coach's ability to be helpful. As you can see from the stories above, Steve's attempt to show everyone the same image of his style was unmatched by the reception from the various potential clients who saw Steve's approach as more or less helpful depending on their own form of mind and their own experience. This might be fine in the audition, where clients are looking for someone whose style fits and coaches are looking for someone they'd like to coach, but it would probably be to Steve's advantage to be aware not only of what his style was like but how it might be interpreted by clients at different forms of mind.

Most coaches, for example, have a style and approach that are better suited to some forms of mind than others. Steve, while he might not have the theoretical words for this preference, has the sense that there are some clients who have a set of needs and hopes that run counter to what Steve most wants to offer. In many ways it makes good sense for him to avoid stepping forward to impress clients who might be unsure about—or even hostile to—his approach. You might have noticed that Steve would appeal most to someone with a clear sense of herself, someone like Soo Jin who believes that we create and choose our own stories. That someone would necessarily have to be at least mostly self-authoring in order to have this perspective on the world before Steve walked in the door. Someone more socialized, like Shannon, might find this strange or confusing, but, as you can see from Shannon's reaction, a person with a more socialized form of mind might be drawn to the new vision the coach offers—and it might, under the right circumstances, be a bridge to a more self-authored perspective. A potential client who currently had more of a self-sovereign mind, like Lien, might find this approach totally foreign and absurd. If his perspective is too far out of someone's range of understanding, that person is likely to feel threatened by the strange and mysterious perspective and might be hostile to it.

This means that as long as there is one kind of mind a coach would like to work with, having Steve's highly targeted approach is perfect—it does an excellent job at pulling in those who are ready for it and repelling those who are not. In fact, it would be possible for Steve to get even better at targeting exactly the right kind of client for him if he so chose. Perhaps he is most fond of clients in the middle of the socialized/self-authored midzone, and he lives in a major city, which allows him a wide variety of potential clients from whom he can select. To ensure he got clients in just the right developmental space for his skills, he could even begin to ask questions about their perspective and become a partner in selecting the clients he thought he could best serve. If, on the other hand, Steve is interested in working with people from a variety of developmental positions—or if because of circumstances (e.g., working in a smaller market or working internally) he doesn't have any choice—he might seek to develop a more psychologically spacious approach.

No matter which approach a coach might take—a targeted approach or a psychologically spacious approach, it can be helpful to understand the various forms of mind the client might have, the benefits of coaching that client might experience, and the particular coaching challenges the pair might face together. With this focus, a coach and a client can together explore the client's *growth edge*,[2] that space where the client reaches the edge of her current capacities. With a focus on that edge, the coach and the client can create more powerful and helpful working relationships.

COACHING AND THE SELF-SOVEREIGN MIND

The collaboration between a leader who sees the world through a self-sovereign form of mind and a coach can be both difficult and extraordinarily rewarding. Those who see the world mostly through their self-sovereign form of mind can bring an unusual level of clarity and certainty about what needs to happen next. Because ideas of cause and effect are so tightly drawn, these leaders are unaffected by the nuances that might concern others. While this clarity can be appealing for some people in some circumstances, it can also be both frustrating and dangerous, as this leader's vantage point tends to be too black-and-white and too tightly focused on the immediate for most leadership situations.

The self-sovereign client is unlikely to be common among leadership ranks, because people with this mind have not yet developed many basic leadership skills and characteristics. This makes it unlikely that they will be promoted to leadership positions in the first place. There are cases, however, where their brains or their particular skills (or connections) might land them in a leadership role.

Also important to remember is that all of us who have moved beyond the self-sovereign form of mind still have remnants of it inside us, and those remnants can come out during times of stress or exhaustion—or during times when people are learning something for the first time and feeling uncertain or insecure about their new knowledge. Because we all revisit the self-sovereign mind sometimes, it is vital that coaches and others who would like to be helpful in organizations can take note of the particular characteristics of the self-sovereign mind so that when it appears, they can recognize it and help expand it into the qualities and characteristics more useful for leadership roles.

Key Coachee Characteristics

The key thing to remember about the self-sovereign mind is that its focus may seem narrow: on what that person experiences or thinks directly. This person can have control over his own impulses and desires, which means that he can see them without acting on them (as opposed to the earlier time when seeing a thing he wanted necessitated reaching out for it). He cannot gain a distance on his own psychological inner functioning, however: He has little sense of his own psychology or, for that matter, anyone else's. Many coaches ask their clients to look for patterns in their reactions to other people; those with a self-sovereign mind cannot see those patterns at all. Many coaches ask their clients to take responsibility for their own actions when they have strong reactions to others; those with a self-sovereign mind cannot control their reactions any more than they can control their heartbeats. Similarly, they cannot see the connections between subtly different events that show a pattern. In order to see a pattern, you have to be able to step back from the events in question and look across at them. If you are inside the events, all you can do is be inside them and reflect on this event from where you are right now. Looking for patterns is not only something someone with a self-sovereign mind *cannot* do, it also is something that someone with a self-sovereign mind may not know *can be done*.

This means that people with this mind can seem unreflective; in fact, in many ways they do not reflect, because they cannot gain enough distance from their own thinking in order to reflect upon it. You can ask someone, "What were you thinking when you made that decision/took that action?" It is likely that the person with the self-sovereign mind will not be able to tell you, asserting that that was just what was clear at the time without any sort of rationale attached to the reasoning. Further probing can either lead to shrugged shoulders or a flare of anger from the client (e.g., "Why do you keep asking this ridiculous question! I was doing the obvious thing!"). This can be very frustrating, and can seem to coaches like those clients with a self-sovereign mind are hiding something or are unwilling to work with the coaching relationship. Neither of these is a fair assessment of the sensemaking of the self-sovereign person; he is simply doing the best he can without being able to see the pieces that are obvious to others with a larger perspective. Simultaneously, though, the person with the self-sovereign mind may well think others are being slippery or deceitful when they talk about an image of the world that is especially complex. Because things look fairly straightforward to the person with the self-sovereign mind (or incomprehensible—"Why would you even *try* figuring that out?"), those with more-complex images can look like tricksters or overcomplicators to these folks. Because that happens a lot, the world can seem to be filled with people who are trying to deceive them.

Take Lien at the beginning of this chapter, for example. She doesn't understand what Steve wants her to do because he is naming issues that feel abstract and unhelpful to her. He wants her to look across the pieces of her life and name a pattern; even more, he wants her to know that she authors the story of her life and that she could author it differently. These concepts require Lien to be able to do a thing she cannot yet do, which means that she can't make sense of them at all. Lien, like so many of us faced with something that makes no sense to us, pushes it away—with some anger—and figures it's Steve who is wrong or limited or manipulative.

Key Coach Fit Characteristics

People with self-sovereign minds may be among the most difficult coaching clients. Most coaching strategies are developed for those who have socialized or self-authored minds; a coach might try strategy after strategy and find that they all fall flat. Yet, because the demands of the modern adult world ask for sensemaking beyond the self-sovereign mind, developmental coaching is an important and valuable gift for these clients. The difficulty lies in finding a way in with these clients—not because the clients themselves are necessarily so tough (although they are sometimes very tough) but because our coaching techniques tend to be designed for other situations. A careful combination of trust-building and targeted skills-coaching can lead to good results for these clients. The most helpful skills are those that support the client in taking on new perspectives, for example—helping people understand new ways to give and receive feedback or to engage in some kind of reflective practice. The best coach for these leaders is one who is patient and flexible and not given to thinking about clients in judgmental or pathological ways.

Transformational Benefits and Costs

The major developmental challenge for a person with a self-sovereign mind is to get a window into his own mind and emotions—and then to use that window to begin to imagine the inner workings of others. It is not possible at this time for him to distinguish his inner voice from the inner voices of others. This is a central point for anyone interested in coaching developmentally. Many coaches focus on drawing out the inner voice of a client and helping to separate that from the noise of other important stakeholders. This is a key task of coaching a client with a socialized mind but is a wrong approach for coaching someone with a self-sovereign mind. Those with self-sovereign minds, remember, have not yet *internalized* the voices of important others. This means that they cannot *disentangle* themselves because they have not yet been entangled in the first place—it feels like all their own voice. It is possible for a client to hear a coach's urging for her to focus on her own opinions and ideas as a mandate to ignore her growing awareness of her own connectedness to the group. This can be anti-developmental.[3]

Instead, the key developmental challenge is to find that her own inner voice can merge and blend with the voices of those around her. She does this by beginning to take the perspectives of others and understand how similar their perspectives are to her own. Or perhaps she comes to desire a closer affiliation with an important institution in her life (like her own organization) and becomes convinced of the merits of having the organization really believe in her and feel loyal to her as she believes in and feels loyal to it. A coach can help her begin to understand that there are times when it would be better for her (and in her own best interest) to put the needs of others before her own needs. Because this idea is clearly obvious to people who have left the self-sovereign mind behind, coaches and others may forget how paradoxical the idea is in the first place. Because it is unlikely to make logical sense, coaches can build a logical case by pointing to those times when others put the needs of the larger group above their own needs and were successful. In this way, the idea of selfless action or generosity can be built from the material of a person's own self-interest. (Notice that this is often the way we teach children about these rules.) The person with a self-sovereign mind may begin to understand the merits of putting someone else first so that they'll put her first another time (in a tit-for-tat way). A coach can carefully support this and then help her extend to see that she becomes a better team player and is more emotionally accepted when she helps others without thought for herself. With this mind, it is the key learning that "other peoples' voices can be even more important to me than my own." This is a hard thing to feel good about supporting if you're a coach who believes your role is to help someone discover her own inner voice.

The costs to development from this form of mind, while certainly worth no-ticing, are less likely to be at the forefront of a coach's mind, because the leader-ship consequences of leaders seeing the world through this form of mind are so troubling. The psychological cost to development in this space tends to be about the disorientation that comes from understanding that the world is far more complex than this person had ever imagined and the beginning of some of the hardest of life's questions: How do you know this is the right thing to do? What will I do in order to move forward? Who/what will guide me when I am confused or lost? These questions are markers of a world turning into a very un-certain place, where cause and effect are not necessarily closely connected, where my perspective is too limited to explain the mysteries of the world I once thought was straightforward.

Coaching Processes, Strategies, and Mindsets

The few cases I've seen of leadership coaching at the self-sovereign order were quite difficult. The leaders tended to be highly resistant to the idea of coaching and found it difficult to get a good match with a coach. Often these leaders are intelligent and technically skilled, and the world has built scaffolds around them to support them in the absence of their perspective-taking skills. These scaffolds—which have allowed organizations to get from these self-sovereign people just what the organization wants—finally begin to break down as the organization wants more leader-like behavior from those who had been protected from developing such behavior for years. Now—often near desperation—the organization hires a coach to make up for this long pattern of "misbehavior" (although the organiza-tion tends not to realize that it has a piece of responsibility for this situation, as it has protected this person from growing, often for years).

Clients with this mind may have their coaches thinking about personality dis-orders or other pathological forces. A reminder that it's possible the issue is de-velopmental rather than about fixed personality offers a new set of strategies, as well as a new set of ideas and metaphors the coach to use for making sense of the client's behavior. Still, much about the coaching experience—even if the cli-ent has a coach with a strong developmental perspective—might have the feel of attempting to *push* the client from one form of mind to the next. While pushing someone else's development may occasionally work, it strikes me as more helpful and respectful to offer an opening rather than trying to force someone through it. This means that perhaps nowhere else is it more important to anchor the bridge at both sides, as Robert Kegan tells us.[4] No one would put a foot on a bridge that was tightly anchored only to the far side of the chasm they want to cross; this would be lunacy. Yet many of us describe the far side of the bank and ask our clients to leap over the precipice.

I often get asked how to tell the difference between people with classic personality disorders (like narcissism) and those who have not yet developed to a place where they can easily do things like have empathy and take the perspectives of others. I believe that our perception of a "disorder" comes from our expectations about what is "normal," and lots of those perceptions are about our own developmental expectations. If we found a 3-year-old who was terrified of the monsters under her bed, we'd think that was normal. If we found a 33-year-old who was equally terrified, we'd think that was a disorder. I tend not to think of development that's disordered, that's "slow" or "fast" or "arrested"; I think of development as the space a person currently inhabits. How do I know whether I'm dealing with a developmental issue or a less-mutable personality issue? There are two ways. First, I begin with a belief that it's a development issue, because development offers more hope (and different tools) than something more stable. Second, I pay close attention to the difference between *capacities* and *practices*. Someone who does not listen well because he is not interested in others' perspectives is different than someone who does not listen well because he does not fully understand that others have perspectives. If you believe that your coaching client is making sense of the world from a more self-sovereign space, though, these techniques may help you be supportive:

Listen without judgment. A colleague, while reflecting on clients who had some of the above characteristics, told me that when he sees someone with these sort of capacities, the only thing he can do is listen as hard as he has ever listened in his life. Leaders at the self-sovereign form of mind often have been pushed into coaching by some crisis situation or another, and they can feel quite battered and over their heads in their organizations—often after having been rewarded for their technical skills. This means that it may be harder to gain the trust of these potentially embattled clients, and even more important to listen without judgment or the immediate hope of changing the client's actions. Indeed, because listening is one of the core skills that a leader at this order cannot master *because* of her development, giving her deep experience with the process can be transformative.

Attack the tactical. With a client in a more trusting space, coaches can offer tactical, skills-based coaching. A coach with a more developmentally oriented perspective might focus on scaffolding the skills in ways that a client with a *developing* capacity to take the perspectives of others might be able to master. This could be a clear case where people around the client (including the coach) might be talking about wanting the client to *act* in particular ways while actually wanting the client to *think* or *believe* in particular ways. A coach with a developmental perspective can understand that the skills for acting in particular ways can sometimes come *before* the change in thinking or beliefs.

Change your mind before trying to change others. It might be that one of the most important minds to change about what is possible during a coaching conversation is the *coach's* mind. A coach can use a kind of rubric to see whether she is asking the client for a change in mind or a change in action, and whether her questions require that the client stand on the balcony looking at her own pattern of behavior or her own psychology. Any of those things may be too difficult for a client in this space, and so the coach can modify her techniques.

For example, if a client seems captured inside her own perspective, a coach might want to get her to take the perspective of an important other. This holding of conflicting perspectives may be too difficult for her, initially. A more developmentally appropriate task might be to get the client to take notes—capturing direct quotes when possible—about what the other person actually *says*. Then, with the coach, the client can begin to piece together the alternative perspective.

No matter what pathway you find toward coaching someone in a more self-sovereign space, the rewards can be significant. Keeping your eye on the real possibilities for this person's growth—rather than the more stereotypical growth you'd expect to see in another client—can help the coaching engagement feel more successful for all.

COACHING AND THE SOCIALIZED MIND

Leaders who see the world through their socialized form of mind are capable of great loyalty to people, organizations, and ideas. Once they have adopted a particular mission or vision as their own, they are likely to hold on to those ideas in powerful ways and champion whatever cause/belief/set of theories they have internalized. The shadow side of this strong support, however, can be a lack of flexibility around editing or adapting this internalized idea/belief/change initiative, which can lead, for example, to strongly-held ideas about what success looks like even in situations where that definition needs to move around. This means that in many leadership positions, seeing the role through a socialized form of mind has limitations, depending on the size and scope of the role (and the organization). As a leadership coach, I have found that the demands of leadership positions tend to put such pressure on people for self-authorship that those who do not yet have self-authored minds can be at a disadvantage; and that disadvantage causes these leaders pain and distress on the job. This means that when a client or a colleague describes someone who might have some strongly socialized ways of thinking about the world, I often think developmentally about how to help that person. Because of the large percentage of adults with socialized minds, there is no shortage of leaders who are in some kind of developmental distress.

The good news is that coaching is a fantastic developmental support for someone who currently sees the world through a socialized form of mind. The bad news is that coaching at this stage can either support development or hold it back in important ways. At this form of mind as with many others, positive behavioral change can come about without any developmental advance, so it is possible that a coach will feel successful in helping the client *make changes* without actually helping the client *develop*. People at this form of mind can have difficulties because of their developmental capacity in addition to wishing for a new set of skills. It is therefore especially important for a coach to have a sense of the difference between the client's developmental needs and his skills need—and where they intersect.

Key Coachee Characteristics

We have many stereotypes of people in the socialized mind in organizations. We know them as "yes men" or as those who need to follow company guidelines to the letter or who want you to think inside a particular box. But the socialized mind is not just found in the company loyals, the rule-followers. There are also the mavericks with a socialized mind: the dot-com folks who stereotypically like to play ping-pong or sit on beanbag chairs as they have their brilliant technological thoughts; the marketing department that as a rule breaks all the rules; those in academia who are ritualistically postmodern; or any other group that is uniformly disloyal or uniformly different. The thing that shows them all as having a socialized mind is the way they do not author their roles and choices, and are written by their circumstances instead of writing those circumstances themselves.

Take Shannon at the beginning of this chapter, for example. The idea of Steve's naming her story as either hero-in-victory or hero-in-defeat seems to her to be a kind of external judgment about a condition that exists in the world—the way she might discover her blood type from a doctor's visit. If she doesn't like the answer, it doesn't matter because she's stuck with it (just because you don't like having rare—and thus more difficult—AB-negative blood doesn't mean you can change it). Shannon doesn't see herself as the creator of her own story enough to believe that knowing about the story gives her particular power. This means that Steve's offer has something of a peek-at-the-last-chapter feel about it: If there's nothing to be done about it, why give away the ending? People with socialized minds can seem to be stuck in their powerlessness: They will tell you they cannot stop getting angry (and thus need other people to stop enraging them), cannot change their minds (and thus need others to change the conditions), cannot take on issues they consider to be outside "who I really am" even if they wish they could. When a coach tries to point out that these are choices (saying, perhaps, "You don't need to be late to meetings; we could work on that"), those with a socialized mind may well push back (saying, perhaps, "I've always been a late person—that's just who I am"). This may feel to the coach like an intentional shirking of responsibility or agency, but the person with the socialized mind actually cannot yet imagine a way he might change those things about himself. To imagine himself as the author of his own personality is a characteristic of the self-authored mind into which he has not yet grown.

Similarly—but differently, too—people in this space can be trapped in a sense of their powerfulness. It is with this mind that people often feel the need to control everything so tightly—because they believe that's what is necessary for them if they are to be real leaders. Just as people with this form of mind can sometimes feel overly powerless, they can also take on too much responsibility and feel overly powerful—and then be shocked (and dismayed with themselves and others) to find out that they are not in control of everything.

Key Coach Fit Characteristics

There is a paradox involved in finding the perfect coach in these situations. Often people with a socialized mind are apt to want their coach to tell them what to do and solve their problems, so they tend to look for a coach who can be tactical and directive. This can be useful in the short term, because a tactical coach (who happens to offer the right directions) can offer some short-term but major improvements. But it may be the wrong strategy for the long term, because it does not grow the clients' *capacity*—just his *skills*. If leadership roles demand more self-authored ways of seeing the world, then skills-coaching alone is unlikely to do more than make the coach a central part of the clients' success story, the vital lieutenant who is always on call. While we all want to contribute to the success of our clients, most of us would like to do that from the sidelines and help clients hold their success without us. Coaching for skills and not transformation at this stage risks having *the coach* become a central voice in her clients' sensemaking, without helping the client learn to question all such voices and eventually replace those exterior voices with an internal, self-authored voice.

There are coaches, however, who quite enjoy being in the center of client decisions and becoming indispensable. These coaches may have unmet desires for power or influence and turn to coaching to satisfy those needs. A coach who wants to be more powerful is a danger to the development of someone with a socialized form of mind, because that coach might seek to be the external voice for the client rather than helping the client build that voice for herself.

The other aspect of the paradox is that coaches who dislike having central roles, who are more likely to never state an opinion, are also not likely to be ideal for people with a fully socialized form of mind. The person with a socialized mind is, in part, looking for expertise, for authorities who will help direct his growth. In those cases where a client is looking to a coach for guidance, the coach who withholds all guidance in the hope that the client will listen to his own internal voice is not noticing that the internal voice of the client is searching for an external voice to follow. One developmentally minded coach I know becomes an expert on behalf of her client's growing expertise. She offers herself as an external expert (which, of course she is) in order to help develop the client's inner expert and thus makes more suggestions and gives more direction than she would with other clients. Her goal, however, is to be sure that she is giving those assignments in order to increase the client's capacity to listen to his own voice. As she listens for her client's voice or urges its strengthening, he feels both supported where he is and also supported to grow.

Transformational Benefits and Costs

As is probably clear, developmental coaching can be extremely helpful for someone who sees the world through a socialized form of mind. Many coaching interventions have been created to support people in this way. This is because the transformational benefits are so commonly understood by the coach, the leaders themselves, or those around them (or all of the above): Leaders are more likely to be able to see the world and themselves in ways that others imagine are more "leader-like."

Perhaps less understood are the costs to people at this form of mind. There are costs to development at each form of mind, but because the benefits can be most obvious and well-expected to the socialized form of mind, it is perhaps the form for which the costs are most often ignored. They can be severe, however. People may find that they lose their grounding in former beliefs—the general experience of those who are developing from one form of mind to another. However, whereas the move from the self-sovereign to the socialized form of mind is often widely celebrated by those around the person who is developing, the move from socialized to self-authored form of mind can stir up mixed feelings in others. Even when others have hoped for the development of the person to something more self-authored (usually experienced as wishing the person were more autonomous or less reliant on the opinions or desires of others), the actual movement itself can leave others feeling pushed away or confused by the erratic wishes and perspectives of the developing person.

Those around the socialized person who are not interested in his growth may have even more difficulty. As I mentioned in Chapter 2, there may be others in the life of the person with a socialized mind who feel abandoned or betrayed by this person's growth and development. This time can be hard on all sorts of precious relationships: between parents and their grown children, between colleagues at work, between teachers and their adult students, and between those in romantic relationships. Issues of love, loyalty, and power shift and change during this transition, and because they shift in the mind only of the developing person (and do not magically change in the minds of those around him), the transition can be a difficult for all.

I am not in any way discouraging developmental support during this time, but rather trying to offer a perspective about how complex the change may be and in how many different facets of her life a client might need support.

Coaching Processes, Strategies, and Mindsets

The move from the socialized to the self-authored form of mind is, in many ways, the most familiar kind of coaching (or therapy or leadership development). In these engagements, the coach is most interested in helping the client discover and learn to trust his own internal voice. This can be about creating good boundaries for the client, helping him figure out what he really believes and why, and supporting him to hold on to his opinion even in the face of disagreement from important others (or perhaps moderating his opinion to consider the opinions of others without dropping his own perspective in the face of a strong perspective from someone else). In addition to the other tools that are likely to be in your toolkit already to support clients in this space, here are three ideas I find helpful in my work.

Question authorities. A key—but very difficult—developmental space is about helping the client notice those voices he uses as infallible guides to what is the best way to be in the world. Clients who have these sorts of guides are often captive to them and take the opinions and perspectives as the truth about the world (even if these are opinions and perspectives of theories or of mentors who have long ago left the client's life). A coach, gently and over time, can help a client begin to see the ways those externally written guides are not always helpful. Similarly, the coach can help the client make sense of the often-painful tearing that happens when people are caught between the important voices of several important others. Clients who are currently seeing the world through the socialized form of mind can be helped to see that authority comes from a variety of different sources and not only the ones the client currently privileges (like job title or educational background or years of experience or whatever else the client believes is the central well of authority). As the client's sense of the wellspring of authority changes, he is more likely to put himself and his growing self-authored perspective on the approved-authority list.

Write definitions. Another related surprise for clients who see the world through the socialized form of mind is that the definitions they have—for such things as "success" or "competence" or "integrity"—can actually be rewritten, and that the clients themselves can do the rewriting. This notion is often such a surprise to clients in this space that they can almost not conceive of it. They ask questions like, "Why would you think that *I* would be able to change the definition of what success looks like? Everyone knows what success looks like—you can't just go and *change* a thing like that!" Because they are embedded in these externally generated definitions, they find themselves out of control of important forces in their lives. This can be okay when things are going along nicely, but when things become difficult or circumstances change—like when someone is doing well in her career and then becomes a mother and finds she needs to materially change the way she spends time—these old definitions become liabilities rather than helpful supports. And if she cannot change the definitions herself, then she is stuck with old definitions and a new life—and the incompatible nature of the two of them.

Focus on authorship. Rather than working on the work/life balance issues above, a developmentally oriented coach can look to see which definitions the person is embedded inside. A coach can help a client discover what things she thinks she's writing and what things feel out of her power to write, and see whether some of those boundaries can change. Ideas of authorship—who gets to write which things—can become central in this kind of coaching as the client begins to author more and more of the prevailing forces in her life.

Notice how Steve, the coach who begins this chapter, tries to do this with Shannon by helping her think about whether her life is written as the hero-in-victory or the hero-in-defeat. Steve's point is that Shannon can take a look at her story, notice that she's writing herself as a hero-in-defeat (if that's what's going on), and then rewrite the story. Without careful scaffolding around the very *idea* of writing your own story, however, Shannon may be more discouraged by this news than encouraged by it—like hearing she has some kind of stable deficit that will hurt her chances of success in the future. Shannon may believe that if her beliefs are self-limiting, there is nothing she can do to change them and she will simply be limited. Steve's point is that Shannon is able to change the forces of her life and rewrite her story, but unless Shannon can come to recognize this (and be convinced of her ability to do it), she is unlikely to be excited by the prospect.

COACHING AND THE SELF-AUTHORED MIND—AND BEYOND

Developmentally, people who see the world through a self-authored form of mind have, in many ways, exactly the characteristics and capacities that people expect from leaders. They are able to get on the balcony of a situation, can be less emotionally reactive, can choose what response to offer in a stressful situation (rather than believe the response is necessarily written by the situation, as they may have once believed with more of a socialized mind). They can distinguish between their perspective and the perspectives of important others and have a sense of their own "true north" as they find an internal compass that helps them make difficult decisions.

These capacities of mind, however, don't mean that such leaders necessarily have the skills or knowledge needed to do their jobs well. While someone at the more socialized form of mind may have a difficult time listening well to someone else's perspective because she is embedded in her own perspective (and can't gain a distance from it), someone with a self-authored form of mind may just not be interested in the perspective of another or may not have the listening skills to elicit it. As I remind coaches all the time, the *capacity* to do a thing is not the same as the *skill* to do it. And both of those are different from the *desire* to do it.[5]

Take Jonathan, for example. A successful executive at a large IT organization, Jonathan got in deep trouble with his boss, the CEO, for not listening to the perspectives of his direct reports on an issue they cared a lot about—job sharing. Jonathan dismissed their request out of hand and would not return to it, because it was his sense that it was bad for the continuity in the work he was doing in his division. His direct reports were enraged and went straight to the CEO, who had heard this story about Jonathan in other situations and thus recommended Jonathan for coaching. His coach, seeing Jonathan's inability to empathize with the perspectives of the others, wondered whether he had the *capacity* for empathy with such a different perspective. The developmentally minded coach knew that someone who is seeing the world through a predominantly socialized form of mind might be unable to hold the perspective of the direct reports simultaneously with the perspective of the organization in which he was embedded and also his own perspective—it's just too many different perspectives to hold at the same time. After conversations with Jonathan, however, his coach was able to get a sense that Jonathan clearly had the capacity for self-authorship. This meant that Jonathan had the *capacity* to take the perspectives of those others, but in a business situation where he was pressed for time and resources to meet a tight deadline, he had not seen the value in *exercising* that capacity. It turned out to be an issue of skills (to slow down and really listen to someone's perspective) and knowledge (that when people are upset, ignoring them doesn't tend to make the problem go away) that Jonathan needed rather than greater developmental capacities. The point is that capacity and skill are different, and it is here at the self-authored form of mind that coaches may want to help develop the skills that enable leaders to make the most of their sophisticated self-authored form of mind rather than necessarily helping them develop in ways that both build skills and expand their minds (as you may when coaching clients with self-sovereign or socialized forms of mind).

The developmental space for someone who sees the world through a self-authored form of mind is potentially twofold. She can work to consolidate her self-authored form of mind, to stretch it into more domains, and to have it be more consistently available to her (because it may be the case that in some of the domains in her life she has more difficulty sustaining her self-authored mind). Or she can work to expand this form of mind into more of a self-transforming space. I often make this choice clear to those with whom I work and also make the point that for most (but not all) leadership positions, the self-authored form of mind is quite a good match for the developmental demands of leadership.

Key Coachee Characteristics

As with people with the other developmental forms of mind, those who see the world through a self-authored form of mind display all different kinds of personalities and perspectives. What they have in common, though, is the capacity to believe that they author their own perspectives and circumstances. They tend to understand their own responsibility and authority in work situations and take an appropriate share of the blame when things go wrong (as opposed to those with a more socialized form of mind who might take either too much or too little blame).

Just like anyone with any other form of mind, however, those with a self-authored form of mind can get locked in their own perspective and lose sight of the different options. Often this is because their self-authored values and principles are so strong that they cannot imagine alternatives—they are subject to the beliefs they have authored. This begins to shift when the person makes a move toward the self-transforming form of mind. It is at this stage that the strong perspectives soften and open toward the benefit of competing ideas—even when those ideas seem, on the surface, to disagree with deeply held values or principles.

Coach Fit Characteristics

With a client with a self-authored form of mind—or beyond—a coach has to have enough internal authority to receive the client's respect; external markers or credentials are not going to be enough here. It is vital for clients at every form of mind to feel understood by their coaches and to have the sense that their coach can really make sense of who they are. The more complex the client, the bigger the demands on the coach for mirroring that complexity. One key benefit of understanding developmental theory for coaches is the way developmental theories extend your questioning and listening reach beyond your own order of mind; in this way, developmental theories act as a scaffold for coaches themselves as they help their most-sophisticated clients.

Transformational Benefits and Costs

Clearly there are a variety of leadership positions that are best suited to the capacities and perspectives of a self-authored leader. For these leaders, transformation may well have a cost as they become, in some ways, bigger than the job they're tasked with. In other situations, the leadership role itself can grow as the leader grows, leading to a helpful expansion of both the individual and the organization.

There are some leadership positions, however, that from the outset call for a leadership perspective beyond the self-authored space. For example, Mary was the founder and chief executive of a professional services firm that had what it called a "transformational" perspective on supporting its clients. Mary, who had worked in a variety of large firms before starting this one, wanted a firm that lived out its values in different ways than the firms she'd worked in before. She wanted her colleagues to use the firm and their partnership to enact their most precious values and principles and to also challenge each other so that they had ever-growing capacities anchored by the fluid community of people attracted to this kind of work. Mary became enormously frustrated by the fact that all eyes in the firm seemed to be on her, and everyone seemed to be wanting her approval and sanction. Work with a coach let Mary see, however, that she created that dynamic even as she was frustrated by it. She eventually—sheepishly—saw that the values she wanted her colleagues to enact were, in fact, her own values, and she mostly wanted them to enact those values in her way. Mary discovered that she needed to both hold on to the values that had led her to start the firm and hold on to the possibility that if her values were successful, the firm might reflect very different values than hers— a paradoxical request. For Mary, movement to the self-transforming space was the only way she could be the kind of transformational leader she so wished to be, and the only way her firm was going to be the firm she most hoped for.[6]

In every developmental progression there are costs as well as benefits, and it might be in the progression from the self-authored to the self-transforming that the costs need to be balanced most carefully—and the benefits are perhaps the least obvious. In most cases, the organizational and leadership world seeks and rewards self-authoring behavior. Leaders are stroked for becoming increasingly self-authored, and it may well be that the organization and the world agree that the self-authored space is as good as it gets.

To step away from that space and into one beyond it—one where there are few models and little social support—can feel like stepping off the edge of a cliff. One very articulate client, as she considered the move beyond her current self-authored form of mind, said:

> It's as if the world was flat and now, peering off the edge, I see that it's round, and I fear that if I step off into the round part, I'll look back and the flat part I know so well will be round too. And I'm afraid that if I turn around, I'll find that there's nothing left that I understand the way I used to know it. It just changes everything—nothing remains the same, and I'll be at the beginning of my knowing.

This reorganization of who she was and everything she knew before is a powerful and terrifying prospect. As a successful business woman, she was faced with the fear that moving into a new developmental space could make her less effective and less successful. She feared that she would lose "the fire in her belly," and she was terrified of the looming loss of certainty. To move from the self-authored space is to say that the self-governing system you have worked long and hard to create is never going to be good enough, that it's time to simply leave that work behind, give up on ever getting to certainty or perfection, and to move forward anyway. Taking that step, unsupported by most social or work pressures, can be enormously difficult.

Coaching Processes, Strategies, and Mindsets

Clients who see the world through the self-authored form of mind tend to be solidly in control of their coaching. They can name their goals and have a sense of what success looks like. Because of this, a developmentally minded coach can really add value to this coaching experience because she can introduce a set of questions or ideas that this client—no matter how thoughtful—has probably never considered.

A developmental coach working with a client who mostly sees the world through a self-authored form of mind might well have an explicit conversation about development. Those with a self-authored sensemaking system often do not imagine that there is a developmental space beyond their own (whereas many with a more socialized form of mind hear others describe a kind of inner voice which they may recognize as missing). The very notion that there are well-charted meaning spaces beyond the self-authored can be challenging for people in this space.

The other big advantage of offering clients a solid theory of adult development is that it assists self-authored leaders to see the potential variety of sensemaking systems in those around them. Leaders—like nearly all other humans—can be convinced that everyone should have the sensemaking approach and capacity that they themselves do. Just as other theories of individual difference (e.g., gender and culture theories, Myers–Briggs Type Indicator [MBTI] personality assessment, etc.) can be eye-opening, theories of adult development can be revolutionary for leaders in how they treat and grow their people. (See Appendix A for a reproducible handout that quickly introduces people to these ideas.)

As in situations with clients at every form of mind, a helpful question to ask is about whether this person's goals sound like they call on a skills or a technical change, or whether the goals call on the more transformational or developmental change. If transformation is most useful in achieving the client's goals, then the key task is to make the self-authored system more of an object for the client's reflection, and to have the client engage with others whose meaning systems might be different—or bigger—and see the value in these. There are several ways to do this.

Explore dichotomies. Track and uncover the dichotomies that the client's self-authored system puts as necessary truths in the world (like Jonathan's above, that if people were to no longer engage in their work full-time, there would be a continuity loss and the work would decline in value). Holding out these created dichotomies and asking about the shade of gray in between is useful at every form of mind, but is particularly helpful for those who are self-authored, because it encourages them to write and rewrite their own narratives—enlarging them or potentially even deciding that a single self-authored narrative is not enough for them and moving more into a self-transforming space.

Uncover assumptions. Even in the self-authored space, people are governed as much by the assumptions they hold about the world as by the principles and values they experience themselves as authoring. These assumptions—about which things necessarily go together, about how people are in the world, about how relationships work or what leadership looks like—create the shape of the world the leader lives in. To help leaders expand that world, a coach can listen for the assumptions—masquerading as truth—which underlie the questions and actions the clients report. For example, one executive I worked with believed that the senior leaders in his organization were good enough—and were not going to get better. His hopes were all pinned on leaders several layers deep in the organization, which was where he wanted the organization's resources directed. Because he believed—unquestioningly—that people at the highest levels of the organization were impossible to change, he did not invest effort in changing them (thus sustaining his initial belief). Once he challenged his belief and began to invest in his top team, small improvements began to take place in those senior leaders. This helped the executive see and question his initial belief, opening himself to the possibility of making other choices.[7]

Seek wise mentors and thinking partners. While it's useful for all clients to find mentors who support and value their work, it is especially important at this developmental space that the mentors have a kind of wisdom—or advanced development—that models new ways of being for the person who is looking at a transition beyond the self-authored space. Because of the serious costs of development from the self-authored space, and because of the dearth of models of highly developed people in most organizations, I urge clients to seek out people they consider "wise" and analyze what creates that sense of "wisdom" in their minds. Leaders may reasonably resist the loss of the self-authored mind (e.g., loss of clarity, loss of the conviction of a one best way), and having mentors who model the space beyond the loss can be enormously helpful. Similarly, leaders at this place need thought partners—people who ask good questions and help leaders see things they haven't seen before. While this is often what good coaching looks like anyway, leaders moving beyond the self-authored form of mind may find that their hunger for thought partners increases just as the pool of available partners is at its lowest.

Question certainty. Finally, one of the most useful habits of mind to develop for someone wanting to grow beyond the self-authored form of mind is a questioning capacity. Especially in those cases where clients are feeling certain about things and thus are the least interested in learning new things, I urge them to question what it is they think they know and to wonder how they could find certainty in such an uncertain world. While leaders would of course have pieces of their jobs they could be certain about, it has been my experience that a leader's certainty is more likely to come from an absence of curiosity about a range of positions rather than the presence of so much data that uncertainty is no longer an option. Leaders who begin to notice their own certainty and ask, "What am I closed off to learning in this space and how could I open myself to learning?" are putting their strongest-held notions at risk, a key marker for growth beyond the self-authored form of mind.

TABLE 4.1   Summary table of key characteristics and coaching interventions

Form of mind	Key characteristics	Core coaching interventions
Self-sovereign	Little or no sense of psychological functioning or of abstract concepts. Can be resistant to coaching if it seems too psychological.	• Listen without judgment • Attack the tactical • Change your mind before trying to change others
Socialized	Sense of self comes from others or from their role. People can either seem powerless to change themselves or can seem to take on too much responsibility, thinking they can solve anything.	• Question authorities • Write definitions • Focus on authorship
Self-authored and beyond	Sense of self internally created. Depending on where in the self-authored trajectory, could be tightly defending boundaries or loosening them to include other perspectives, principles, or values in their thinking.	• Explore dichotomies • Uncover assumptions • Seek wise mentors and thinking partners

Table 4.1 summarizes key characteristics of the different forms of mind, and coaching interventions to help them develop.

THE COACH'S GROWTH EDGE MATTERS, TOO

This chapter has focused on the developmental form of mind of clients and on particular coaching interventions that might be most effective for different people at different places in their development. It is fair to wonder, though, about the growth edge of *coaches* as well as their clients. When we are trying to help others, how does our own form of mind organize our experiences so that we see particular possibilities and do not see others? Probably quite a lot. What do we need to know about our own development, as coaches, to make the most of our opportunity to support and help our clients?

My sense is that coaching, like leadership, makes a particular developmental demand. This demand is for us to be clear about what the difference is between our opinions, positions, and feelings and that of our clients. We need to have nuanced understandings of the different perspectives that people might have inside the organization. We need to be able to understand the difference between being liked and doing our job well. We need to be able to use a variety of theories and tools and not be used by them—to pick and choose when to use particular tools rather than being disciples of one system of ideas or another. Each of these is a demand for some of the capacities and characteristics of a self-authored meaning system (or beyond). But given that the self-authored meaning system is not abundant in the world at large, do we withhold coaching certification or permission from those coaches who have not yet arrived at the self-authored form of mind? Even if we could do this (which we cannot), the idea of it is strongly at odds with the greater perspective of this book: That we can grow into the demands made upon us, and we can support the growth of others into those demands. So the question then becomes: How do we cope with the difference between our own highest hopes and aspirations and our current capacities—and how do we support ourselves to grow?

A little self-diagnosis goes a long way. For many coaches, simply learning about the theory itself is developmental, as we begin to ask ourselves the developmental questions the theory asks, and we begin to listen in a different way to our own answers. As we struggle with decisions or strong emotions—or anything that might show an edge to our own sensemaking—we can look inside ourselves and begin to understand which ideas we're most attached to, how we are weighing our options, who is authoring our response. Asking the series of boundary questions from Chapter 3 is a good beginning, and there are a variety of developmental supports throughout this book. Merely bringing focus to the key concerns of development brings it from subject to object and is in itself a developmental space.

Rub theories together. Coaches—like other reflective adults—tend to have particular theories or beliefs that guide our work on a day-to-day basis. We have common patterns and ways of engaging. We use particular tools or ideas to understand a situation and offer insight to clients. As we do this, we are sometimes intentionally using our tools and perspectives, and sometimes seeing through the lens of those tools and perspectives without understanding that we're doing it. This book is meant to be a useful but partial look at the world—and any developmental theory will be limited in lots of important ways. Taking new theories and putting them together—especially theories, practices, or ideas that are contradictory—gives us practice in holding the paradoxes of what it means to be human. For example, holding theories of individual development (like this one) along with theories of the way systems and groups work to influence each other can offer conflicting— sometimes directly competing—reasons for a particular approach or quite different explanations for the same event. While these differences are confusing, they are also helpful for keeping a kind of mental flexibility around issues that matter.

Listen to be unsettled. I teach leaders about how to listen to learn and expand the solution space—and to expand the number of people who are creating the solutions. Generally coaches are excellent listeners already, but those with whom

I work point out that they are excellent listeners *in their own particular way*. What this means is that they generally listen to learn about their clients and those clients' perspectives, thoughts, and actions, but they tend to do that listening through well-traveled paths, filling in a familiarly patterned landscape with this particular client's thoughts and needs. A theory of sensemaking like this one asks us to listen differently, to listen to be unsettled rather than to simply fill in common patterns. When listening for sensemaking, the core question isn't simply, "What do I think my client is making of this?" (although that's quite a good question). Rather it's, "How could I be really wrong about the sense I think my client is making about this?" The first question leads us to ask questions of our clients, the second requires that we also ask questions of ourselves.

Put yourself at risk for growth. Coaches are constantly supporting the growth and development of their clients; it's one of our central jobs. We ask our clients to try new things, to question their beliefs and assumptions, to see a bigger picture with a different set of possibilities. Part of being a developmentally oriented coach is remembering to do all those things for ourselves, to question our own assumptions, to put treasured ideas at risk. This means seeking out those parts of our own sensemaking that may frighten us. It means going toward the demons and questioning our most cherished beliefs. Often those who are in fields like coaching are attracted to growth and learning in many different ways. But those different ways tend to be patterned as coaches seek out particular areas of resonance and areas they feel they do best, that scare them the least (or at least scare them in a way that is most manageable). To be really facing the question of our own development is to also keep our eyes on what things scare us such that we *don't* want to do them.

CONCLUSION

In this chapter, I have offered developmental tools and practices and also cautioned about the costs of development for our clients—and thus for ourselves as well. I haven't made the point that simply *listening* for our client's growth edge can be an enormous gift. Because we tend not to have any way to gain distance on the structure of our thinking, simply having a structural set of theories in mind as you work with a client can open up new ways to help the client gain perspective on her own inner workings. I offer these ideas to clients not to pigeonhole them or to find ways to force or artificially manufacture their growth, but to give them access to a new sense of themselves and a new set of choices about who they want to be next. A developmental perspective is a fundamentally hopeful perspective, always seeing the way we can become bigger. By valuing clients—and ourselves—for their sensemaking and their journey, we honor what it means to be magnificently and imperfectly human.

5 TRANSFORMING PROFESSIONAL DEVELOPMENT

Diane came into a professional development program as a career-changer, someone who wanted to learn a new profession and take it into the workforce in a new way. She enrolled in a practical master's degree program, taking classes and working in the field. While she enjoyed the program, she was frustrated by what she saw as the hammering of a single philosophy and skill set rather than a grab bag of philosophies and skills for her to pick and choose among. She thought that as a professional adult, a program should give her a wide variety of things from which to chose so that should could forge her own way.

Phil had a different problem with his professional development program. While he too was making a career change, his program was too diffuse, the philosophy uneven and all over the place, the skill sets disconnected from one another and from his practical concerns. Phil thought that because this was a program for adults changing from one career to another, it should give the simple and coherent model needed by a new professional, and cut through the overcomplexity of too many perspectives and models.

There would be a variety of things those of us interested in creating learning experiences for professional adults might focus on in this pair of stories. We could try to find the sweet spot between too much theory and too little, too much of a grab bag of ideas versus too much complexity for the learner. The reason the sweet spot feels elusive in this case is that Diane and Phil were both going through the same program, both sharing the same classes, doing the same professional internship, and working for the same ultimate goals. If you had been sitting next to them in their classes, you'd have known they were enrolled together; if you heard them talk about their classes, you'd have sworn they were in entirely different programs.[1]

In the first four chapters of this book, we've looked at the way an individual's form of mind influences the way that person understands and relates to the world.

But many of us have responsibilities that are collective rather than individual, and we often have to think of our work in collectives rather than just one-on-one. How can thinking about a developmental theory—which is after all a theory of individual sensemaking—help us in these collective situations?

A key part of my own identity is as a teacher. I think of myself as a teacher when I'm working one-on-one with a leader in a coaching or consulting situation, when I'm teaching a long-term leadership development program to a collection of middle or senior managers, when I'm making a speech to 250 people, or when I'm here in my study writing a book, the dog at my feet as my only companion. In each of these domains, thinking about development helps me reach an audience—no matter how large—differently than I might be able to reach them without this theory in my head.

In Chapter 1, I made the distinction between learning that helps us learn new *stuff* (e.g., a new computer program or accounting system) and learning that changes *how we think* about the stuff we already know (e.g., a new organizing framework or theory that helps us reframe things we already know and see new patterns in old information). This is the distinction between informational learning and transformational learning. *Informational* learning is about increasing your stores of the content you know—the facts and the procedures and the content of your field. Transformational learning changes the form of your knowing—it makes you able to rethink about the things you've previously thought about and see them in a new way. Learning the concept that people have different sensemaking systems that change the way they understand and experience the world is *informational* because it gives you a new distinction about what makes us uniquely human. Actually considering these sensemaking systems as you go about your day can be *transformational* because it changes what you might notice as you talk to others or run ideas through your own head. As you continue to make this move, your scope of understanding grows, more things move from subject to object, and you become bigger as you see and understand more and therefore have access to choices and ideas you didn't have before. But in this case as in many other cases, the kind of information and the way the information is used are what can lead to transformation.

Transformational learning is what I'll talk about in this chapter, not because informational learning isn't important (it is!), but because transformational learning is what adult developmental theories help us understand.[2] Adult developmental theories help us know what we mean when we say transformation (the *form* of mind is changing) and how to encourage that change (with techniques that help move ideas from subject to object). These theories give us an organizing framework that helps people who are interested in transformational learning think about the ingredients that make learning truly transformational. For me, there are two key pieces to look at when we design transformational professional development experiences. The programs have to be psychologically spacious, and they have to be oriented toward changing the form of thinking. Whether you're designing leadership development experiences or trying to give teams support to work together more productively, these two ingredients can be woven through a program to make it transformational.

PSYCHOLOGICALLY SPACIOUS

Sometimes we use theories of individual difference to tighten our design, so that the learning will be as targeted as possible to the specific needs of the group in front of us. For example, if a facilitator[3] is working with a group of engineers who, he has been told, have a strong preference for specifics and examples, he might design a different learning experience than the one he did last week for the poets collective. This targeting of techniques and curriculum to the learning needs of the group we're working with is a time-honored and respectful way to help people learn.

When dealing with adult development, however, there are unlikely to be helpful guidelines to give you a shortcut that helps you discover what developmental forms of mind are represented in the seats in front of you. Dealing with a group of engineers? They might be all over the place developmentally. Poets? CEOs? Social workers? Shop floor workers? They might be all over the place developmentally, too. In fact, in most adult settings, you're likely to minimally have some blend of socialized and self-authored forms of mind, and it's possible—given the age and other characteristics of the audience—to have a single room of people who span self-sovereign to self-transforming forms of mind. With this potential range, targeting your teaching for one or another form of mind is not usually a helpful enterprise.

Instead, developmental theories call on us to *expand* our design and teaching to be psychologically spacious and to include as many different sensemaking systems as possible. This means that we need to think in new ways about things like how we make a beginning with a group (entry points), how we help them relate to our knowledge (relationship to authority and the truth), and how we judge our success (successful outcomes).

Entry Points

The first thing I consider when I try to create psychologically spacious professional development is to imagine the entry points my content might naturally have, and what entry points I could add to enlarge the space available to participants. Here, as in so many other pieces of human interaction, we often plan for others to enter the content in much the same way we ourselves do—or, if not in exactly that way, in the way a particular person or group of people who are well known to the us might enter it. This is natural, but it is not fully helpful if we are trying to get *each* person to learn and not just those who share characteristics with which we are most familiar or comfortable.

For example, I recently attended a workshop that focused on organizational culture. The consultant clearly and articulately laid out a version of a theory designed by the founders of her company, lined up the various ways this theory has been tested and found true in a variety of cultures and settings, and then used the theory to show the executive team something about the difference between the way they understood their organizational culture and the way others in the organization saw it.

From my perspective, this session—which was well-conducted and well-received—offered entry points for quite a small range of sensemaking systems. In Table 5.1, I outline some of the key elements of the workshop, and their relationship to the different forms of mind of potential participants.

You can see from this set of ideas that the entry points for this workshop were open to those who were hovering near the self-authored mind—transitioning to it or not much beyond it. This might be a fine mark to strike, as many leaders are in this space. As with Steve in the previous chapter, however, a facilitator in this space might find her approach broadened by looking at the different possible entry points for a wide variety of forms of mind. It can be especially helpful to look at the ways self-sovereign and self-transforming minds might open to these ideas, because these are so often neglected in the designs of organizational learning programs. Creating these open spaces isn't just good for those who might currently see the world through these two forms of mind, but also makes space for all different kinds of perspectives—and the sometimes temporary excursions we might make to sensemaking systems either more limited or more expansive than our usual system.[4] People who are seeing the world through different forms of mind need different questions answered right at the outset if they are going to engage.

Self-sovereign forms of mind. What's in it for me? What is the concrete reason I need to learn this? How will I be better off at the end in clear and tactical ways? How can this exact thing show me what I need (rather than having to transfer from one set of ideas to another, or from a game or a simulation to real life)?

Socialized forms of mind. What is the authority behind this information? Has an authority I can trust supported this and said it is true? What is the authority

TABLE 5.1   Entry points in culture seminar

Element of workshop	Assumption about sensemaking	Form of mind most suited	Form of mind most left behind	Form of mind too sophisticated
Described a theory of culture that was stable and enduring but could be changed with work.	That people understand that cultures are definable and malleable.	For those in the transition between socialized and self-authored to those with fully self-authored forms of mind, this theory about culture may feel familiar and able to be held and understood.	Self-sovereign. Culture is too much of an abstraction on its own without lots of clear examples; culture relies too much on the internal and abstract sensemaking of others. Similarly, someone with a predominantly socialized form of mind will often be too much inside the internalized organizational culture to be able to see it—or even know it exists.	Self-transforming or those with certain kinds of belief systems held by self-authored forms of mind. These people may believe that culture is lived in the moment and cannot be described as a universal; they may see culture as interconnecting mosaics (at individual and group levels) and want to approach it as a whole picture and also in ways that cast light on different pieces at different times.
Culture named as aggregate of opinions of others on either desirable or undesirable elements like aggression, warmth, etc.	That people can understand that cultures are created by collections of abstractions.	Socialized and self-authored forms of mind may be drawn to these ideas.	Self-sovereign will be potentially confused, which can be helped by the content a little. On one hand, there are too many abstractions of abstractions; on the other hand, the clarity around good and bad and the associated rules might be useful.	Those with socialized minds that hold in a very unified view of culture may also see this idea as simply wrong or misinformed. Some self-authored minds may have theories that are in conflict with this one. Self-transforming forms of mind may resist the dichotomous nature of the positive elements vs. negative ones, seeing more gray, more interconnectedness.
Theory offered by expert with data that told the truth about the organization.	That enough experience giving cultural surveys gives the authority to describe this particular culture.	This is a roomy assumption. Self-sovereign, socialized, and some self-authored forms of mind may be comfortable with these ideas.	These assumptions backed up by recognized authorities and offered as a kind of data-driven truth may well appeal to even self-sovereign leaders.	Some who are self-authored and simply hold different theories about cultures, or those who have more self-transforming ways of seeing the world, are less likely to believe in the ability of individuals to measure culture in a stable way, believing instead that the cultures are born in the moment.

of the person who is offering the information? (Remember that some people who see the world predominantly through their socialized form of mind do not trust conventional forms of authority and therefore the facilitator might need to have a range of authorities behind him to make a connection. Sometimes authority comes from practice rather than theory, sometimes from street smarts, or other sources. A facilitator who can use the various authorities he possesses is more likely to reach a wide variety of people in the socialized world.)

Self-authored forms of mind. How does this square with my own internal beliefs and ideas? Where is the room for me to edit or adapt what's being offered in order to hold it against my own beliefs and take (and leave) what I want? How open is the facilitator to lifting up the hood on these ideas or concepts and showing me the inner workings so that I can make my own decisions? How attached is the facilitator to thinking this is the one best way (which would be fine as long as I also believe it's the one best way but is otherwise a problem)?

Self-transforming forms of mind. How much does this program come from a view of the world that is consistent with or might add to my view of the world? Is there room here for nuance and subtlety, or do I get the sense that the facilitator has a hammer and sees all ideas as nails? What can I learn here? Is it possible for me to understand these ideas in a way that helps me see that they can be both true and not true simultaneously? How might we, as a group, generate additional ways of seeing these ideas? Will the facilitator play with me in that space or will he become defensive there?

So in the example above, the facilitator reached well into both the socialized and the self-authored spaces—as many good facilitators do. How could she have reached for those who might be seeing the world with a more self-sovereign mind? She could have come in and made really clear the connection between culture and other measurable, concrete features (e.g., productivity, attrition rates, sick leave). She could have had the group generate some specific examples of the different abstract categories, using those in the group whose forms of mind support their transferring from one context to another to generate examples across context. All of these small changes would have enlarged the space for those who were seeing the world through a self-sovereign mind, but would also have made good conversations and connections with others who had a variety of forms of mind.

Starting with the group's experience is also a good way to create entry points for those with self-transforming ways of seeing the world. Creating spaces for people to name and get grounded in their own experience is an important technique from a wide variety of perspectives (from learner-centered theories to brain-based learning practices), but it is also helpful in a developmental sense. Getting people to name their own connection to the core concept (whether it is an abstraction like culture or a more concrete set of procedures like performance management systems) makes space for each person to enter the content in his or her way. It also helps the facilitator understand where different members of the group are coming from. It is not all effortless, however, because if she finds out at this point that the group has a wide range of developmental styles, she has to be even more careful with the way she holds issues of authority and the truth, and the way she understands and describes potential outcomes.

Relationship to Authority and Truth

There are ways that other theories of individual difference suggest creating spaces large enough for many people to enter. Often these are about expanding our sense of what is possible and opening our eyes to the fact that our own way is not synonymous with The Best Way. Cultural theories, gender theories, theories of personality type—each of these contains recommendations for how someone might make space for those who are different from him. Using these theories of difference as your lens, you can often have different techniques side by side that remind you to do a variety of things: Use the body as well as the head, use connected forms of logic alongside more-objective forms of logic, pay attention to the variety of beliefs or customs or cosmologies in the room.

This is excellent practice for any number of reasons—it makes sense to shape your teaching to the needs of those you're trying to teach and to sprinkle a little of that idea here and a few of those ideas there in order to reach the widest possible audience. The problem with the appreciating-diversity technique, when you consider developmental ideas, is that you are dealing with people's hidden and fundamental assumptions about the world and about the way you hold those assumptions yourself. These are not just different ways of processing information or different sorts of language or different processes of learning; this is the way we make sense about *everything*. In no area is this more true than in the space of authority and ideas about what is true in the world. Earlier in our developmental journey, it is not just that we are uncomfortable with ideas more complex than our grasp; it is that we do not see those ideas as *possible* in the world and thus make judgments about our own capacities or the capacities of others. As we keep developing, it is not just that we come to add to what is possible for us; it is that we may no longer believe in the relationship to truth and authority that we once held dear.

To be most comfortable for those earlier in the adult journey—in the self-sovereign and socialized worlds—authority needs to be held in a way that is consistent with their beliefs. People who see the world through one of these forms of mind don't have *particular beliefs* about authority, but these different ways of making sense of the world lead to *different relationships* to the idea of authority or the truth. I'll take each one in turn.

Self-sovereign forms of mind. Authority from this perspective comes from identifiable sources and is generally closely associated with power. The person seeing the world mostly through a self-sovereign mind believes that truth and authority lie together. If the professor says that something is true, and it is the professor who is grading the papers, then that something must be true. If the boss says this is the one way it must be done, and the boss has power, then this is the way it must be done.[5] Framing things as expert-based is a help as long as the expertise is valued by this person (some people value ideas that come from practice, others ideas that come from theory or people in management or people not in management—it matters which is the authority in whom this person believes). Truth can often have a capital T and be held with ironclad certainty. When we are seeing the world through a self-sovereign lens, there are clear categories of things that are knowable and things that are not knowable. Those that are knowable are mostly known by experts and learned by others; those that are not knowable are not worth exploring very much, because it is a waste of time investigating that which cannot be known. A world described as full of gray is confusing and potentially frustrating when we see the world in black and white—or else there is the possibility that we simply won't engage with that world at all, ignoring the complexity we cannot see.

Socialized forms of mind. Authority from this perspective comes from identifiable sources and is attached to different roles or forms of community. Because the socialized form of mind deals more in abstraction than the self-sovereign, the connections to authority can be less concrete (e.g., to my boss, my teacher) and more abstract (e.g., to a particular theory, those in leadership positions, those who have X years of experience). When we see the world through this form of mind, power tends to come through role (e.g., manager) or community agreement (e.g., an informal head of a social group, a generally recognized thought leader). We hold ideas about the truth in the ways the rest of our group holds ideas about the truth. For many of us, when we see the world through the socialized form of mind, the truth looks like something *created* by experts and *learned* by ordinary people. More complex than the view we probably had when we held a more self-sovereign mind, the classic socialized view of truth has some categories that are known (and justified by experts or those with lots of experience or prestige) and other categories that are not yet known (but are being worked out) alongside categories where there might be multiple ways to think about what is true constructed by multiple authorities, none of which seems any better than any other. That third category—of hyper-relativism—means that we might believe that anyone with any opinion can have a valuable say, but no one could be right or wrong. It can be important for those who offer training on complex ideas not to wander too close to this boundary, because the strong relativism of this boundary means that there is no reason to learn very much in these spaces, as there is nothing better than anything else. (There are also, as I've mentioned elsewhere, socialized postmodernists who believe that the Truth is that there is no Truth.)

Self-authored forms of mind. Those with more self-authored forms of mind make their own decisions about what is true and where power comes from, and they tend to have a more eclectic approach—picking the ideas of one expert in one regard, relying on their own experience in another regard, and combining a series of ideas in yet another. One of the strengths of this form of mind is that we have the capacity to look at our own decision-making process and make choices about how we want to do things, such as choose who we believe in as authorities or what we'd like our relationship to truth to be. This means that what we want when we see the world through this form of mind is the permission and the space to pick and choose when we're faced with developmental opportunities. In learning events, we want to forge our own paths rather than follow a predetermined path, and we want the facilitators to mirror back to us a reflection of the world that is complex enough to be familiar to us—or to explain why they are mirroring a simplistic picture.

Self-transforming forms of mind. Truth and power are all contextual to us when we see the world through this form of mind. This can look like the hyper-relativism we experienced when we had more of a socialized mind; the difference is subtle. In the socialized form of mind, we throw up our hands and believe we cannot get at the truth because no truth is known—everything is as good as everything else. With more of a self-transforming form of mind, we believe that each truth is valuable and each offers a piece of the world that is helpful—and also that there are still ways to get better and worse decisions/outcomes/processes based on useful criteria. Instead of throwing up our arms in dismay, we reach out to hold as much as we can in our arms—often with delight. What we resist is someone who tries to back us into a particular corner or tie us tightly to one belief or another. When we see the world through this form of mind, we know others have certainty and others have truth, and this is fine for them. If someone offering training tries to make *us* own that certainty and truth, we may become difficult.

Holding these various perspectives in the same space is extremely difficult. To expand the reach of professional learning toward people who have at least some capacities beyond the self-authored mind (or very open self-authored systems), a facilitator has to allow people to hold her expertise lightly. To support the learning of those who have tighter ties to ideas of truth and authority, she has to hold on to her expertise strongly enough so that those who need the authority can see it. This is a very tricky balance, indeed.

This is because the facilitator, in order to hold the attention of those who are more self-transforming, needs to offer shades of gray. Talking about shades of gray might, if she's not careful, bewilder those who are less able to see the nuances—and might undermine her message. So the facilitator needs to allow those around her to have different sorts of relationships to her ideas—to allow some of them to use the ideas as The Truth and some of them to use the ideas as a metaphor or one among a variety of useful lenses. Perhaps the most difficult part of this task is that the facilitator herself, then, needs to hold the ideas as possible in each of these spaces. She cannot be attached to the notion of her content (whether it is about the best performance management system or the best personality descriptors or the best systems-design software) as The Truth if she wants to hold on to the respect of those who experience the world through their more self-transforming minds. She cannot believe that her content is simply one among a variety of equally good ideas, any of which she'll play out for people, if she wants to hold the respect of those who experience the world through their more socialized or self-sovereign minds. In this regard, it is *her own* relationship to her ideas that may create the psychological spaciousness that allows for entry points from people in a variety of different developmental places. While this is a natural perspective for many people with growing self-transformational forms of mind, it can be a learned perspective for others of us who aren't there yet. Knowing about this particular path and set of decisions makes it possible for us to act in ways that are beyond what we might spontaneously think about on our own.

Successful Outcomes

A final consideration when I'm creating psychologically spacious professional development is about how we make sense of the possible outcomes a person might have after going through the experience. This idea, while in many ways an obvious one, is something I have to learn and relearn as I work with different groups in different circumstances. Even though I study and teach about individual differences of all kinds, it can still be hard for me to remember that the kind of "learning outcomes" that many ask me to describe and plan for are unlikely to be actual "outcomes" for all. Learning outcomes, like everything else inside adult learning spaces, need to allow for developmental and other differences if they're going to mean anything.

For example, one of the things I teach about a lot—mostly with executive teams but also with others in organizations or schools or universities—is deep listening. Because there has been so much written on the connection between listening and leadership, creativity, teamwork, teaching, and so forth; and because listening is not something that almost anyone is naturally good at, I try to get groups of people to increase their skills at listening carefully to the content and intent of another person. In the earlier days of this work, I tried to accomplish the same goal for all of the people in my workshops: That people would be able to hear a statement and then offer a response that was a listening response, by actually saying back to the person the sense that they thought that person was making to herself. I tried to distinguish this from the most common responses—telling about themselves and making suggestions for improvement.

To help them get a handle on this idea, I'd play a fictional role and say something like, "I can't believe we had to deal with all that trivia at the meeting today! Do they know how many of our hours they waste and what a loss to productivity and morale those meetings are?" I'd ask participants to give me back something of the *sense* that person was making of her situation. They would struggle not to fix or tell, but to do this thing I called "listening." For the first years I taught this, I was struck again and again that some people simply *can't* get this. Not only can they not generate a listening statement on their own, but they cannot differentiate between the different types of statements when their classmates or I offer them as examples. Even with a variety of sentences in front of them, they cannot hear the difference between a listening statement ("So you found that meeting really frustrating?") and a telling statement ("I hated that meeting, too!") or a solution statement ("Have you talked to them about how stupid their agenda is?").

This happens consistently enough—not for very many participants, but for participants in workshops all over the world—that I know this kind of listening requires some capacity that not everyone has.[6] It's a particular developmental demand to ask someone to listen, because it requires separating out the meaning *you* make of something someone said from the meaning *that person* has made of what he has said. That distinction is difficult for someone who approaches the task with more of a socialized mind, and it is nearly impossible for someone who approaches the task with a more self-sovereign mind. Therefore, in my listening workshop, what outcome could I actually say I provide if some of the participants may not yet be able to get to that place I would normally think of as deep listening?

I have had to learn (and to continually keep learning) to think of outcomes as a walk from one place to another rather than as a walk to a particular, predetermined place. If you come into the workshop not knowing how to actively and purposefully listen, you should learn something about listening and should be better prepared to do it than you were before. Some people may learn how to make those distinctions between what is listening and what is telling. Others may learn how to make more subtle distinctions—between the *content* of what was said and the *emotion* that stands behind the content, for example. Still others might not be able to do any of that, but can realize that at least some people hear a kind of listening tone that they cannot yet hear—that there are others in the room who can see shades of gray which do not exist yet for this person, but which might exist in the future.

This openness to a wide range of possible successful outcomes can sometimes leave me a little lost about what it is I am really accomplishing, anyway. If I keep the major developmental goal of each form of mind in my head as I teach, I can begin to imagine what my particular content might look like for the range of people probably in the room.

Self-sovereign forms of mind. The key developmental outcome in any curriculum for someone seeing the world through a self-sovereign form of mind is simply to begin to see that he is part of a bigger world than he understood before. One element of this is for him to understand and take in the perspectives of others. This is a time to learn the benefits of subordinating your own needs to the needs of others, and so any teaching that asks this person to take and hold a really different perspective than his own is extraordinarily helpful. Similarly, any picture that unsettles a simple cause-and-effect view of the world can be developmental, like showing that different effects can come from the same cause or that the line between cause and effect is not necessarily a solid one. For example, someone in this space might have a solid cause-and-effect relationship between hours spent working on a job, and the reward that should spring from the job's completion (whether in financial or other ways) and not think about quality as an abstract concept as removed from concrete elements like hours invested. Or a person might hold the views of someone with whom she disagreed as simply stupid or bad rather than considering that the other person might have principled or well-reasoned rationale for disagreeing. Opening up the space to make these discoveries is developmental for someone with a self-sovereign form of mind.

Socialized forms of mind. The key developmental outcome for those seeing the world through the socialized form of mind is to begin to differentiate from the ideas and perspectives of others and to self-author these guiding concepts and principles themselves. In order to do this, she needs to listen carefully to what she thinks about things, balance her listening to others, and begin to separate out her sense of agency. Any outcome which has her thinking about and contrasting her idea with the idea of an authority in whom she had previously trusted—or which gives her permission to begin to author things for herself—will be developmental. Similarly, anything that makes object for her some of her internal assumptions, some of the connections she is making between abstract concepts to which she might be subject (like loyalty or success or happiness) and a possibility for her to create more-nuanced values or felt experiences around these abstract concepts will also be developmental. For example, if the image of leadership she has adopted requires always appearing to be certain, she might have to slowly understand the ways she is often uncertain, and then may need to look at her own experience with leaders who were thoughtfully uncertain. Then she can begin to build a more-nuanced relationship with her own uncertainty.

Self-authored forms of mind. The key developmental outcomes for those seeing through the self-authored form of mind are either around growth (toward self-transforming) or consolidation[7] (to bring more of their sensemaking into the self-authored space and to enlarge and hone that space). People who see the world through this form of mind often can make decisions about whether they want to be really challenged (and see the world in a different way) or whether they simply want to consolidate what they know. For the goal of consolidation, the key outcome is to make the self-authoring system itself more expansive, more compassionate, more whole (in whatever way the course objectives or personal objectives of the leader might suggest). Here the challenge is often about helping the system become more coherent, smoothing out internal inconsistencies, adding new behavior patterns that are more helpful than previous ones. For the goal of growth, the key outcome is to begin to come to terms with the fact that no matter how expansive and carefully crafted the self-authored system might be, it will always be partial, always be coming from a single set of eyes and a single perspective. It will never be fully coherent because humans are fundamentally incoherent. It is only when someone begins to see that in at least some circumstances a self-authored system is too small that he begins to reach toward a more self-transforming system.

Self-transforming forms of mind. (Note that because research has not convincingly discovered or described a form of mind beyond the self-transforming mind, and because there are so few people actually there in the first place, this will just be about deepening and consolidating in the self-transforming space.) For those in a more self-transforming space, growth is a part of everyday life and so transformational learning experiences take on a different flavor. Here the powerful outcomes are less about helping a person enlarge herself. Rather, the experience might be more about helping her gain a perspective she had not seen before. People at this space are eager for new lenses through which to see the world, and they thrive on complexity, ambiguity, and possibility. A key delight is to take multiple perspectives on an issue and then be challenged to take perspectives on those perspectives. Another possibility can be to simply hold up a mirror to the complexity of this person and support her to feel known in the fullness of this form of mind. Because that is a rare experience for people with this sensemaking system, the feeling of being well-seen can be powerful and lasting.

In Table 5.2, I offer to facilitators a quick glance at what outcomes you might seek, developmentally; how you might reach for those outcomes; and questions you might ask yourself about your success with people making sense with various forms of mind.

No single program or activity will encourage everyone to grow in similar ways. The point here is to begin to think about success—yours and theirs—in new ways so that you can set realistic goals for transformation, and so you can be gentle with yourself and others along the way.

One way to keep anchored in a large range of possible outcomes is to focus on the difference between informational learning (which might have one kind of definable outcome) and transformational learning (which might have another).

TRANSFORMATIVE PROFESSIONAL DEVELOPMENT

If what you want is for people to *understand new kinds of content*—what the procedure is for managing a supply chain and making decisions about ordering, for example—then information is probably what you would need to offer. You'd probably be interested in having everyone in the group understand the same content in the same way, and you would likely be able to develop an assessment that tested people's achievement in that regard.

If what you want is for people to *think about things in new ways*—for example, to weigh the various systemic needs when managing the supply chain and making decisions about ordering—you need to create a transformative learning space. For something to be transformative, it needs to change the shape of people's thinking—they need to be seeing some piece of the world in a new way. This happens in a variety of ways, but using a developmental theory helps us understand a rough five-stage process.

Step One: Getting It on the Table: Making Things Object

Transformational learning—by the definition I'm using here—needs to help promote a subject–object shift. I think in these cases about participants getting things out on the table. This happens when people see something about themselves that they were previously blind to: an assumption, a mental model, a belief about role

TABLE 5.2 Key outcome, design elements, and questions that support people at different forms of mind

Form of mind	Key outcome	Pieces to consider including in the design	Questions for a facilitator to ask himself about successful outcomes
Self-sovereign	To broaden her perspective and learn that she is part of a bigger and more complex system than she previously understood.	Opportunities to have people understand the complexity of various situations by giving concrete contexts and examples. Giving people real experiences of being broadened and assisted by the thinking of others.	Have I given people the opportunity to show that they can hold the perspective of another person? Have I made room for people to demonstrate a capacity to subordinate their interests to the good of the group in some way?
Socialized	To focus his perspective on his own thoughts, ideas, and principles, to give him the sense that he can *create* his experience, context, and reactions rather than simply *having* them.	Opportunities to have the time and permission to author key ideas for themselves. Time and space for people to find their own path, connecting the content to their own experience and feeling the freedom and encouragement to adapt rather than adopting.	Have I given time and space for people to express the distinctions between what experts think and what they themselves think? Have I offered the idea, repeated more than once and with examples, that people can author their own path, write their own contexts?
Self-authored	*For consolidation:* To improve upon and enlarge the self authored system. *For growth:* To begin to recognize some of the limits of the self authored system and the need to be co-creating systems with others.	*For consolidation:* To reflect on the self-authored system, make it object, and make decisions about how it could be extended or improved. *For growth:* To look at complex or ill-structured problems and come to the understanding that no self-authored system will ever be complex enough to make real traction in a world filled with ambiguity and uncertainty.	Have I given people the time and space for reflection on their own sensemaking? Have I helped people see parts of their internal assumptions about the way they have authored their lives that they might want to change or adjust? Have I offered the opportunity to have people interact with a variety of complex and very different viewpoints (none of which is obviously better or worse) and hold those viewpoints together with their own perspectives?
Self-transforming	To continue to learn and grow—taking a larger and larger view over time.	Opportunities for people to walk around the full edges of an issue, to compare with those who are dissimilar, and then to take a perspective on the multiple perspectives.	Have I allowed the world to be as complex as possible without allowing people to simply throw up their hands in dismay? Have I offered chances for people to find multiple perspectives on a single issue and to discover all that is right (or wrong)—and partial—in each of them? Have I allowed people chances to find ways through the complexity of an issue, to try to construct pathways that fit the context?

or focus or procedure. Once a belief/assumption/idea becomes an object for your reflection, you can place it on the table in front of you, walk around it, make decisions about it, and decide what other things to have on that table (or indeed, whether to have anything of this variety at all).

Because we tend not to see what we are subject to (which is how we have remained subject to it), a facilitator often has to use some technology to make this hidden thing become more object. This technology can be literally technological—like a video camera. It can be relational—like when you talk to a respected colleague about a perspective she holds which is quite different from yours. It can be fictional—like watching a film or reading a book and comparing those lives with your own. It can be internal—like keeping a journal. It can be a particular exercise, like Kegan and Lahey's "Immunity to Change" exercise (from their 2009 book of the same title). In any case, it needs to bring to the surface some piece of our sensemaking that we are subject to and give us a good look at it.

For example, to prepare for one leadership course, participants were asked to pay attention in the weeks leading up to the course to problems in their teams that seemed to need solving again and again. Supriya noticed that she spent far too much time engaged in doing the work of her direct reports—answering questions that they should have known the answer to, redoing work that came in to her half-finished way, and so forth. She had not articulated this to herself (she laughed and said she was far too busy to notice this pattern!) until she began to pay attention to it. Once she started to notice, she realized that she was spending most of her time not working at the level of her role because she was tidying up the work of her direct reports. Getting the issue on the table was a major discovery for her as she paused just to take stock of her situation.

Step Two: Walk Around the Table Curiously

It's not enough to hold something out as object just for the sake of doing it, though. Thinking, "Hmm, isn't that interesting that I do too much of the work for my direct reports" doesn't get Supriya very far. Just putting something on the table doesn't mean that you'll understand or be able to deal with it differently. Instead, it's important to walk around the table, to take a variety of perspectives on the issue and to ask a variety of questions about it. Supriya's program required her to wonder why she was spending time in this way. Was it because that was the work she liked best and felt most confident about? Was she really a terrible teacher, so unclear in her instruction that her people couldn't achieve the proper standard? Was she actually afraid of doing the work at the level of her role because she feared she wouldn't be good at strategy and long-term planning and other more leaderly tasks? As she examined the issue, some questions hit home (yes, she was anxious about the strategy stuff) and others fell flat (she was actually a fantastic teacher, and she wasn't particularly glad to do that more tactical work again). All of this wondering gave her a bigger sense of why she had been so stuck.

Step Three: Invite Others to Your Table

Bumping up against people who are different or who hold different assumptions or solutions or ways of thinking about the world is one of the most powerful ways to make sense of your own perspective—and hold it as a perspective rather than the truth about the world. Transformational work can be done with individuals (as the coaching chapter suggests), but it is very powerful to make use of the diversity of a group to get many different ideas on the table—to all be examining these perspectives together.[8] This is obviously helpful in situations where assumptions are at the root of the issue (as in a change process where people's assumptions about what is necessarily true and constant may be getting in the way of their imagining new possibilities). It is also helpful in tackling some of the most common—and most seemingly intractable—leadership issues, like Supriya's. Because a group of leaders will often acknowledge that they, too, struggle with some core issues, the loneliness and shame of making the same mistake again and again decreases. Because each person thinks about these difficult issues in a different way—and because each of these different ways is partial but useful—putting many versions on the table offers more options for each individual to select from.

Step Four: Don't Just Do Something, Stand There

One of the most counterintuitive pieces of transformational work is the need to avoid solutions and action—at least in the beginning. Many people have written about the potential loss associated with creating solutions too quickly.[9] In transformational work, it's not just that people need time to get the problem well-defined, but that the *problem itself* is instructive and useful. Those things to which we are subject are, in many ways, the signposts that point toward regions of greatest possible growth for us. If we simply fix the thing on the table without being curious about it and wondering how we could make different forms of sense about it, it might make the problem go away (momentarily) but wouldn't help us develop.

Step Five: Keep the Table Set

The final thing to remember about transformational work is that we generally tend to forget about what's on the table, have the things that used to be invisible to us return to invisibility, and just move on to what we were doing before. Even after understanding and paying attention to multiple perspectives and options in the transformational space, it is still important to keep reflecting on the issue at hand. Once Supriya worked to put systems in place that would enable her direct reports to do their own work so she could get on with hers, she was on the alert for any falling back she might do—when a new person came on the team or when the context changed enough for the systems she had put in place to break down some. Keeping the issue as an object for her reflection, rather than as a force she was subject to, helped her learn and change—transforming her practice and her leadership.

These five stages are useful in a professional development context because all of them can be designed into the setting of a program. Once you begin to understand the ingredients for this type of transformation (because you understand this version of the "form" which changes), it makes a variety of calls on program design. For example, having people do the inner work to get elements of their knowing on to the table is rarely a key element in professional development workshops; often, we want to tell people how to be different rather than beginning with the assumptions and habits that make them who they are today. Similarly, if we are to keep elements on the table in company and over time, we need to design group experiences into the programs—and we need to avoid the one-day transformation that many of our clients still crave.

Combining both psychologically spacious and transformative professional development practices is not always possible—and doesn't always match client interests. In those cases where clients and program participants are interested in making long-term, substantive changes, however, these techniques might help us be better company for their journey.

People sometimes ask what the difference is between those who seem to use potential growth opportunities to grow, and those who seem to ignore the potential for growth and instead solidify their former forms of mind. We probably all know people who have turned away from potentially transformational opportunities, and people often want to know what makes that so (and how to keep from falling into that trap themselves). While there isn't any magic wand that helps people transform, there are particular habits of mind that seem to not only encourage growth now, but also to encourage growth well into the future. This chapter has been about the kind of seeds you might plant and how you might plant them; there's still the very real question of the soil in which those seeds get planted.

Are there particular ways of thinking about the world that lend themselves to growth? My partner, Keith Johnston, and I have found that there are three distinct but related "habits of mind" that seem to contribute more to ongoing growth than any others. These habits, whether sprinkled into professional development programs, encouraged in coaching, or practiced in the course of a workday, seem to help shift forms of mind over time. They help prepare the soil for growth for this season as well as the next and the next. I turn to those in Chapter 6.

6 TRANSFORMATIONAL HABITS OF MIND

At every organization I know, people are stretched to their limits. They are asked to do more with less, to operate effectively in roles that used to belong to two people (or three), to cope with changing demands and keep up with ever-increasing complexity. They are so busy *doing* the work that they have little time to *think* about the work, and even less time to step away from the work to learn new things. Learning that takes place on the job is rushed and uneven, and learning that takes place alongside the job (in programs or coaching sessions) is compressed and sometimes disconnected from real work. Is it any surprise that these busy people aren't absorbing more of what they want to be learning?

In fact, I bet we all have the experience of a program or event that seemed powerful at the moment and disappeared quickly when we got back to our real lives and our real jobs. *Sustainable* professional development means that the learning doesn't disappear but is connected into the fabric of someone's sensemaking, changing what is possible for that person into the future. In this chapter, we'll look at the way developmental theory, transformational learning theory, and the new and expanding world of neuroscience—taken together—help us find ways to support people's development into the future. These theories suggest that the key way to support lasting change is to create *habits of mind* which do not only support this change but also make future changes more possible. This is to not just change what *content* people make sense of, but the *processes and procedures* with which they make sense.

This sort of development is organizationally sustaining, because it means that the individuals in organizations are better prepared and able to learn. In an organization with ever greater numbers of people with these habits, there would be a fertile and growing appetite to continually learn and grow, and each job would turn into its own learning engine. Because, in the long run, the point isn't to simply design excellent coaching and group interventions that support growth; the point is for organizations themselves to support growth. Systems thinking expert

Peter Senge (and others) talk about the "learning organization," but here I am talking about the *learners'* organization: a place where learners show up to work, not just to do their jobs but to learn from the doing of their jobs so they can do the job better tomorrow and the day after.[1]

When we learn at work, it should not only benefit organizations but also be personally sustaining. I'm not talking about offering scuba lessons at lunch time or asking about your relationship with your mother at the quarterly retreat. I'm talking about the need humans have once our more basic needs are met: to make something of our lives, to leave a legacy, to connect with others and ideas and actions. Our learning should allow new things to happen for individuals and get them closer to their deepest goals—even as we are moving the goalposts to new and bigger hopes and dreams. Learning at work should be about making possible tomorrow things that were not possible yesterday—both for the benefit of the organization and the benefit of the individual. And, if we are to take this idea of the learning organization seriously in a new way, the context that nurtures development must change as the people change.

Of course, our developmental context matters for our entire lives. When we are babies, the developmental force within us pushes us to grow, to constantly learn and explore and try new things. We are learning machines. As we age, we lose some of that push until, as educators have widely bemoaned, by the time we are in secondary school, most of us are bored by the whole prospect of formal learning. Some people rediscover the love of formal learning at a university; others in vocational or trade programs where they learn an art or a discipline or trade that will be important to them into the future. We don't yet know why some pieces of our life support our learning better than others. Maybe when we're young and we are surrounded by so many mysteries, we push ourselves to learn and grow. Maybe we are wired to learn and grow like crazy until we are old enough to produce offspring, who then take over learning and growing like crazy. And of course there are individual variations as well. Who knows why one toddler who falls and falls while learning to walk turns into the executive who won't take a single risk and another toddler—falling just as much—turns into the sort of person who continues to grow and develop her whole life?

Developmental theory shows us that as we grow, we become more aware of the losses associated with our growth. A baby does not know that when she learns to crawl, she is giving up a lovely developmental time when she can be content watching the world from a single seat (although her parents may understand this and face her crawling with a kind of delighted ambivalence). A toddler does not know that when he learns to speak, he is giving up a world that is unbounded by language, a world filled with nonlinguistic possibilities he will never get back. And in some ways these characterizations are absurd. The baby's life is surely more fun and exciting once she can crawl over and get what she wants, and the toddler's must be less frustrating once he can communicate fully with those around him. Still, many parents mourn these key passages as they celebrate them, knowing that each new stage is both a beautiful set of new possibilities and also the end of an era that will never return.

Our losses becomes more alive to us as we become more able to think in abstract ways, and we begin to hold more tightly to our old meaning systems and do not crawl toward the unknown future with such abandon. Child psychologist Jean Piaget talked about the effort children put in to making new information fit with their old sensemaking—trying to assimilate new data points into old (and very implicit) theories about the way the world works.[2] It is only when it becomes too difficult to assimilate these new data points that children finally change themselves and begin to accommodate—to grow bigger ways of thinking about the world to fit the bigger world they now have access to. This process does not get easier as we age; in fact, in some ways, we get more caught by our own sensemaking and more invested in the current way we see the world. Brain scans show that our brains often simply ignore unexpected data, showing us only what we were expecting to see in the first place. Scientists all over the globe ignored the first years of data showing there was an expanding hole in the ozone layer, dismissing the data they weren't expecting as meaningless computer noise. Our adult brains and psyches seem to have a cottage industry set up to prevent our (emotionally costly and disorienting) learning.

And yet some people do naturally go toward growing. What is the core difference in these people and how can we share that around more evenly? Research in creativity and flow suggests that it is curiosity that breaks through to this, and that through curiosity we can recover some of the delights of learning without so many of the fears.[3] For this to happen, people have to be seriously engaged in learning that is helpful, where the payoff for the learning is not just disorientation but increased capacity to do something useful or something for which they will be rewarded. In my own work (with many colleagues, but especially with Keith Johnston), I have tried to develop sustaining and sustainable habits of mind that meet my requirements: They are teachable, they are psychologically spacious (e.g., any adult might get better at these no matter where he had started), they are useful in organizational settings, and they are inherently developmental (because they move a variety of different things from subject to object). There are probably a variety of habits of mind which meet these criteria, but the three Keith and I focus on are: asking different questions, taking multiple perspectives, and seeing the system. We've found that these habits can be built into coaching and professional development programs, and can also be knit into the fabric of work itself (as we'll show in the next section). As we develop these habits, we grow.

ASKING DIFFERENT QUESTIONS

Asking different questions is perhaps the most underrated of all learning skills. People ask the questions they know how to ask whether or not those are the most helpful questions. We are so used to asking these familiar questions, in fact, that we do not recognize that they are familiar and that we know the answers. Some of the most familiar questions come from the perspectives available to the form of mind which created them. You can see from Table 6.1 that we don't lose the questions

TABLE 6.1   Questions most associated with particular forms of mind

Form of mind	Classic questions
Self-sovereign	What's in it for me? Do others have to do exactly this same thing? What are the consequences of this for my getting more of what I want in the future? What are others doing that will affect me? Who is in charge and enforcing things here? What are the rewards for something that meets (or exceeds) the standards? What is the consequence for something that does not meet the standards?
Socialized	What will others say? How will this change my standing in my core group/role (in which I am embedded)? Is it the appropriate thing for me to be taking on given my role/experience/education? Am I doing this right? Are others doing this right? Who can tell me whether I've done it right or not? How will I know?
Self-authored	How does this forward my bigger goals/values/principles? What contribution do others make to this? With whom do I need to coordinate or collaborate? How do I know that this is the right thing for me to be doing? Have I really thought hard enough about this? Is it within my scope to do it? Is it a good problem to take on? How might I interact with others on this? How do I develop the standards to judge my success?
Self-transforming	What can I learn from this? What assumptions about the world underpin my actions or opinions about this? The actions or opinions of those around me? Is the framing of this issue compatible with the way I see the world? How does it connect to the other things I am working on and care about? How do I work with others to shape and reshape this issue? How does this issue shape and reshape us? What is lost if I succeed here? What is gained if I fail?

from a previous form of mind as we grow—it is always important to us to know "What's in it for me?" We do expand our questions as our form of mind grows, and this expansion opens us up to new questions. These questions shape our reality because they shape the data we seek and thus the data we find.

If we are to really grow on the job, though, it becomes vital for us to not simply ask our regular questions again and again, but to ask questions that move us beyond the frontier of our current understanding. This is paradoxical because we are often rewarded at work for knowing the answers rather than asking the questions. We are generally not rewarded for uncertainty, yet having the courage and the ability to ask different questions, and being open to a wider range of possibilities, is key to equipping us to manage complex issues. What many people do not understand is that the questions we automatically ask—the questions that our brains form without much effort from us—are questions that keep us on the same path, questions whose answers are unlikely to surprise us. In fact, we have found in our practice what neuroscientists find in the brain: When we are the most surprised, we are the least likely to ask good questions. Rather, in conditions of uncertainty, we tend to ask questions that will move us back into familiar ground. When the time is most ripe for our learning, our reflexes push us away from learning and into something that feels more comfortable. To be able to ask different questions, questions that will keep us learning, is a habit of mind that stretches the brain, makes possible new discoveries and new connections, and creates a distinctive learning system.

It is not just our form of mind that shapes our questions. Our background, our gender, our culture, and even the particulars of our jobs and our educational experiences all shape the questions we automatically ask. While it would be helpful to understand the wide range of questions that come up for you naturally, in Table 6.1 I chart the questions that emerge from different forms of mind. These aren't the only questions someone at this form of mind might ask, and people at many forms of mind might ask these particular questions at different times and in different contexts. These questions, though, are the ones that might arise naturally for these different sensemaking systems. For any individual, less-sophisticated questions might arise in a more-stressful situation, and more-expansive questions might arise in a more-supportive situation. In the table, see whether there are some groups of questions that seem to you to be most like the ones you might ask at your best, and some that represent the questions you might ask when you're feeling smaller or more self-protective than usual. Play around with them and see whether asking yourself some of these questions takes you to a different space—whether more open or more closed.

It is useful to understand these typical questions for two key reasons. Knowing what questions you are asking automatically shows you something of the internal operating system you're using for a particular issue. Perhaps more exciting, it's also helpful to have a sense of these questions because they can support you to grow. It turns out that by asking questions that are typical at the next form of mind along the developmental path, you can have transformational experiences and intentionally grow yourself. I'll show you what I mean.

Knowing Yourself

Clare was the chief executive of a nonprofit with an excellent reputation in its field—much of it based on people's belief in Clare's leadership. To most issues she brought a set of questions that were about questioning assumptions, continuous learning, and bringing a strong and clear vision into the world—a mix of self-authored and self-transforming questions that arose naturally from her sophisticated form of mind. On one particular project, however, a partnership with a key community stakeholder group, Clare's questions were much less sophisticated. She was anxious about whether the community partner would think her people were doing it right, and she was much more concerned than usual about reputation. Talking with a coach about this, she realized that it was the presence of her first boss and mentor—who was now the chief executive at the partnering organization—which was pulling on her attention and, she discovered, making her questions less sophisticated. Once she understood this pattern, she could consciously break it and return to her more-sophisticated questions—and more-sophisticated and inquiring form of mind.

Growing Yourself

Sean was a middle manager at a prestigious financial firm. With a primarily socialized mind, Sean was asking questions about how he would know he was doing his work right, when he would achieve a kind of externally oriented vision of success, and how he would ever live up to the standards of important others who had different values and gifts than his own. Work with a coach on asking different questions—questions more typically associated with the self-authored mind—offered him a new set of perspectives and ideas. Rather than asking himself how he could meet the externally oriented set of values he had adopted from the world around him, Sean began to ask about how his work forwarded his bigger goals/values/principles. This meant that he had to first come to some understanding in himself about what those goals/values/principals really were and how he would make choices between the many options of what is good in the world to pick those that were most important to him. Then he was ready to ask another question he had not asked before: How do I develop the standards to judge my success? This was in a different realm from the questions he had been asking himself, and the answers both surprised him and took him to a new place. He discovered that in fact he had very different ideas about what was important in the world than those of his role models, and he began to exercise his creativity in new ways rather than simply trying to be one of the company men he once thought he wanted to be. This change opened up new career pathways and allowed Sean to come to new places in his thinking and his action—and to achieve success along his own lines. As he began to strengthen his self-authoring form of mind, he found that those questions which had been so difficult for him to entertain six months earlier became possible for him to ask on his own. Over time, he came to have the self-authored questions as his default questions.

The questions we ask change what is possible for our learning and our understanding. By asking different questions, we open to a new world. These questions move ideas from subject to object, and allow new thinking with new thoughts.

TAKING MULTIPLE PERSPECTIVES

Taking multiple perspectives enables people to see a wider range of possibilities, be able to empathize, make deeper connections, and understand the views of others. Even with these benefits, taking multiple perspectives isn't natural for most people. Once again, the brain acts as a filter, keeping from view any perspectives or ideas that might be disconcerting—or that might actually teach us a thing or two.[4] Learning the habit of intentionally taking other people's perspectives stretches the mind and makes it possible to see new options. And when someone has the habit of taking multiple perspectives for herself, others begin to sense the openness and begin to offer information that a person with a more closed perspective and affect might never hear. This means that the multiple perspectives begin to be fed from within and from without, and people have greater access to the broader views they need in order to address complex issues.

Because of this, one key to transformational and sustainable professional development is the degree to which taking multiple perspectives becomes a habit. One way to ensure this is to work opportunities for taking other perspectives into learning and work experiences. It is perhaps this habit of mind more than any other that benefits so strongly from having a group experience; giving people an opportunity to have their own perspectives enlarged by the perspectives around them can help them grow.

TABLE 6.2   Perspective-taking capacities when people agree and disagree about important issues

Form of mind	When you have a perspective that agrees with mine	When you have a perspective that disagrees with mine
Self-sovereign	You have the right values and perspectives—you see clearly and you put the facts together appropriately.	You're either with me or against me—if you're against me, you are incorrect and are not seeing things with a logical (or moral or correct) perspective. Because this shows a flaw in you, it seems unlikely to me that I will find common ground with you on anything.
Socialized	You are one of "us." If you share my belief about this issue, it is likely that you'll share my belief about other things which are important to "us."	You are one of "them" and perhaps could become one of "us" in time if you changed your actions. There might be some ways we agree, and depending on how vital this issue is to me, I might be interested in finding common ground.
Self-authored	You and I share perspectives on this issue—which does not necessarily mean we will share perspectives on future issues.	I seek to understand your reasons for holding a different opinion because often it is the people who disagree with me who help me hone and shape my argument the most. I can judge—and perhaps admire—your logic irrespective of your view on this one issue.
Self-transforming	You and I may agree on this issue, but my guess is that we probably have a whole different sense that we make of the issue and we probably agree for a variety of interestingly distinct reasons. I'm curious about the differences in why we might agree about this.	I am interested in all views on all issues because they push my thinking around and help me learn. Your disagreeing view might change the way I think about my own opinion, adding nuance and complexity. I recognize, in fact, that the only reason I can even hold one perspective strongly is because someone else holds the opposite perspective strongly—that in some ways, your opposite perspective creates and enables mine.

Perhaps it is not surprising that at every developmental form of mind, it is easier to take the perspective of someone who agrees with you than someone who disagrees with you. In fact, increasing capacity to cope with differing perspectives is perhaps the hallmark of growth. In Table 6.2, I offer a quick look at this changing capacity.

Obviously, people in organizations—like people in families and communities everywhere—disagree with one another and need to deal with that disagreement. Understanding our natural differences helps moderate hopes for the ways people might handle conflict. It also helps support people's growing capacity to take the perspectives of others by offering different images of what is possible. It's not that we intentionally make a decision not to take the perspective of another person—that just happens. We simply don't notice that we're not taking another person's perspective. Or, equally common, we take another person's perspective in the most basic and limited way. When someone seems impossibly self-serving to you, you try to be generous and think, "Well, that person thinks that being so self-serving is important for some reason" (and often our perspectives go downhill from here). If we work in collectives to stretch our perspective-taking capacity, we can be encouraged not only to take the perspective of another person, but to check that perspective-taking with those around us, to ask, "Does this seem like a reasonable view on Jim's possible perspective?"

To get this point across, one exercise in a leadership development program asked participants to focus on the person they found to be most antagonistic to their making progress on something important to them. Participants talked about the idea that each person was the hero in his or her own story, and that what they saw as divisive or troublesome in some way, the other person saw as some form of heroism, some protecting of their integrity. In groups of three, they had to come up with three different possible—but heroic—reasons for the action of their antagonist. Coming up with the first one was not so hard, but other group members tended to point out that that first one was not so heroic after all. Coming up with the second one was easier. By the time they discussed the third possibility, on participant called out in a loud voice, "Oh damn! Now I have no idea why she is doing what she is!" When the facilitator asked him what he was going to do about that, he gave a shrug and laughed ironically, "I guess the last resort is to actually talk to her and find out!"

In this way, the habits of mind are interactive and mutually reinforcing. When you take the perspectives of others, you come up with new questions to ask. New perspectives create new questions which create new perspectives. The third habit of mind, seeing the system, helps you see the relationships between the questions, the perspectives, and the enabling and constraining forces of the wider system.

SEEING THE SYSTEM: MANAGING PATTERNS AND POLARITIES

The media is filled with accounts of how much more connected we are to one another: through our technology, through our social networks, through the miracle of air travel. It's true. I can instantly find out the current temperature nearly anywhere in the world. I can have clients in New York and New Zealand. I can eat breakfast with a colleague in Sydney and have a late dinner with a friend in Bangkok.

Because of this, there are patterns available for us to see that we never could have seen before: cultural differences, geographical differences, economic or fashion or mindset differences. We can look across large swaths of time or place and think about how things are different, how they're the same. So because we have access to more data, we have access to more patterns. But a pattern isn't a thing that actually exists in the world; it's a construction, a made-up clumping and analysis. It's about constructing and sensemaking. So it's not as though patterns just *are*; it's that they come into being when we *notice* that they are.

For example, what is the pattern in this series of numbers?

2 4 6 8 10 12 14 16 18 20 22 24 26 28 30 32 34 36 38 40 42 44 46 48 50 52 54 56 58 x.

What does x equal?[5] Easy, right? We agree on this sort of pattern and learn it when we're young.

How about this one:

1 2 3 4 5 6 7 8 9 2 4 6 8 10 12 14 16 18 3 6 9 12 15 18 21 24 27 4 8 12 16 20 24 28 32 36 x.

What does x equal?[6]

How about this one:

7 0 6 4 8 1 8 3 2 1 6 1 7 5 7 6 0 0 8 5 2 0 2 2 4 8 6 3 7 3 6 4 4 2 9 2 7 9 6 x.

What does x equal?

In this case, x equals 6. Did you get it? I'm betting that you didn't see the pattern here. It was utterly obvious to me, however: These have been my phone numbers over the last 20 years. There is a clear pattern here, but you need to have a particular set of information or perspectives in order to get it. Without that, the pattern is meaningless (or maybe some of you found a different, more general pattern which my not-so-mathematical mind didn't see).

The human mind is a pattern-making device. We think and see and clump into patterns. We do not have to *try* to see patterns; our brain sees information and clumps it for us. You can probably think of the different ways different people see patterns: Men and women might see things differently, city dwellers and country folk might see things differently, Westerners and Asians might see things differently.[7] But another set of the experiences/knowledge/skills/capacities that shapes the different patterns you can see is your form of mind. And, like the other transformative habits of mind we've considered in this chapter, intentionally stretching to see things you've not seen before is not only helpful but transformative.

One set of capacities and perspectives that grows over time is our ability to see progressively more-complex patterns. Seeing how things are connected to one another makes the world in some ways seem less mysterious (because we see the interactions between things that once just seemed like an assorted collection of unconnected events). In other ways, it makes the world seem more complex, with tangled threads that go in every direction. It is this progression from simple—but mysterious—to complex—but potentially overwhelming—that is the core growth in this regard.

It happens, too, as we think about polarities or what we might sometimes think of as opposites. At first, the opposites seem disconnected from one another—black is one thing, and white is another.

Then gray gets introduced, and you get three possible options.

Gray has a relationship to the black and white but is mostly distinct from them, and they are still distinct from one another.

Then more grays come along and more and more, and there are so many choices between black and white that it can begin to feel slightly overwhelming.

Then, as the choices are just out of control, the relationship between them all becomes clear and suddenly black and white are connected to each other with a long stream of grays.

Now what seemed like opposites to you at first now seem like connected edges of a single pole (polarities), and you see that white and black create gray, and in many ways they create one another as well.[8]

When we're talking about meaning rather than color, this shift turns out to be at least partially related to your form of mind. There are some forms of mind that see connections between particular poles effortlessly, and others that would claim there is no connection at all. In a world as connected as ours, filled with as much data—and as much noise—as ours, it can be a real benefit to see those connections.

Let's take a common organizational issue as an example—filled, as most of these issues are, with many grays—and see how it plays out for people with different forms of mind.

The leadership team of the small business division of a financial services company wanted its people to be more customer-focused and make more-independent decisions about what individual customers need. For the leadership team, this translated into a practice where the employees would give more-personalized service and be more discerning about which products and services to recommend to their customers. As they considered this new direction, the leaders thought it was a fairly straightforward set of ideas—if difficult to support. The HR department created workshops on having client conversations and influencing skills; the marketing department offered lunchtime seminars on the latest suite of more-personalized products and services.

As most people do, the leadership team neglected the different ways people might make sense of issues of patterns and polarities—and the strategies they might try to get a handle on these issues. Like most of us, the leadership team figured that the patterns that emerged for them would be obvious to all, and that any sense of opposites or polarities would be insignificant. Thinking about recognizing and managing patterns and polarities as ways to help people change—to help them both get on board the particular change the organization wants to make and also to help them grow to be more complex in their sensemaking into the future—was not a thing they considered. Let's look at the different ways people may have made sense of this particular issue, and the way that their sensemaking could have been expanded over the process.

Self-Sovereign Forms of Mind

Jessica understood the directive this way: We weren't making enough money the old way, so try selling people more in this new way. She didn't understand all the talk about having conversations and giving more individualized attention, and so forth. For her, the patterns were clear: Move from selling one thing to each person to instead selling at least two things to each person. While Jessica attended the various sessions, they mostly left her cold; why would she want to have a different set of conversations with her clients? And why was there all this talk about listening? Even in the influencing workshops, there was talk about trying to understand what your client needed by careful listening. It seemed to her that what she needed was to *talk* better—not to *listen* better. No one could sell things without talking. More helpful was the set of products and services seminars, but those were too confusing, as well. Jessica found it hard to keep all the products straight and needed to make lists of them. Sometimes she thought that the marketing group was just making up different packages to be confusing to her and to make it look like they were really working in some way, earning their big paychecks. In many ways, the marketing people were like the senior leadership team itself: always making work for others in order to keep their jobs. Jessica knew that it was only the folks in direct sales (and maybe some of the people in IT) who were actually doing the work which paid the salaries. To that end, Jessica invested a lot of her time in this change at first: The bonus plan was enticing! She'd know she was on the right track when she saw the results in her paycheck.

Patterns. At a self-sovereign form of mind, people have a hard time constructing complex patterns. They boil down the complexities of an initiative into what they think of as "the real deal," which eliminates the possibility of seeing some of the key patterns. For example, Jessica does not see the connections between the various products and services—nor does she see the connection between listening and selling. The patterns she sees are causal in a simple way: The new program is designed to sell more products. Her time-span reach is relatively short: She does not think about the effects of things far into the future, but weeks or months away.

Polarities. At the self-sovereign form of mind, people experience the world through many sets of opposites. Jessica focuses on the opposites, such as talking and listening (unconnected), and employees who are not customer-facing versus those who bring in the money (unconnected). When people try to explain the connections between these opposites (explaining, perhaps, that while the marketing people are focused on internal communications right now, they are working to increase revenue together and need to all work together to make the initiative succeed), Jessica senses that people are not being fully honest with her because they are connecting pieces which, to her mind, are clearly *not* connected.

Managing patterns and polarity. Because people who make sense with a primarily self-sovereign mind do not see the patterns and the opposites as malleable, they do not try to manage them; what would be the point of managing something that wouldn't change? (It would feel like trying to "manage" something that just *is*—like managing gravity or managing our need for oxygen.) Because there are not many shades of gray in their reasoning, there are not many shades of gray in their options, either. Jessica looks for payoff in what she's doing, and if she doesn't find it, she may reject the entire package. This approach might frustrate the senior team and those who believe in this change, and they may see it as "shallow" or "self-centered," but really it's simply about Jessica engaging in the world she sees. Unless they help her understand the connections between the different pieces she sees, it wouldn't make sense for her to act differently.

Socialized Forms of Mind

Jamal understood the new initiative as coming from the latest research on financial services, and he liked being in an organization on the cutting edge. The connections they were making between the personalized service and the increased sales made perfect sense to him, and he set out to understand and make sense of the various principles of this change. Jamal found the marketing seminars useful; he liked that they had created lots of flexibility inside the main products and services. He was still somewhat anxious about how to know when to offer which piece of the package, but he trusted that as the roll-out continued, they'd provide better direction about that. Jamal had a harder time with the HR seminars. The HR people didn't think like folks in sales and marketing, and it was harder to transfer their lessons and messages into the actual work he did. It was all very well to look at case studies, but the whole point of the initiative was that every customer is different and every situation is unique. That seemed to make it unlikely that you could use these case studies helpfully unless you had a customer who just happened to fit inside those exact examples. Otherwise, it seemed to Jamal like he'd just be making it up as he went along, which wasn't the way professionals operate. As Jamal worked away at implementing this new style, he found he had mixed success. Some of his customers really did seem to have a variety of needs once he began to look for them. But what he really thought was that the clients he'd always gotten along with were now in even better shape, and the ones he hadn't been able to reach well before were still pretty unreachable. He was confused about what value this change was really adding and how he'd know that he was doing it right.

Patterns. More pieces of the world become objects of examination when we develop toward a socialized form of mind, which means we can put more things on the table and thus can see more of the patterns going on around us. Jamal can see the patterns in the different products and services in a way that Jessica could not and so he is better equipped to hold the many distinctions in his head. (This is because when you show someone a pattern with more distinctions than they can currently hold, it simply doesn't look like a pattern to them but a series of unconnected dots.) At the same time, Jamal is unable to generalize from one *situation* to the next, which means that he cannot make sense of the way one HR case study might help him in another, different situation. With a socialized form of mind, we prefer to have exact parallels between one situation and the next in order to make use of the ideas in multiple contexts. Patterns are available to us when we can see them from inside the space of our previous experience; patterns generalized into the future are much more difficult to grasp.

Polarities. Those who make sense with a primarily socialized form of mind have increased their sense of the connections between things that used to look unrelated when they had more of a self-sovereign mind. This means that the unconnected opposites they used to see are now getting connected into polarities, perhaps with grays in between them. While some things are still right/wrong as they were in the more polarized self-sovereign mind, now more have gone into the modified buckets of "sometimes" or "probably." In addition to increasing their level of nuance, people with this form of mind can also see different elements going on around them and name those elements as paradoxical: In this case, Jamal notices that the focus is on *customization,* but they are teaching collections of skills that are meant to be used with *all people.* This is a subtlety that he probably wouldn't have noticed with a more self-sovereign mind, but it is also something that probably won't trouble him when he has more of a self-authored perspective. Right now he can't make sense of what he sees as an inherent conflict, but later he'll see that actually there are techniques that help you be more specialized which can be used across different situations in different ways. What he can see are the specifics and the way the specifics are in conflict; he cannot yet see the principles underlying the specifics (that would resolve what he experiences as a paradox).

Managing patterns and polarity. The socialized mind can see more patterns and polarities than it did when it was more self-sovereign, and it can also be trapped or confused by what it sees. The world becomes a more sophisticated place than it was, but it also becomes less certain and more confusing—and without the self-authored capacity to feel like we can intervene in what happens. This means that for people with this form of mind, it is a gift to have specific coping strategies around the complexity of patterns that people might be noticing (for example, organizing tools like two-by-twos, which help people map the full complexity). Tools to help uncover patterns are not of much use without tools to help manage them; this is not a form of mind where *creating* such tools seems particularly possible.

Self-Authored Forms of Mind

At first Miri shrugged off the new initiative the leadership team was rolling out. She had strong principles about how to treat her customers, and she didn't think that simply following the latest and greatest financial services fad was a useful way to go. She was surprised, then, when she went to a couple of the trainings and found that there really was lots for her to learn; she had been simply going by instinct when there were more-useful tools and skills for her to develop—especially during those difficult times with clients she didn't naturally get along with. She was impressed, too, with the nuances in the suite of products and services she could now offer to her customers, because in the past she had had to do a lot of retrofitting of their previous products. This new set of offerings, while complex, enabled her to specifically fit the needs of her customers. Miri was not interested in changing everything she did—why would she be, when she had been quite successful already? But she saw that there were opportunities to tweak her thinking and actions in ways that might offer big changes down the road. As she tried out these new techniques and tools, she noticed that they were especially effective in those situations where in the past she'd have gotten stuck. There were a wide variety of those situations, but they tended to be with a specific kind of client who had no interest in partnering with her but rather in simply ordering her around. It wasn't that she minded being ordered around so much as it was that she felt she could not add value to these clients. Paradoxically, Miri was finding that, when she listened most carefully to the more-demanding clients, they often began asking for her opinion and seeking her advice. There were still parts of this culture change that she didn't intend to follow (why was the leadership team always talking about "transformation" when these were important but not sweeping changes?), but the parts she did intend to follow were already making a big difference in her relationships with her clients, in her sense of satisfaction at a job better done—and in the bottom line.

Patterns. By the time we have a mostly self-authored mind, being able to get on the balcony is a familiar skill. This means that patterns emerge for us effortlessly; Miri didn't need to try to see the patterns in the new products and services; they just seemed obvious to her. Similarly, complex interpersonal patterns are also available, so Miri can see just what kind of client it is that she struggles with and also understand why that struggle might exist. Notice all the shades of gray available to her, and all the connections she sees. At the more-socialized form of mind, this insight would be either unavailable or less helpful. Because the distinctions get more specific and the individual events more connected into patterns, more possibilities become available and more solutions emerge. Even if someone with a more-socialized form of mind could make sense of the specific features of the kind of client who was most difficult for him, it is unlikely that he would be able to understand, as Miri does, that it is *his own reaction* to the person that's the problem to fix rather than the way the other person is acting (which might be annoying but is not solvable).

Polarities. People with a self-authored form of mind see fewer opposites, because there are more shades of gray that connect opposites into polarities, which then get connected by grays into wholes. The largest set of polarities comes from those areas where the self-authored self has created values or principles or ideas about what the truth is and should be. Because these self-authored ideas are part of the engine of the self-authored system, we are subject to them and thus have a hard time understanding the nuances around these principles. Notice that Miri first dismissed the new change out of hand because she thought it was just a fad. She has a set of notions around what constitutes her own, time-tested practice rather than the fads of the day, and she couldn't at first see that there was a connecting space between the two. As she began to see the connections, however, she was able to pull back from her thinking about the new initiative and accept it in a different ways.

Managing patterns and polarities. At the self-authored form of mind, patterns become much more readily available just as a matter of course. Part of the flexibility of the self-authored mind means that because more things are held as object and can be examined, more pieces can be moved around on the table. Miri can step back from her own opinions and try to make sense of them in a new way rather than being subject to them as she would have been when she saw the world through a more-socialized form of mind.

Self-Transforming Forms of Mind

Lester was curious about the new initiative, but as anyone would tell you, Lester was curious about everything. At the first workshop—which he found really helpful—he also wanted to be clear about what things they were giving up or moving away from as they tried to make this change. The workshop leaders tried to explain to him that he didn't have to give up anything but less-successful ways of working, but somehow that struck Lester as a partial answer. Was it even possible, he wondered, to get something new without giving something up? He talked to a variety of people in the office to try to figure out what they were having to give up in addition to the clear benefits they were getting. At the next workshop, Lester offered a list of what he had heard people thought they were giving up, and the list was strange: Lester said people were giving up a sense of themselves as people who could rely on their instincts, a sense of mastery over their profession, a sense of hopelessness when they got into trouble, a sense that there were some clients they couldn't (and therefore didn't have to try to) help. The workshop leaders told Lester to focus on the positive of those things they were giving up, and urged him to speak to folks from the executive leadership team.

It became clear to Lester, the more he worked with the new tools and products and services, the more he talked to his peers, the more he engaged those responsible for the change, that this was a real transformation. He saw that there was a demand for them to think differently—about their clients, their products, their entire role. They had thought of themselves as working for the financial services company and selling things to customers. This initiative, from Lester's perspective, meant that they were to think of themselves as working to create a partnership between these clients and the company—that folks like Lester were actually working in the space *in between* the client and the company. Lester saw that this would change his actions dramatically, and that it's true that he might, paradoxically, be more successful at selling the organization if he were not actually trying to sell anything. He wondered, though, whether people had actually given much thought to all the changes a person would have to make in *himself* to change his thinking to such an extent.

Patterns. By the time someone sees the world with a self-transforming form of mind, he has the agility to draw patterns out in a wide variety of ways; harder for him is to *not* see patterns. And because seeing patterns of all varieties gets easier and easier, he can have a hard time remembering that others don't see them (this is true for all of us, but the more easily patterns arise for us, the more difficult it is to remember how hard it is to see patterns sometimes). Notice that Lester wasn't confused about any of the pieces presented to him—he didn't even think to ask the questions the others asked because he was not puzzled. The questions he thought to ask were at a larger scale of pattern, looking at the overall impact of the change on the system of the group and the individual's thinking. It was hard for him, even with examples, to connect the pattern he was seeing in such a way that the workshop leader could see it as well.

Polarities. Ironically, while it's fairly simple for those with a self-transforming mind to see patterns, it is difficult for them to see the polarities that other people see. Everything becomes connected to its opposite, and it can be difficult for people in these positions to remember that these connections look like distinct shades of black and white to others. For example, Lester could not follow the direction of the workshop leaders to focus only on the positive pieces of the data he had uncovered about what this change would mean to people. It's not that Lester was unwilling to change his focus—it's that at the self-transforming form of mind, these two different pieces (the good things and the bad things) arrive in people's thinking as wholes. Separating the two pieces from each other makes them less whole (as opposed to earlier in our sensemaking, when they form two different wholes—the whole of the positive and the opposite whole of the negative).

Managing patterns and polarities. Here the task is more about managing communications to others than it is about trying to create a kind of coping mechanism or tool that will help get a handle on these things. If Lester is going to be able to get his own questions and concerns met, he'll need to be able to communicate them in a way that allows other people to have a glimpse of what he sees—but through their different forms of mind.

PICKING UP THE HABIT

Each of these habits of mind—asking different questions, taking multiple perspectives, and looking at patterns—will take on a different form and shape depending on the person who uses them. These differences are part of what make the habits psychologically spacious—useful both for kindergartners and CEOs. The tricky part is in finding ways to adopt the habit, to have it become a part of who you are and what you do. Coaches and those responsible for learning experiences can weave these habits into their coaching or their programs as one key way to help people begin to create their own development over time; I now design these into all the work I do. More difficult, but perhaps more transformational, would be if we could weave these habits into the work itself. Part Three takes up that challenge.

PART THREE CHANGING ON THE JOB

7 CULTIVATING LEADERSHIP

WITH KEITH JOHNSTON

If we're really going to make a difference in the way workplaces support people to grow, we'll have to make a difference in the way leaders think about their work. My partner, Keith Johnston, and I spend most of our time helping leaders make those shifts. Keith is also a leader himself with a long history managing in the New Zealand public service and now as the chair of Oxfam International, a global aid agency committed to helping end poverty and injustice (and if aspiring to reach those goals isn't a good reason to support development, I'm not sure what is). Keith is joining me on this chapter because—as we'll argue throughout—we need to practice thinking together about leadership, not just to support individuals to grow, but also to help leaders create contexts where everyone can bring their biggest self to work.

The specific context we'll look at is leadership inside organizations and workplaces. We are taking leadership specifically because it is so filled with developmental ideas—so bound up with sensemaking about authority, control, and perspective-taking—that having a developmental perspective offers a whole new lens on how we think about and exercise leadership. We also know that leadership is a helpful anchor-point for other things that matter in organizations, such as culture, values, and structure. We are not naïve enough to believe that leaders create these things—in fact, we know that quite often the cultures, values, and structures are what create the leaders. But the interaction between these different forces gives us a helpful tension and allows us some new ways of looking at and making sense of life inside organizations.

We'll begin by looking at some of the key pieces of a leader's job, and then at what happens as the role increases in scale and scope—along with the demands on the leader's sensemaking. Then, having painted a rather daunting picture, we'll show how the habits of mind help support leaders to both meet sophisticated demands today and also grow to be better able to meet them tomorrow. We'll try to do that in a way that supports you to grow your own practices, too (which we hope you'll share with us and with one another). Finally, we'll look at the ways that organizations can create systems and structures that cultivate leadership, as well.

LEADER WORK

Leadership has become one of those words that means everything and nothing. Different authors will tell you that it's primarily about managing conflict or change or motivation. Looking across the vast literature, we think that most of the pieces of a leader's job boil down—perhaps blandly—into three key elements: vision, people, and tasks. We won't talk about these extensively (because you could read whole books about them), but they tend to go a little like this:

- Vision: Often the great distinction between management and leadership is that leadership is about the future state and not about the status quo. This means that leaders need to have a vision for the future and also have some way of connecting that vision to actions that might take you there.[1] This requires the managing of many polarities: task and people, head and heart, big picture and detail, present and future. It requires supporting and requiring people to change, which can be uncomfortable and anxiety-producing.

- People: Without other people engaged, there is no leadership. These people might be direct reports or managers, colleagues inside or outside an organization, key stakeholders on every side of the issue. Even thought leaders who don't have any classic organizational leadership responsibilities still need to enroll people in their ideas, shape conversations and thinking, and support others to take on new ideas and new actions. Inspiring and motivating people, supporting them to do their best work, helping them learn, connecting them across difference, working with conflict—all of these are pieces of the mosaic of a leader's job with people.

- Tasks: Most leaders are charged with accomplishing something—or getting others to accomplish things. While a good manager might support people to stay on task and get things done, the leadership space is about selecting tasks, connecting them to people, and supporting people to achieve and to learn how to do things better—for a larger purpose than crossing an item off a leader's to-do list or accomplishing some disconnected goal set by someone else.

As you can probably see, each of these requires the other—it's vision that helps lead people and decide on tasks, people who create the context for the vision and accomplish the tasks, and the tasks that bring new things into the world, whether they are new products or concepts or opinions or relationships. You can probably see that if each of these elements is relatively bounded, a leader's job is difficult but learnable. As roles increase in scale and scope, however, these three elements interact to give rise to new forms of complexity that require a kind of paradoxical element to add to the leader's to-do list:

- Know where you're going and how to get there (so people will follow you) and also be open to the ideas of others (so that others add to your thinking and are engaged in a purposeful way). In other words: be a leader and a learner simultaneously.

While the combination of these different pieces is complex on its own, each feature gets more difficult, as well, as the leadership task grows in scale and scope.

THE COMPLEX INTERACTION BETWEEN LEADERSHIP AND SENSEMAKING

None of these leadership elements is unexpected, obviously. People tend to take leadership roles because they have some sense of the future (although sometimes it's a hope to protect or to return to a better past), some idea of the people they're going to lead, and some sense of the most important tasks. Often, however, they have their eye more clearly on one of those pieces than others. We have one client who picks her next position almost solely by looking at the people involved, and another client who doesn't need to meet the people but just needs to understand the core work. Often our clients tend to enter senior leadership positions because of the intersection of the organization's mission and the clients' view of a possible future—and in those cases, both the individual people and the tasks they might do are less interesting than the possible role of the leader in creating a vision for the future.

Whatever reasons people might have for selecting their next leadership position, most of the leaders we have worked with have been surprised, as they've moved into leadership roles with a greater scope and scale, that things are not as they expected them to be. The expectations they carry with them into new and bigger roles—that finally they will have the platform to make the difference they have wanted to make—are often flattened along with the moving boxes by the end of the first week on the job.

The Paradoxes of Increasing Leadership Scale and Scope

We are often called in to support people who are moving from one leadership role to another one with a larger scale or scope. Perhaps they are moving from leading a team to leading a division; perhaps they are making the move to the same role in a larger or more-complex organization; perhaps the size and scale of the issues with which they are struggling is bigger. (See Figure 7.1.) In any case, we have seen that oftentimes people feel they have been thrown in at the deep end and they do not have what it takes to perform the new role. In part they are talking about the *skills* involved in making the transition to a different type of work: They may be doing less of the job they knew how to do well (developing software, for example, or running community programs) and more of a job they know less about (coping with budgets and spreadsheets, creating strategic plans, or setting up and running meetings of software developers or community organizers). They may need to work on their public-speaking skills, their delegation skills, their translation from theory or insider jargon to ever wider communities of interest.

Often, though, people are talking about the different *sensemaking demand* of leadership that arises from the role: They are expected to take a bigger view, to put the work into a wider context, and to understand the forces that shape this context. All of these are not just calls for what a leader needs to *know*, but also for what she needs to *think* or *believe*. With our adult development lens, we can see that as the leader progresses up the career ladder, she doesn't just have a bigger job title—she probably has a bigger scope and scale to look after, which may well

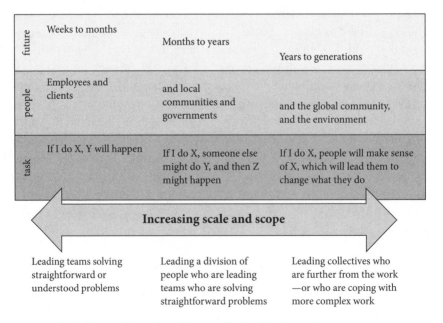

future	Weeks to months	Months to years	Years to generations
people	Employees and clients	and local communities and governments	and the global community, and the environment
task	If I do X, Y will happen	If I do X, someone else might do Y, and then Z might happen	If I do X, people will make sense of X, which will lead them to change what they do

Increasing scale and scope

| Leading teams solving straightforward or understood problems | Leading a division of people who are leading teams who are solving straightforward problems | Leading collectives who are further from the work —or who are coping with more complex work |

FIGURE 7.1   Increasing scale and scope of leadership demands

make demands on her for increasing self-complexity. Because your form of mind doesn't change as quickly as your business cards, it is vital for leaders to be supported so they are able to do the new jobs they are promoted into. This requires that we understand what we're asking of them in the first place. As the scope and scale of a leader's work increases, the pressure for a bigger perspective increases in each of the core leadership elements.

Take vision, for example. We've talked about how leaders need to think about the future, but the size and distance of that future changes as the scope and scale of a leader's role increases. A leader with a smaller role or scope might be thinking about a relatively close-in future. Leaders with a more-significant scope and span need to think about longer timeframes and project farther into the future—developing strategies and plans that might cover years of possible actions and lead to significant future outcomes.

The demands for dealing with people also increase. As the scope and scale of work increase, leaders have to connect with—and understand the perspectives of—a widening group of stakeholders. With a relatively small scale, leaders connect with those immediately engaged with them and often don't need to bridge enormous divides (although we all know that conflict can come into any team, no matter how small or united in focus). As the leader's reach expands, the number of perspectives and priorities of an increasingly diverse set of stakeholders also increases, building complexity into every interaction.

It may be that the leader's relationship to task and outcome is more complex—even to write about—than the other two. In its simplest form, the connection between what you do and what happens is clear and repeatable, and leaders in the most straightforward contexts can take advantage of these simple connections. If a leader assigns a straightforward task, others will know how to accomplish the task; and then, once the task is accomplished, everyone knows what the result will be. Imagine, in the most simple case, telling another person to clean a room or weave a basket or make a meal. The person assigning the task knows what he wants and why, he can support the person to whom the task is assigned to do the thing well, and once it's done, they'll both be able to look at the outcome and know that the task was accomplished (or not).

The combination of a longer timeframe and more stakeholders leads to more-confused cause-and-effect interactions, as there are more people in the system and greater lag times between the thought and the action. This makes tasks harder to pin down and the effects of a task harder to judge. It becomes more difficult to tell which actions cause which reactions.

For example, take the widely researched and examined case of New Coke, which was released in 1985. If the task assignment was to create, field test, and market an improved cola drink that would stop Coke's dropping market share, it was a failure. Amid much fanfare, New Coke was released and then, with more fanfare, Coke Classic was returned to the shelves less than three months later and New Coke ultimately disappeared from most of the planet. Yet the publicity around this "fiasco" was so significant that Coke products were outselling Pepsi's quite quickly; the release and then abandonment of New Coke ended the eroding of Coca-Cola's market share. That looks like a success—some kind of Coke drink was beating the Pepsico drinks—it just wasn't the Coke formula they had thought it would be. The actions of the senior leaders have been written about extensively. But the leadership lessons here (which have been pulled out in different ways by different authors[2]) go in all different directions—perhaps because the cause-and-effect lines go in different directions and are measured differently with different time scales and different stakeholders. From our vantage point 25 years afterward, it looks less like leadership and more like luck; the outcome was so unlike what the plans were meant to do. At these higher orders of scope and scale, it can be hard to know when or how to measure success or failure; the connection between task and outcome gets less and less clear.

The expanding complexity of timeframe, stakeholders, and task means that the demands on leaders become more intense as their scope and scale increase. You can probably see some of the implications for development that arise just from this little list. But add to that list the major *paradox* of this increasing scale and scope:

- Leaders are looked at as being more in control and able to make changes and see the big system, just as they move so far away from the actual work of the system that they feel themselves as having less and less control.

The combination of these issues is made more difficult by this final paradox, which weaves through every aspect of a senior leader's day and makes serious demands on sensemaking in general. In the next section, we turn (carefully) to how these demands might be experienced by people who see the world through different forms of mind.

Leadership and Forms of Mind

We believe there is a relationship between orders of mind and capability of performing particular leadership roles, but it is not a direct fit, and there are real dangers in drawing too close a relationship. Political scientist Shawn Rosenberg (2002) has described the "potential serious and noxious ramifications" of the use of these theories to label and critique people.[3] A colleague of ours laughs ironically about the misuse of such theories in organizations where people make snap judgments without good data or thinking. It is as if people are saying, "That guy has got a socialized haircut," and then boxing him into that space forever. So we know we're on unstable ground here, and we hold our hands out to you to join us, not because we think there's a firm surface underneath, but because a careful look at some of the implications of these ideas might help us all create more sympathetic and supportive workplaces—where we can grow into the challenges with which we are faced.

In essence, this will not be news to anyone reading this book: Leaders with different forms of mind will experience the demands of their roles through their sense-making systems and thus will see and understand their jobs in significantly different ways. There may be a degree of fit (or not) between the demands of the leadership role and the form of mind of the leader—we might think of it as leaders being more or less inside a comfort zone when their form of mind and the leadership demands coincide, and outside their comfort zone when the leadership demanded is not challenging enough or is way too tough. We won't walk over old ground here, but a quick look at the leadership challenges shows that some forms of mind are more able to flexibly understand and make sense of the leadership challenges of longer time spans, more stakeholders, and increasing complexity in the cause and effect of tasks. The paradox of the role is an additional demand that comes with the change in scale and scope. We'll quickly look at these core issues below.

SELF-SOVEREIGN LEADERS

- *Increasing time span:* Self-sovereign leaders are likely to struggle with the demands of increasing time span, especially in those cases where there are short-term losses that lead to long-term gains.

- *Increasing stakeholders:* Because those of us who see the world through a self-sovereign form of mind struggle to hold diverse perspectives—especially when those perspectives conflict with our own—the more stakeholders a leader has to manage, and the more divergent the perspectives those stakeholders might have, the less someone with a self-sovereign form of mind will be able to hold and manage them.

- *Decreasing clarity of the connections between cause and effect:* This idea simply doesn't make sense to someone with a self-sovereign form of mind. Cause and effect are relatively sophisticated concepts already; and at the self-sovereign form of mind, holding the connections between cause and effect is a major milestone. Leaders who make sense of the world with this form of mind cannot see or make sense of the increased complexities of cause and effect.

• *Paradox of the appearance of increasing control and the experience of decreasing control:* This paradox is unlikely to be felt or noticed by leaders with a self-sovereign form of mind. It is likely that if a colleague described feeling this way, the leader with more of a self-sovereign form of mind might think the colleague was incompetent.

SOCIALIZED LEADERS

• *Increasing time span:* Socialized leaders can hold the abstraction of an increasing time span, although they'll need help drawing out the implications of this increase. They may be unsettled by it and look for rules or other forms of guidance to proceed.

• *Increasing stakeholders:* Because leaders with a socialized form of mind can understand multiple perspectives, making sense of these increasing stakeholders is more possible at this form of mind than it was for the self-sovereign leaders. However, leaders who see the world through this form of mind are likely to unquestioningly privilege a particular perspective as "correct" and thus are likely to be unable to see the merit in the perspectives of those who are different, making it difficult to build new possibilities together.

• *Decreasing clarity of the connections between cause and effect:* A leader with a socialized form of mind may have a more-complex vision of cause and effect and discover that particular causes may have perverse and unintended effects. How she makes sense of this complex view may depend on the leadership culture into which she has been socialized (either at this or another organization). If the organization (or the organizational theories in which this leader believes) espouses this lack of clarity as a by-product of complexity but not as the fault of either the leader or the system, this may feel like a complex but normal piece of the role. If there is no clear frame to put these ideas in, these unintended effects may well feel like either incompetence of the leader ("I was wrong in having this idea or else this wouldn't have happened.") or of someone else ("They carried out this idea badly or else this wouldn't have happened."). With a socialized mind, leaders may search for new guides to leadership or to more technical information in order to avoid such mistakes in the future. They will likely assume that a clear cause-and-effect relationship can be established even when the situation is too complex to be knowable.

- *Paradox of the appearance of increasing control and the experience of decreasing control:* The leader who sees the world mostly through a socialized form of mind is less likely to see this as a paradox and more likely to see it as a problem with the control environment or organizational procedures that can be fixed. Again, with organizational cultures of theories to put this into perspective, a socialized leader may come to believe this is part of a senior leader's role.

SELF-AUTHORED LEADERS

- *Increasing time span:* Self-authored leaders have a greater capacity to understand and think across increased time span, and they have the capacity to model potential interactions out into the future.[4]

- *Increasing stakeholders:* Self-authored leaders are more likely to have the capacity to manage the perspectives and ideas of multiple stakeholders and be able to get up on the balcony and look for similarities and differences among the different individuals and groups, although they may tend to see them as competing demands rather than interdependent and co-constructed. This *capacity* for seeing many perspectives does not necessarily mean that leaders with self-authored forms of mind have the *desire* to see multiple perspectives, or the listening *skill* needed to draw out different perspectives in the first place. It means that with the open mindset to value multiple perspectives, and the right skills to uncover and explore the perspectives, these leaders have forms of mind which allow them to hold the complexity of the many perspectives.

- *Decreasing clarity of the connections between cause and effect:* Those with a self-authored form of mind are more comfortable with the idea and practice of long lags between cause and effect, although they can still get frustrated by the difference between what they want to happen and the actual outcome. Because this ambiguity is common throughout their experience, the leadership demand does not seem to be particularly unsettling; it seems, rather, as if leadership, like life, is complex and messy, and those with a self-authored form of mind work to make sense inside the complexity. This does not necessarily dissuade them from wanting to find the best answer and working away at that answer until it appears to be perfect.

- *Paradox of the appearance of increasing control and the experience of decreasing control:* Leaders with self-authored capacities are able to recognize this as a paradox to be managed, not a problem to be solved. The capacity to recognize this paradox doesn't necessarily translate into the belief in the paradox, however. Leaders still might have a mindset that pushes them toward believing that the perfect structure or communication system or leadership group will create the conditions for the leader to actually be in control of the situation.

SELF-TRANSFORMING LEADERS

- *Increasing time span:* Self-transforming leaders naturally think across a longer time span or carry a perspective that circumstances can evolve to be very different over time in unknowable ways.

- *Increasing stakeholders:* Self-transforming leaders naturally take multiple perspectives and can see how their ideas, hopes, and values are represented in the perspectives of even those who are very different. They can therefore hold the divergent perspectives of different stakeholders and find the larger patterns of agreement, disagreement, and multiple commonalities among the different groups.

- *Decreasing clarity of the connections between cause and effect:* Those who have something of a self-transforming form of mind are less likely to believe in linear cause-and-effect ideas in general, turning their attention more naturally to nonlinearity and emergence.

- *Paradox of the appearance of increasing control and the experience of decreasing control:* Leaders with self-transforming capacities are likely to have complex notions of control in general and to believe that control is likely illusory.

The conclusions that live in this short description could be overwhelming. Increasing the scale and scope of leadership positions means that in the most-complex roles, even those with self-authored forms of mind have to reach hard—and learn a lot of skills—to take in the complexities with which they are faced each day.[5] There are two key problems here that face all of us who are concerned with leadership anywhere. The first is that self-transforming people don't marry, mate, and produce self-transforming babies, so if organizations seek people with these capacities, there has to be something organizations can do to first support leaders who might be over their heads developmentally and then to help them grow bigger over time. The second issue is that in our research, we've found that often those who are on their way to a self-transforming form of mind find organizations the wrong context for their work lives—so that even if we support people to grow, they leave organizations before the organization can get the full benefit of the self-transforming mind.[6] We'll try to address both of these questions as we suggest practices—individual and organizational—that would support people to grow and stay growing at work.

CREATING CONTEXTS THAT HELP LEADERS BE BIGGER

Throughout this book, you've seen the image of a scaffold pop up from time to time. Let's stop and really look at that image here, because it's going to help us do the two things that need doing: (1) to support people to do something beyond their current capacities and (2) to give them time to build internal supports so that external scaffolds aren't so necessary. In maybe no place is this core idea so useful as imagining how organizations can think about cultivating leadership. We hear people in organizations around the world talk about developing "leadership bench strength," and we imagine a long line of eager, uniformed leaders waiting patiently for their turn at bat. We think building leadership scaffolds is a much more helpful metaphor, which doesn't just increase the strength of the bench at particular levels of the organization or particular periods in time (like when the senior leadership team looks around and notices that they're all 58), but supports leadership as a resource—by growing particular leaders and also by creating the systems and structures that support leadership throughout the organization.

Scaffold-Building

We don't want to just sell you a prebuilt scaffold, though. We want to teach you to build one yourself. That way you can take the model scaffold we've built and you can tell us about the ones you're building and we can eventually think of thousands of ways to support people at work as they grow over time. So, here's the scaffold-building exercise.

Leaders (and all of us, really) need to be supported to grow over time if we're going to reach for our highest capacity. We can do some of this growing through the coaching and professional learning interventions we've described in the earlier chapters. But those interventions are likely to be a tiny percentage of our actual working time. This means we have more time and space for development if development is inside the work we have to do anyway. One easy way to do this is to focus on the pieces of a leader's role and then pay attention to the ways his job can be completed while also intentionally making use of some of the habits of mind from Chapter 6:

- Asking different questions
- Taking multiple perspectives
- Seeing the system

Remember that these habits of mind are inherently developmental—and that they continue to create development into the future. If the leadership practice you create both gets work done and also flexes the habits of mind, it's a developmental work scaffold. Table 7.1 shows how we put those ideas together.

TABLE 7.1   Scaffold building

Leadership demand	Habits of mind	Practice
Shape the future	• Asking different questions • Seeing the system	Make a map
Lead people	• Asking different questions • Taking multiple perspectives	Think about and give feedback to others in new ways
Accomplish tasks	• Asking different questions • Seeing the system	Draw boundaries on purpose

Notice that we're not saying that these three practices are all leaders need to do well—nor that they're even the secret pieces which, once you do them, will make everything else fall into place. Rather, we're trying to show you some helpful practices (that will both do the work and also help support leaders to grow) as well as how those practices are developmental (and thus support you to create developmental practices, too). So if you practice these three—whether you're leading ideas or families or companies—you may find yourself growing at the same time.

Shape the Future: Make a Map

"Becoming more strategic" is one of the most common goals leaders have as they enter our leadership development programs or engage us for coaching. They want to learn how to escape from the details of their day-to-day work and try to focus on—and energize other people around—a desired future worth striving for. Being strategic isn't a personality trait some of us are born with (although clearly some people are more naturally strategic than others). It is something we can all learn to do better, and it's a place where we can bring others in as helpful supports.

The first piece of the practice of shaping the future is recognizing the limits of shaping it—and also recognizing the benefits of trying. People who believe that they can create whatever future they want just by wishing it were so tend to be disappointed in the end; people who believe there's no need to try and create a future because it'll never happen tend to be disappointed the whole time. But as soon as we recognize that drawing a map—of the present and of a hoped-for future—isn't a solo sport, we are able to amplify our capacity for future-thinking by the capacity of others around us which helps us all.

Asking different questions about both the present and the future. Executive coach Catherine Fitzgerald recommends finding thoughtful people both inside and outside your particular industry and asking questions like these about the present:

- What would customers (or other key constituencies) love for us to do differently? What might they demand we not change?
- What is the biggest potential opportunity we're not paying enough attention to? What is the biggest area of risk or threat?

And questions like these about the future:

- How do you imagine our business being different a year from now (or two years or five years or . . .)?
- If we were bold, what might we do? What might we stop doing? If we were five times as bold, what might we do or stop doing?[7]

Asking these questions of yourself and others gives you the terrain of a possible map.

See the whole system of these responses and your experiences with them. Once you have gotten these multiple perspectives, it's time to put them in conversation with the entire system. We suggest that you actually do this in writing (or drawing), because it's important to both get the ideas out of your head (and move from subject to object) and also capture them so you can track the changes along the way and remember the journey. We've found that one helpful way to do this is to write themes or ideas on large sticky notes and put those on a wall or whiteboard, so that you can move them around and find different patterns. In any case, you're on the lookout for patterns.

- Where are the connections between what different people (or you) have said?
- Where are the dis-connections?
- What might be some causes for the connections or dis-connections?
- Where is the relationship between the current state and the future direction?
- What does that tell you?

As you play with these different questions and the multiple perspectives you have gathered on them, you can begin to see connections that you did not see before. You may question the pieces to which you were once subject and see new sets of possibilities for the future. And you may develop a more-open style as you include others in your exploration.

You may be able to see that this simple approach can help leaders develop a more-strategic and inclusive approach to the path between the present and the future for their organization. What it also does is intentionally support the growth of the leader's mind (as well as the minds of others involved in this process over time). This double benefit—good for the business and good for the mind—is most important.

Lead People: Think About and Give Feedback in New Ways

One way to quickly change the culture of what leaders do and are expected to do is to change the way we think and teach about giving feedback. Nearly every leader with whom we have ever worked struggles with giving difficult feedback (and they may not notice it, but they tend not to do a good job giving positive feedback, either). There are endless books, blogs, management workshops, and feedback models people can use to make this go better. The mindset which underlies most of these models is, as Kegan and Lahey critique in their 2002 book, of a "supervisor" who has "super vision."[8] Nearly every book with a shortcut about how to organize and give feedback is probably coming from this perspective—that the leader (or feedback giver) has access to a powerful truth that the receiver (who needs to have feedback) does not have access to. If the leader can give the feedback in a way that the receiver can hear it, the problem will be solved.[9]

As long as we hold this image of feedback being something that one person (often a leader) gives to another person to educate that other person, we've missed the ultimate point of the feedback system, and we've limited the power of the organization to support the growth of the leader (ironically because the organization is attempting to support the follower). If you build *asking different questions* and *taking multiple perspectives* into the giving and receiving of feedback, it not only becomes a helpful support for the person receiving the feedback but also for the person giving it.

Feedback as a concept (or as the thing that happens when you talk into your microphone too close to the speaker) is simply information that goes into a system (and comes back at you with a high-pitched squeal). What happens next is where things get interesting—the postfeedback learning, which is the point of the feedback in the first place. The postfeedback learning can look obvious but sometimes really isn't. Consider these examples:

- *The issue:* Jack is giving a speech while standing 2 feet from the loudspeaker, and the speaker is making a big noise. *The learning:* Here things are pretty straightforward: The learning is to back away. This fixes the problem and Jack can go on with his speech.

- *The issue:* Jack is watering his plants every day, and they're droopy and unhappy. *The learning:* Because he's dealing with a living thing, the learning gets slightly more complex. Maybe he should water them less. Or it might be that the plants need to be watered less often but more deeply, or that they need more or less sun, more or less heat. Jack can experiment and try to get it just right (and save the plants).

- *The issue:* Jack is yelling at his direct reports and they're antagonistic and disengaged. *The learning:* What should Jack think? What is the learning here?

Well, that depends on your vision of cause and effect. Simple vision says that cause follows effect in some discoverable way (as it does with the first two examples). But people are not mechanical systems nor are we simple biological ones. Leaders who believe that the learning from the third example is as straightforward, linear, and testable as the learning from the first two have missed some of that increasing confusion between cause and effect. Is Jack yelling at his direct reports because they're antagonistic and disengaged, or are they antagonistic and disengaged because Jack is yelling at them? Or are Jack's yelling and their antagonism different symptoms of the same cause that is affecting them all? You can't be sure by yourself, and probably can't even be sure by talking to Jack. In this case, feedback isn't something you should give to Jack to fix his yelling, because you simply don't know enough about the connection between the causes and effects.

A feedback model that begins with asking different questions means everyone can learn. In our experience, the "questions" people ask in a feedback situation tend to not be genuine questions at all. Rather they're leading questions (e.g., "Do you think yelling at your people is the best way to motivate them? Do you feel motivated when people yell at you?") or open-ended questions to which you already know the answers (e.g., "So how do you think the team is getting along?"). Asking different questions in a feedback setting is about understanding what it is you don't know about the situation and about which you might be genuinely curious (e.g., "I noticed that there was quite a lot of tension and I heard your raised voice as I walked by your unit earlier today. I have some opinions about that which I'm happy to share, but I'm most interested in how you're thinking about the working relationships in your team right now and how they might get improved."). Teaching question-asking as a core piece of the feedback process changes what is possible for everyone. It is not only a better way to actually solve problems together, but also it's a way to help people grow.

In this case, it's not enough to ask different questions, however. It's also vital to *take multiple perspectives* when you're dealing with a feedback issue, so that you can keep from being locked into a single story or option. In order to hold open enough possibilities to really help both of you reach a helpful way forward, you need to try to take the perspectives of multiple people in the situation. One way to do this is to list all the folks implicated, and then come up with not one but several different ways each person might be making sense of the particular incident or topic.[10] Once you and the person with whom you are having the conversation have asked all the different, curious questions and taken the perspectives of various others, then you can begin to form solutions that take the larger system into account—and in this way you both might actually learn as you go.

Teaching a feedback model that resists simple cause and effect (and rejects the requirement for the supervisor to have super vision) scaffolds several things at once: It helps the leader get socialized into a system where he doesn't need to have all the answers. It helps the leader understand some of the confusing spaces around cause and effect. And it helps the leader get others to think alongside him, increasing the number of folks who are trying to diagnose the problem and come up with a solution. It helps the leader grow while he helps his direct reports grow. If an organization adopts a more-complex feedback model, that complexity can support people in the organization to be bigger today (by relying on the scaffold of the new model) and grow bigger over time. It is an organizational practice that is psychologically spacious and conducive to growth. Everybody wins.[11]

Accomplish Tasks: Make Connections and Draw Boundaries

If you're just setting out to do the tasks others have assigned to you, that's not leadership (although all leaders still sometimes just have to do the tasks that are assigned to them by others). Accomplishing tasks in a leadership frame isn't about only getting things done, but also about the whole range of elements from deciding what needs to be done to selecting the person or people to do that and then giving support and feedback along the way until the task is accomplished. Each of those steps is a leadership task (and you'll see that each of them involves some sense of a desired future and a way to think about and deliver feedback).

Here we're suggesting a practice that will support leaders to be more thoughtful about various aspects of getting things done, focusing specifically on the first step—deciding what needs to be done. We think of tasks as the solution to a problem you (or someone else) has defined. The problem might be that there is too much diversity in the business units about the way they handle budgeting. The task (solution) might be to create and roll out a new budgeting policy and procedure. One leader would have been in charge of defining that original task as the solution to the problem, and other leaders through the organization would be given the job of doing a piece of that work. In any case, though, the work that gets done needs to connect in some meaningful way back to the problem it set out to fix—and often this gets lost along the way as the solutions take on a life of their own and don't ultimately solve anything after all.

No matter where a leader is in this task-assignment chain, she needs to figure out how to get her team to understand and complete the tasks in a helpful way.

The leader in question could stay in the particular vantage point that is most comfortable for her. She could describe and assign tasks in the ways she generally does, and she would not put herself at risk for learning much about the work—or for growing her mind at all. If she were to take a different approach, where she asked different questions and looked at the system, she might find that the task assignment and support gets better—and that she learns a lot in the process.

In this case, the first thing to do is try *to see the system.* A surprising number of leaders forget to step back and look at the system which has generated the particular tasks that the leader and his team are responsible for achieving. The most-sophisticated leaders keep the original problem in their mind—the one that led to the task assignment in the first place. In this way, it's not "create a corporate budgeting policy and procedure," which is the task for which she's responsible. It's "people are confused and resources are unfairly distributed when different areas use the budgeting system in different ways." With this bigger problem in mind, the leader can see the system of the whole issue and see that it's more than creating a watertight policy and procedure that matters. Rather, a solution requires getting people to use and understand the new policy and procedure as a resource rather than yet another bureaucratic requirement that comes from working in a large organization. Anyone at any level of an organization can trace the task back to the problem, and can hold on to the piece of the problem their task was made to solve. Having a leader see the relationship of this task to the problem and also this task to the other tasks that are underway (or planned) can change both how the task is undertaken and also how the leader learns and grows from her part in the work (and, as she helps others see the system, how their minds grow as well).[12]

In addition to seeing the system and making the connections for himself and others, a leader needs to *ask different questions about what is to be done.* In this case, we're suggesting a set of questions about the boundaries of the issue, because boundaries are by their nature both important to the delivery of tasks and important to the growth of peoples' minds. Again, the boundaries of the issue are often not well discussed—each person makes assumptions about where a boundary should be, which separates my work from yours or this task from the next. Asking different questions can make that boundary an object for exploration rather than something to which different people are differently subject. For example, about any major project, a leader can ask:

- Who is drawing the boundaries on this issue?
- What happens when the issue boundary gets bigger or smaller?
- What happens if different people are involved?

- What happens to the issue and to our options when the boundaries get moved in our out?
- Who can move them?

For example, in the issue above, a key question will be about who has defined the problem and set boundaries around this particular structural solution to it. What would happen if the team opened up the boundary and thought about how to get all necessary financial and budgeting information more clear and available to the whole organization? What if they narrowed it to see a single check step at the end of the budgeting process rather than a whole new system? They could ask about the people. What if it were the human resource team rather than the finance and policy teams which were tasked with this—how would that be different? What if it were the organizational learning group? How would they think of the task differently? What are the ways that this group could include some of that sort of thinking it as works through the issue?

It's not that these questions need to be asked and answered every day. If a leader would schedule time for these more systems-seeing conversations at least once a month, she might find that her productivity increases—as does the sophistication of her thinking and the thinking of others around her. Like the other pieces in this section, it's simply to suggest that using the habits of mind in the day-to-day work of the leader can support more-thoughtful, helpful, complex understandings of the people and the work, and also grow minds.

ORGANIZATIONAL SUPPORTS

So far, we have concentrated on how leaders can lead in ways that support their development and the development of people they are leading. We want to take this one step further and consider how work and organizations can be designed to better support the development of leaders and adults. As we have done elsewhere, we start by asking: What is needed to do the work well? How can we create tools/systems/procedures that support the work and also scaffold an individual's development? Are there whole systems or structures that organizations could create to make development more possible?

Asking these questions leads us to three related hopes. We want organizational scaffolds to:

1) Help people to do their work more effectively;
2) Help teams and/or leaders and their direct reports to respond to those factors that increase complexity in the workplace—longer time spans, larger

numbers of stakeholders, and less clarity about the links between causes and effects; and

3) Create opportunities for individuals to reflect on their own sensemaking and development, and thus get a bigger perspective.

With that set of criteria in place, we have three core ideas about creating developmental organizations: They need to be clear about roles and how value is added; to connect supports to the challenges; and to explicitly use structure to support development.

Be Clear About Roles and Adding Value

Lots of organizational books will tell you it is critical to be clear about roles. In many ways it makes obvious sense to be clear about what people are expected to work on, how they are expected to know whether they have done a good job, and how their roles fit together with others. Both our own experience and historical records are filled with the times this didn't happen. Famously, Franklin Delano Roosevelt would on occasion set the same task for different members of his cabinet and not have them discover they were duplicating their efforts, working on the same issue from different ends, until later. He may have thought that having competing approaches was the way to get the best solutions and test these ideas through the internecine conflicts that resulted. Unfortunately, in the process there was also confusion, waste, and ongoing hostilities.

While role clarity makes sense from an organizational theory perspective, it makes a different kind of sense from an adult development perspective. The more unclear or overlapping work might be, the greater a demand it places on individual sensemaking. If there's a clear task to be done, anyone with the brains and skill can do it. The more ambiguous a task becomes, the more you have to rely on people's form of mind in addition to their brains and skill. People who see the world from different forms of mind will react differently to ambiguity, but those reactions take time and attention you might not want used in this way. Instead, clarity about roles—and the demands they make on individual sensemaking— may create the supports for people to do the job well.

It is also important to be clear about the boundaries set around work and where and how other people add value to my work. Remember that our understanding of boundaries shifts and changes as we grow, so creating clarity—especially creating clarity I can either rely on or push around a little—is a gift. Helping me know what I can expect in the way of others adding value to my work (and letting me know what value I can add) is a support that helps me do my job well.

Take the case we worked on recently of a group of software designers each pushing to solve a problem in the design of a new program. For expedience, two teams were set up with overlapping work but different programming paradigms, each of them going down a different path as they sought the fastest and most reliable solution to this issue. As the stress level rose (which may have temporarily diminished their developmental capacities), they increasingly lost sight of the larger goals of the project and lost perspective on how their roles and responsibilities played into those larger goals. Some took responsibility beyond their scope; others sat back and waited for the worst of the storm to pass. The leader, who thought he had delegated a clear issue to them, was left unclear about how he would add value to their work by helping them see the big picture again—in fact, some days he lost sight of the big picture himself. As his boss asked him questions about how the team was going, he was uncertain about whether he was adding value to the work by asking questions, whether he needed to cut off the least-productive work stream (and how would he decide which was which), and what decisions he could make and which ones should be made by his boss or by his teams. The lack of clarity was hardest on those who had more of their identity tied up in the work, but all of the muddiness created a situation so layered and complex that it became unclear how they'd get any software developed at all.

The point here is not that every piece of the work needs to be described and nailed down. Nor are we restating what you'd find in any management text book. Rather, we're pointing to the developmental implications of getting the roles right—and the developmental risks of getting them wrong.

In this particular case, as each group was left to create their own roles, they created them without a view of the big picture, and they lost their ability to collaborate inside the vague spaces. Those with more socialized or self-sovereign forms of mind were unable to hold the whole picture and ended up lost and angry. Neither the role clarity nor the leader could provide the scaffold for them to be clear about their interactions with the other team, and the project was left in shambles, as the two teams needed to be disbanded and a new leader—with more clarity of direction—brought in to save the project.

So it is not just for expedience or efficiency that organizations need clarity about roles and how people can add value to each other's work; it is also a vital support for sensemaking. You could create this in a conventional hierarchy, where each additional level of management has to be able to add value to the work of direct reports by placing their work into a bigger (and coherent) context. In matrixed and networked organizations, these bigger pictures come from different places in the matrix or network, but it still needs to be clear how these bigger views are going to emerge and be held for the benefit of those who cannot yet create them for themselves. If leaders are not adding a bigger picture which takes the work of the unit and the organization forward, they are too often subtracting rather than adding value. If people don't know how to add value to one another across a network or through a matrixed organization, then too often the unit or organization is spinning its wheels to little effect other than to add to the frustrations of those involved. While this confusion might create a dissonance that supports development, it's more likely that it would create a tangle of uncertainty that sends people back to their most familiar patterns rather than opening new possibilities.

Connect Supports to Challenges

When organizations create roles and structures, they do it with any number of things in mind. Some organizations create structures based on the particular work that needs to happen and the most efficient and effective hierarchy that can support that work. Smaller and newer organizations might organize around individuals already in place (e.g., "We need a role to handle more of the people stuff because Janice will never be able to do that"). Sometimes roles and structures form around clusters of related work streams or geographic connections. Sometimes they just solidify informal networks and connections. We have found only a few organizations, however, that even considered the idea of the sensemaking demands and supports as they were creating roles.

Most organizations agree that knowing what your job is and how to do it successfully are key drivers of effectiveness and satisfaction. We are arguing that it is more than just knowing what *work* you're supposed to do but also knowing what *sense* you're supposed to make of that work that will help you be effective and satisfied with your job. To this end, we can imagine that those of you who support organizational structures from the inside, or who are charged with helping organizations reshape their structures from the outside, could spell out the demands on sensemaking capacity for each role. You could be explicit about what is expected of each leader in the role and support them to lead in the ways required and also hold them accountable for this. Leadership roles are often designed around competency models, which are useful in their own way. But many competency models ignore the notion that competencies can arrive in bundles as sensemaking systems shift.[13] As you get really clear on what sorts of thinking and relating people will need to do in each leadership role, you'll be better able to develop scaffolds to support their development.

This means that when you see the most complex jobs, which will make a hard-to-match complex sensemaking demand, you could create supports that help someone live more comfortably into the job. Imagine asking these questions about a role before filling it:

- What is the time span we're hoping this person will think about?
- How large and diverse are the stakeholder groups this person needs to work with?
- How far removed are the effects from the direct control of this person?

Now you can have some sense of how demanding the role is of complex sensemaking. If, in fact, you find the role is particularly demanding, the leader who moves into that role is either going to need to have sophisticated sensemaking capacity, or she is going to need a variety of supports—individual and organizational. The most sophisticated demands (especially at the top of the organizational charts or in organizations with large amounts of diversity or very sophisticated core issues) need to arrive with the biggest and most powerful supports.

These supports can take the shape of all of the things you'd generally think about in leadership development contexts, and they can also be built right into the organization itself, to support people in new, difficult roles, and also to support everyone to grow.

Structure Organizations and Systems to Support Development

There are many things to consider when structuring organizations. You have to think about what is most effective in achieving the mission; the need for flexibility, innovation, and speed of response; the exercise of control, quality, and accountability; the extent to which functions and information need to be integrated; and how much need there is for centralizing or decentralizing aspects of the work. But there's also the question of structuring for individual development. How much does the organization need to develop its people? How much might the people wish to develop with the organization?

If you believe that individual development matters throughout the organization, you need to build developmental supports right into the structure of the organization. To create a structure that will deliver the organization's mission and also support development requires careful thought, but we think the long-term outcome is well worth it. Individual development requires at least three factors to be present in the organizational mix: reflection, experimentation, and time.

First, people need space for reflection. They need to be able to get up on the balcony and see how they are in practice, to begin to understand the ways they make sense of the world and change these things to which they are currently subject into objects that they can engage with and perhaps seek to change. They need feedback, in terms of data, and ideally a companion for the journey—a manager, mentor, coach, peers—who are able to put their ways of making sense into a wider perspective.

Second, people need to be able to try out different ways of operating and of making sense of situations. They need to get back on the dance floor and try out some new steps. This is another form of spaciousness at work. It could involve doing the same work in different ways or trying out different roles in different teams. Learning from this experimentation requires the time to be able to reflect on the experience, again preferably with someone else.

Third, reflection and experimentation take time in the moment, but most important for development, people need to be able to see how they have changed over months and years. It is most helpful to have a long view, to be able to look back over a significant time span and notice how your thinking (and sensemaking) has changed. This can be a challenge, particularly in those organizations focused on innovation, speed, and flexibility, which morph regularly to better meet the needs of the market (although there are also large hierarchical organizations that restructure regularly and may be less focused on innovation and flexibility).

By making time for conversations *about the work* a regular, scheduled, and formal part of our work, we create two powerful opportunities for getting the work done and for supporting growth. First, a regular formal conversation gives talking and thinking about the work a new status. It recognizes that there is a lot about the work we do not know; and by meeting, as a leader with direct reports or as a team, and really inquiring into how work is going, we can better forward the work and also create a space for learning and reflection.

Second, this can be a personal development opportunity for all those involved. Reflecting on the work also enables us to reflect on ourselves at work. It enables us to ask questions about what we might learn from the specific situation, how we might do things differently, and how we might *be* different. It also enables us to note patterns. The lessons we might highlight from the current situation might be novel (and all the more powerful for that), or perhaps they are familiar and we can ask ourselves questions about why we might want to learn this thing over and over. In either case, creating formal opportunities for discussing work and reviewing the major issues involved—if done well—can both get work done and also help us grow (for more specifics about how to structure learning-meetings, see Exhibit 8.3 in the next chapter).

Finally, there needs to be clarity about how people contribute to—and add value to—one another's work. In a well-focused, hierarchically arranged organization, ideally the roles of the different sections and staff should be clear, and the levels of the organization should enable value to be added from each level, with leaders at each level able to contribute a markedly bigger picture than the one below. As we have seen, at the higher levels, leaders are dealing with longer time spans, more-complex stakeholder relations, and less clarity in the relations between causes and effects. At each level in the hierarchy, this means more abstraction in much of the work and more-complex demands on sensemaking.

A thoughtful organizational hierarchy enables work to be managed effectively. It can also create a frame for conversations about an individual's development that go beyond the addition of specific skills to chart an expanding pattern of sensemaking. This is not easy to do. It works best when leaders have enough of a basic development awareness to be able to make the linkages between the complexity of thinking that the work requires and the possible range of forms of mind of the people on the team. At its most sophisticated, an organization could create different leadership steps that would increase in complexity in a clear and stepwise way—and, of course, it would include the supports people need in order to meet the growing requirements of their positions.

In matrixed or networked organizations, these levels are less explicit and the developmental requirements are likely to bleed through a variety of job descriptions—and to pop into someone's role during one project and leave it during the next. To help people make sense of the growing complexity in these more-flexible organizations, we suggest three key components.

First, there must be leaders who are responsible for the development needs of individuals, both for the skills people need to learn and the transformation in sensemaking their role may require. Second, leaders need to be explicit about the complexity of work that is being carried out across the matrix. They need to understand the developmental demand of the work and how people will get supported to achieve that level of complex thinking and engagement (e.g., Do they have the skills already? Are senior members of the team expected to mentor or coach others? Is the team expected to lift the game of all its members by bringing multiple ways of thinking about the issues to the table?). Third, someone needs to put the first two things together and create spaces that allow reflection on both individual development and the developmental requirements of the work.

When we think about structuring development into an entire organization, however, we begin to leave the realm of leadership and imagine whole workplaces that would help all of us grow (and not just the leaders). If we can create practices that help leaders to develop while getting work done, surely we could do that for us all. Chapter 8 makes a beginning.

8 CULTIVATING WISDOM

We have traveled together through time and perspectives, and we've looked at the way different people make sense of the world—and the way we ourselves have made sense of the world in the past and the way we might make sense of the world into the future. We have explored how to support one another on this journey through coaching, facilitation, and developing the core habits of mind that support growth. We have looked at the ways leaders might develop—and the way organizations might change to make that development possible. Now it's time to step back and think about ourselves.

This book does not mean to convince you that adult development is the most powerful idea the world has ever had, or that it is a unified theory of everything, or the answer to all the great secrets that puzzle you. It means to offer a lens through which you might view the sometimes mysterious terrain of human behavior, and to see whether we might use that lens to create the conditions that support our growth—and the growth of others. I would be lying to myself and to you, though, if I did not admit that there was a thing I was trying to convince you of: the need to take our growth seriously across the lifespan, and to create spaces where adults can stretch into their full potential. I am convinced that *we must begin to think of workplaces as places where people grow, and not just deliver the goods.*

In the previous chapter, Keith and I made the claim that one of the key forms of leadership development involves creating ways for leaders to do their jobs and grow simultaneously. In this chapter, I'd like to broaden this out another step. It's not just our leaders that our workplaces should be supporting to grow—it's all of us. The core idea I have been asking you to take seriously for the hours it has taken you to read these pages and the years it has taken me to write them is that we adults need to think about our own change contexts, and we need to support ourselves and others through these changes. We need to grow our own human potential, and growing wisdom is as important as making cars or delivering the mail. The first step is just believing that's our job.

I am not naïve enough to believe this is a small shift. We are used to thinking about growing and nurturing our young in schools (and even there we are not doing well enough). While increasing numbers of organizations have an espoused orientation to learning, their practice is almost always at odds with their words. We really mean to get around to developing, but who has the time? And who has the money? If we finally find some extra money lying around, and we can find people with time on their hands, we're committed to using that for development. That will probably happen—next year or the year after.

This propensity to put development off until tomorrow stems from two related difficulties. The first difficulty is our core belief about what an organization is meant to do. We tend to believe that an organization's core mission is to deliver more of what it says it will: shareholder value, food for the hungry, services that increase the common good. These are some of the outward purposes of for-profit, non-profit, and government organizations. But what if all organizations shared a common *second* core business? That their job was to grow the workforce, grow the force of human capability, and the possibilities for human potential in the world? What if it was every business's job to create not only their expected outputs, but also to develop people who were more capable when they finished work than they were when they started?

This leads us to the second difficulty that keeps us from supporting people to grow at work: We believe that helping people grow is a *cost* to the organization and we will have to give up resources (of time and money) for some potential but often distant good. I think both of these core difficulties can be solved by the shifting mindset that says, "Growing our people is our core business, because growing our people makes our core business better. These things are intertwined and impossible to separate; as our people grow, our capacity to do good work grows as well."

Is this some kind of idealistic, liberal hope? I don't think so. Our sense of work has changed so dramatically over the last 150 years that one more push might actually tip us into a significantly better place—as if the tinkering of seven generations had led us here.

We have been able to think of the adults who spend most of their waking lives in our stores and offices and factories as the hands (and sometimes minds) that are needed to get the core work done. Our relationship to those who might work alongside us has changed dramatically as the context of work has changed. In the preindustrial work world, years of apprenticeships were needed in order to eventually become a master of your work. The apprentice and the master needed one another—one as a teacher, the other as a necessary extra set of hands. In some industries, the apprentices were highly valued because they would put years into learning the craft and then would invest their next years into training others for it. My ancestors were crystal blowers and cutters in Ireland, and there are stories of the generations of craftsmen who would learn a certain way of blowing a vase, a certain pattern of diamond cuts to make it shine. That earlier world was not perfect, by any means—there was no end to the potential for exploitation and misery—but there was the accepted fact that the training and development portion of the job—the building of the capacity of the workers—was inextricably bound to the work itself.

With the advent of factories and assembly lines, the time needed to train someone to do the work became negligible. There were still people who were better and worse at their jobs than others, but the point of the factory was to smooth out those differences and make it so that there was as little individual variation as possible. A few people at the top were needed to manage the work of many people on the assembly line, and lots of that management was about coordination and scheduling, relatively simple both cognitively and interpersonally. As a workforce, we figured out how to get people to do the most work with the least training, which worked out well (economically) until the rest of the globe got connected. These days, the work—which had been designed to be unconnected to either location or extensive training—has moved to where the unskilled workers are less expensive. The Western world sheds the jobs and also sheds the ability to create new jobs. The global economic crisis showed us that when jobs are lost and don't come back, everyone suffers. It hurts us all to have a workforce unable to find employment—it is a drain on demoralized individuals and families, on our social services, on our economic and banking services. It threatens to destabilize whole societies. How on earth can developmental ideas help with that?

These ideas can help us reexamine the connection between work and learning and development, and weave those things back into a single braid—and to do this as fast as we possibly can. There is no shortage of writing about the new "knowledge age" or about the workforce of the twenty-first century and what it will take to get there, but lots of that work is done in the education field and focuses on what schooling experiences people will need in order to get them suited for knowledge work in the first place.[1] It would be fantastic to figure out how to get young adults into the workforce who had the beginning of the capacities that will take our thinking and our organizations to new levels. But while those young people may have spent 16 years in school, they may well spend 36 or even 46 years inside organizations. What could we do to help make organizations the training ground for the workers whom organizations of the future might need? How does rethinking the core task of an organization—and beginning to believe that the development of its people is part of that task—change what is possible?

The shift could happen alongside—and be supported along with—the changes in the way organizations are viewing our environment. Around the globe, organizations will need to rethink their relationship to the environment in which we live. With the increasing understanding of environmental impacts like climate change, organizations are learning that the ecosystem is a fragile thing, and it is necessary for each of us to take responsibility for trying to keep it healthy.

Similarly, as the problems organizations face get more complex and multifaceted, it will be the people who begin to deal with those problems. And it will be the those with the most-complex forms of mind who will be able to deal with the most-complex problems. Highly developed people are a kind of natural resource that can be cultivated, and the organizations in which people spend the bulk of their adult lives will determine whether the pool of those highly developed people is sufficient. It's also no secret that organizations need these highly developed people and are frustrated by their short supply. Here the supply and the demand are all in the same place: In organizations, we can create our own resource of wisdom. Understanding this as a core technology is a vital part of organizational life in this century. Having a leader actually take a mindset that believes in the twin purposes of organizations is also vital.

Merely saying that we should do this has almost no impact, of course, because we might agree that it sounds good and still have no idea how to put these ideas into place. In this chapter, like the previous one, we'll look at three things people need to do at work if they are to be successful, and we'll look at the way the habits of mind help us build those elements right into the doing of work. I've kept them in the same basic style as the key leadership tasks, but you'll see that these are modified for *all* of us, not just those who have leadership roles or responsibilities. Table 8.1 compares these ideas to the ones in Chapter 7. As in Chapter 7, I'm not claiming that these three things are the only things people need to do—nor am I claiming that these three ways of changing practices and mindsets are the only ways to move forward. Rather, I'm offering my ideas about this in the spirit of putting my head together with yours so that we can all begin to think together. Changing the paradigm of modern work is no easy task; it will take all of us working together to figure out how to tip it into a new place.

WORKING ELEMENTS FOR ALL

As a writer at the beginning of the second decade of the new millennium, I have little confidence that I can predict the way the work world will look in 10 or

TABLE 8.1   Tasks for leaders compared with tasks for us all

Leadership task	Task for all	Key difference
Shape the future	Grow curiosity	Leaders have to shape the future and have the vision to do so, but all of us need to be curious about a future that is different and hopefully better than the present.
Lead people	Recognize people as sensemakers	Leaders have to lead others toward particular outcomes, but we all have to get along and actually do things with others. Before we can do that well, we have to actually understand each other better.
Accomplish tasks	Think and create together	This isn't to suggest that leaders shouldn't accomplish tasks with others. It's to say that no matter what you do these days and whether you're a leader or not, you probably have to figure out how to put more heads and hands on it than just yours—and that means improving the way we go about thinking together.

20 years. The world is changing fast and the future is swirling around us in unpredictable ways; I suspect, but don't know, that we'll tip into some different way of thinking about our connectedness, our work, and our world. In that uncertainty, I can offer some elements that I suspect we're moving toward in our work lives rather than moving away from.

The first key task is growing curiosity. I know that it's weird to think of this as a task in the same way that crafting a vision or a strategic plan is a task for leaders, but I think it's just as important (and also something leaders need to do, as well—that's why this section is called "for all"). I'm completely convinced that curiosity—and the way it leads to openness to learning—is a necessary skill that workplaces should be actively cultivating. Some authors link it to happiness and fulfillment[2]; others to willingness to make organizational and personal change happen.[3] It's paired with the future orientation that leaders need to hold, because being curious about the future—about what the possibilities are, what the opportunities and threats might be—is a useful place for us all to get curious. As things get more complex and the amount of information we have to deal with increases, becoming numb to it all seems an antidote, but numbness leads us away from real solutions. Rather, becoming curious is the way to move all of the noise into real growth.

The second task is to understand people as sensemakers. Here I'm not just talking about understanding people's differences in a generic way; I'm talking about understanding what it means to be a person, the various parts of ourselves that compete for airtime, the incongruities of humanity, the way we construct the world and then live inside our constructions. One of the biggest mistakes we all make—and have been making for generations—is believing that people (should) act in rational and predictable ways based on the facts of the matter. Even believing that we'd agree on "the facts of the matter" or on what would be "rational" is misleading and unhelpful.[4] Remembering that we are all sensemakers and acting as if it's true is a second key developmental piece of growing on the job.

The third task is to combine the first two in order to get better working relationships—and better work outcomes—together. If you are really getting to be curious, and you are understanding other people as sensemakers, you will know that your way of putting things together (which feels like the best way) and someone else's will be different. Believing that your job is to think and create together—to make new sense together—means genuinely understanding that you can't do it alone and that nearly every piece of work that requires thinking requires thinking together, just as every piece of work that requires creating something requires multiple creators. In the next section, I extend these ideas give you some tactical ways of changing your practice on the job.

Grow Curiosity

Curiosity is the lubricant of the learning process—without it, learning is possible but meets more resistance and difficulty. Anyone walking down a city street with a 3-year-old sees that kids are nearly made of curiosity—each leaf must be touched and turned over, each car noise must be imitated, each passing stranger must be given a good hard stare, each answer leads to another "why?" Yet as we grow older, we are likely to find that curiosity decreases; perhaps we think we have learned so much that there is so much less in the world for us to wonder about. Early on, we begin to be scolded for being curious and rewarded for knowing things, for being certain. In school, we were rewarded for having the right answer (not a great question); in job interviews, we were rewarded for looking confident and in control. We come to view curiosity as belonging to children (and fatal to cats).

Yet it's also clear that certainty closes down our openness to new ideas, to new possibilities, to learning things that might unsettle us. The economist John Kenneth Galbraith knew this when he wrote, "Faced with the choice between changing one's mind and proving that there is no need to do so, almost everyone gets busy on the proof." In fact, many of us don't even know we've had a choice to change our minds, because we tend not to even notice the opportunity, so focused are we on confirming what we already knew to be true.[5]

EXHIBIT 8.1   Growing curious by searching for the equals sign

One easy-to-remember practice that helps raise our curiosity along each of the habits of mind is to search for the *equals sign* in your own reasoning or the reasoning of others. Math class has told us that the equations on either side of the equals sign always add up.

$$2x = 12$$

There's lots to be learned from paying attention to what's on either side of the equals sign. In this case, we can be confident that x stands in for the number 6, because we have faith that the equals sign is right.

Life teaches us, however, that we often create some seriously unbalanced equations:

Success = owning my own company by the time I'm 50

There's a way that the first equation and the second equation can feel equally true, and that's because the logic seems so clear to us. Becoming curious about the equals sign helps uncover meaning—regardless of someone's form of mind.

To search for the equals sign, just trace the logic of any conclusion: You ask, Why did I/we come to this as the obvious answer? You're looking to be open to those times when you're sure that something *necessarily means* something else: A bad meeting *necessarily means* that people think less of you; the fact that he had two reasons to say no to a date *necessarily means* that he doesn't want to spend time with you; your not making partner this year *necessarily means* that your upward trajectory has stalled and it's time to start looking for a new job. In each case, you might be right: People might think less of you, he might really be not that into you, and you should dust off your CV. Subject–object theory, though, tells us that when you find something that necessarily means something else, you're probably subject to that set of ideas. Sometimes we want to stay subject to those ideas, but sometimes we might like to bring those ideas out into the open, have a look at them, and make a new set of decisions. Tracing your logical certainty opens up a new form of curiosity and helps you decide whether you want to continue to hold a thing as true or whether you might like to open to a different set of possibilities.

How can we come to be more curious, though, when we are designed (by our cultures and maybe also by our brains) to act more certain? The three habits of mind from Chapter 6 will help us here. Each of those is curiosity-generating.

Asking different questions is both curiosity-driven and also curiosity-increasing. Here I am not talking about questions that seek to solve something or fix something or actually *do* anything at all. To be most developmentally supportive of yourself or others, the key is simply to ask questions about anything you're curious about, to ask questions that this set of ideas awakens for you. In this way it isn't about you solving the problem for someone else (or even, if you're asking questions of yourself, solving it for yourself). It's about learning deeply about something without attempting to solve it at all, at least not at first. The questions then become their own purpose, and the insights that you and others find in them are not necessarily the insights you were looking for when you began questioning. Asking a question and hoping the person comes up with the answer you have in mind does not count as a genuine question. Neither does asking a question which could—if you were really honest—end with "you moron!" (e.g., "Have you proofread this sentence really carefully [you moron]?"). Asking questions about which you are genuinely curious is surprisingly difficult and also makes a subject–object move. Asking questions to understand will help you and others grow.

Taking multiple perspectives, of course, is also both curiosity-driven and also curiosity-creating. Your way is the one way of looking at the world you know well—so well, in fact, that if you're not careful, it will feel like the truth to you. Who might you have to talk to so that you can get a perspective that's utterly different from yours? Many groups and individuals are great at parts of this—and there are a variety of ways to engage with other perspectives (e.g., stakeholder analyses, customer surveys). Yet even in places where taking these other perspectives is common, or where there is a system of asking for information and perspectives of others, there are often two types of key perspectives we leave behind: those we discount, and those we never think about in the first place. Generally, in the first category, we discount perspectives when we find them unhelpful or hostile to our own perspectives; we tend to think of them as out of touch or ignorant or just plain batty. Whose perspective do you discount as you go about your daily business? What might those discounted perspectives add if you were to really take them seriously? A harder set of perspectives to take are the silent, missing perspectives—the ones that we neither seek nor that seek us but are simply missing from the field of view. Whose perspectives are you leaving out and how might you shift that? How can you make yourself be open to what there is to learn from someone with whom you disagree? And, maybe more important, how can you bring yourself to actually *care* about those other ways so you go out of your way to find them? Intentionally going toward multiple perspectives both helps you grow and also increases the quality of your work.

Finally, looking at the system always leads to curiosity, because systems are naturally so difficult to grasp and understand. Intentionally seeking out behavior not just about individual elements but also about the interaction of those elements can give you a new set of options—for your thinking and your decisions. You can pay attention to the interaction between different people, forces, or ideas. You can pay attention to the boundaries different people draw around key issues or theories. You can pay attention to the way that ideas, information, money, influence, culture, power, and so forth flow through the system—and look for shortages or surpluses of all of those things. As you begin to wonder about these different features, you get really curious. As you get curious, you learn and suddenly are better placed to find new solutions—and also to find new openings for curiosity. This virtuous cycle helps you grow. (For another quick tool that helps increase curiosity, see Exhibit 8.1.)

Understand People as Sensemakers

Do I contradict myself?
Very well, then, I contradict myself,
(I am large—I contain multitudes.)
Walt Whitman, *Song of Myself*

It's not revolutionary to think that people have different ways of making sense of the world—you knew that. It is revolutionary to *remember* that and to act as if you really believe it is true. I spend most of my time—as a consultant, as a coach, as a leader inside an organization—reminding people (and myself) that people around us are making sense of the world in different ways, and that those differences really matter. It seems to be a key piece of being human to understand that idea with our heads but not put it into practice. Simply remembering that each of us is a sensemaker, and each of us makes sense of the world in our own way, can change the way you react to yourself and to those around you.

By now you've probably seen the ways these forms of mind live in you and others, and, when you're trying, you can probably manage a new level of compassion for the mysterious and beautiful sensemaking of others. You've probably spent enough time with these ideas to think in some kind of shorthand about the different forms of mind (like the one at Table 8.2). It is easy to have patience with our differences during spacious and happy times—but how might we have patience with these ideas even when we don't want to, when we are angry or stressed? This happens when you can feel for the strengths and challenges of others—even as they annoy you—and connect to your compassion for them. Table 8.2 is a handy support when you can't quite remember what their strengths were in the first place.

For example, imagine that Minh seems to change his mind depending on the group he's with. When he's with one group of stakeholders, he tells them one thing; but with another group, he seems to have a whole different set of beliefs. You could do the natural thing and believe Minh is a liar or being manipulative, or you could keep in mind the potential that his form of mind is making some kind of difference in the way he is acting. How would it make you more

TABLE 8.2   Strengths, challenges, and compassion required to understand people as sensemakers

Form of mind	Strengths	Challenges	Compassion needed
Self-sovereign	Clarity of purpose and self-interest	Lack of perspective-taking and empathy	To understand that this is a person who is growing the capacity to take perspectives of others and to see a picture bigger than herself, and that the world—especially inside a leadership position—can seem overwhelming and unfair a lot of the time.
Socialized	Devotion to a cause bigger than himself	Lack of capacity to decide between important others or competing ideas in which he is embedded	To understand that this is a person who is authentically and genuinely living out his values and ideals—with the help of outside experts, relationships, or ideas—and that he may often feel over his head and ill-suited for the leadership task at hand.
Self-authored	Strength of commitment to self-authored ideals and values	Lack of ability to get outside own commitments and perspectives and see the ways a well-reasoned idea might be wrong	To understand that we *are* our values and principles and therefore our possibilities are limited by those values and principles. What might strike us as an unhelpful line in the sand may be a key piece of the identity of the self-authored person, and her certainty may come from these parts of her self-authored system.
Self-transforming	Openness to new perspectives, constant interest in learning, ability to see nuance and be untroubled by complexity	Lack of ability to *not* see patterns; difficulty remembering that seeing the world this way is unusual	To understand that this can be a lonely place and that folks who are here—or on the way to this form of mind—could use good company and deep listening.

sympathetic if you believed he was acting out of his own meaning-making system rather than just placating others? How would you support him to grow? When you keep the development of meaning systems in mind, you have access to a whole new set of questions and opportunities.

We all know from personal experience what research tells us: that we get frustrated with other folks because they do things that do not make sense to us, things we don't like or which strike us as unhelpful in some way. Yet the thousands of people I've worked with—even those who were enraging everyone around them—believed they were doing the right thing, or at least they were doing their best. If you hold an orientation that everyone around you is doing their very best, then their annoying and frustrating (mis)behavior turns out to have its own form of logic and sense in it. You can ask yourself, What would I have to believe about the world for these actions to make sense and seem like the best way for me? And sometimes, once we get the full picture, we see that it's ourselves in the wrong. Those who have something of a self-transforming form of mind can hold on to this idea longer than the rest of us, but all of us can come closer. Keeping sense-making in mind—even if it just reminds us that there is a whole new world for us to explore, and it lives inside the minds of other people—can help us practice a new form of connection and compassion with others.

When we're thinking about ourselves, there's a second set of questions to ask. When something frustrates or unsettles us, or when we are feeling sad or angry or desperate, we can begin to ask, What would I have to believe for this not to be so sad/unpleasant/frustrating/infuriating? Sometimes we find we'd have to believe things about other people. Sometimes we find that we'd have to believe different things about ourselves. Imagine that in a Friday afternoon meeting you got flustered and tongue-tied during a big presentation to your boss and your boss's boss. All weekend afterward you run the commentary of what you could and should have done differently—from preparing more, to being less defensive when they asked questions, to never wanting to be a part of this stupid profession in the first place. By Monday morning you want to stay under the covers and not go to work ever again.

Yet you know that some folks can have a setback like this and feel bummed but then move on without real misery. What do they believe about the world that you do not? They might have a more self-authored perspective and have a sense that their job is only one facet of the value they bring to the world—they are not fused with what they do or how they make sense of things. They might have a more self-transforming perspective and know that often it is the setbacks which, paradoxically, lead to the most wonderful and unexpected outcomes. What would you like to believe about this? How could you do that? Just knowing that you *could* have

EXHIBIT 8.2   Understanding people as sensemakers:
                Separating data from meaning[6]

In everything we see, there is the external event (the facts of what happened that might be objectively measured or described) and the sense we make of those facts.[7] Because of the way our complex brains work, that package of information—facts and meaning—come at us in a blur and we can often have a confused sense about which is which. If someone else is in the picture, that person is making the same leap about you, and might be similarly confused. If you're in a meeting or a group, people are leaping to conclusions all over the room.

One core practice is just to see if you can, on your own, get a sense of the difference between the *facts* of what happened—those things which could be objectively verified and with which other people would agree—and the *sense* you're making of those facts (which are the judgments/thoughts/beliefs/assumptions). This tends to require some stretching.

For example:

Sergio was really gunning for me in that meeting today! He argued with everything I said while totally supporting every world out of Sheila's mouth. He's got a real axe to grind with me . . .

This is often the way our reactions come to us—in a package that combines what we saw and the sense we make of it. Unpicking those from one another gives you a set of questions to ask about an event. Keeping in mind that both you and Sergio are making sense of the world in particular ways means that everything becomes possible to test and explore.

First, you can ask yourself questions about your own sensemaking:

What gave me the impression Sergio was gunning for me? What did he argue with? It felt like everything, but what was it, really—how many things? Which sort of things? I suspect this means bad things about the way Sergio feels about me. What else could it mean?

Then, you could restate the whole idea of it to make your sensemaking separate from what you saw as data and offer them as two separate pieces rather than one lump:

Today in the meeting, on at least three occasions I remember, Sergio interrupted my description of an idea with sentences I found critical:

"That'll never work." "We tried that already." "Your data is wrong on that one." This upset me and made me worry about the state of our relationship and, to be frank, the quality of my ideas.

Once that's clear, you can begin to decide where the open spaces of curiosity might be.

- In what ways is Sergio's assessment about the quality of my ideas? (*Am* I recycling old ideas that haven't worked? *Am* I missing or using incorrect data?)
- In what ways is this actually about Sergio and not really about me at all? (Was he having a particularly bad day? Were these ideas somehow cutting across his authorities?)
- In what ways is it about our relationship? (Is Sergio generally more critical of me than others? How do I treat his ideas? How are we relating to one another outside of this meeting?)

Finally, you could go and talk to the other person and find out his perspective of these events.

When you keep in mind the fact that your vision of the world isn't the truth, it reminds you to practice picking apart the data from your sense of things. This creates a little space between what happens and your reaction to it. That space is where our ideas and our beliefs and assumptions become object, and we get more choices.

Practicing this is like flexing a muscle: What did I actually see? What sense did I make of what I saw? What were my feelings, beliefs, assumptions, intentions?

Lift and repeat ten times a day, and you will develop.

---

a different relationship to anger and frustration is a beginning of developing that new relationship. (For a way to practice this approach, please see Exhibit 8.2.)

Thinking and Working Together

As we pointed out in Chapter 7, organizations can build developmental practices into the structures and procedures throughout their organizations and can think about supporting development. It isn't that folks in organizations don't do some of this thinking already: Most organizations with more than a couple dozen people have human resource structures, development plans, and some idea about organizational learning.

So the problem isn't that we don't know that we *should* do this; the problem is we don't know *how* to do this. Performance management systems, training programs, promotion reviews—all of these tend to be set up to help people learn, and yet the people in the hundreds of organizations I've worked with almost always think these systems are a waste of time, are too low-level, are too confusing, or are just generally misguided. If those who created those systems understood developmentally related differences, we might all find ourselves more clearly and intentionally supported to grow.

We could ask questions about whether people who were more self-sovereign were getting the opportunity to develop loyalty and a bigger picture; whether people who were more socialized were getting enough feedback to know how they were doing and enough permission to know that they could author their own ideas. We could keep the relatively common practices that supported the consolidation of the self-authored perspective, and we could intentionally develop systems and programs that would help create and support a bigger, self-transforming meaning-making system. We could do more than support the growth of individual forms of mind; we could create whole organizational cultures that support growth and development alongside the doing of excellent work.

For example, unless you have a Gallup survey, a consultant, or a psychologist explicitly using a cultural lens, the culture of an organization, a work group, or a family is all part of the water we swim inside rather than a set of choices we think about and make. Culture is not easy to see until you get outside of it. For me, the North American culture in which I was swimming was not visible until I moved to New Zealand and saw the subtle shifts in patterns of thought and behavior. Still, we all know that just getting outside your own culture isn't necessarily enough to put it on the table; people can travel all around the world and work in a variety of very different organizational cultures without noticing those differences. The concern is that culture shapes what is possible for us, shapes what we can see and can't see, what we believe is fair, what we think is possible, and yet it's very hard to step outside and examine. And as we have seen elsewhere in this book, if you can't step outside something, it may be hard for you to change it (thus the millions of dollars spent on unsuccessful culture change projects each year).

To begin to build organizational cultures that enable growth requires that we understand and make choices about our lives. Intentionally questioning the culture of a place (or other hidden assumptions about your thinking and your work) helps you get some distance on the perspectives, habits, and norms which might otherwise hold you tightly and make decisions for you. Core questions you can ask are:

- How do we think about and deal with conflict here?

- How do we think about and deal with affection here? How about mistakes? New ideas? Self-congratulation?

- What things are we not allowed to question? What things are we not supposed to take for granted? How do we know when we have done a good job?

Organizations can work these questions into monthly reviews, families can work them into dinnertime conversation, individuals can reflect upon them in a journal or a conversation with friends. Eventually the culture can become one which seeks to question itself, which is inherently developmental and likely to be much more agile and responsive than cultures which charge on, unreflectively.

In these learning cultures, we could reexamine entry and onboarding programs, building in space for people to be sensemakers and not just decision makers.[8] We could think about the organizational systems that support assumption questioning and boundary pushing. We could help leaders learn how to give feedback in ways that supported everyone's learning rather than simply delivering a message from on high.[9] If we went really far in our thinking and practice, we could transform that most powerful of all organizational events: The Meeting.

Meetings are where many people in organizations spend vast amounts of time, and people in every organization I've ever been in believed that some significant percentage of their time was wasted in these gatherings. I've helped clients calculate how much money is wasted in ineffective meetings, and the numbers tend to make people cringe.

Yet when I introduce the idea of making meetings opportunities for growing and developing as well as for getting work done, people think I'm crazy. If we cannot even imagine how to get *work* done in meetings, how would we ever create a meeting where work gets done *and* people are developed? My argument is this: If meetings were designed not only to do work but also to be developmental, both pieces would be accomplished with more success than either is accomplished now. Right now, the most common thing that most people expect to come out of a meeting is a list of things they mostly already know (and could have been e-mailed) and a date for another meeting. What if people could ask themselves: What did we agree to in that meeting? (the work bit), and: What did we learn? (the developmental bit). If everyone can answer those two questions, meetings will be both practically and developmentally productive.

Imagine how different meetings would be if the point of a meeting was learning from different perspectives rather than the common assumption that team meetings are spaces for us to show our certainty or convince others that we've got things under control. The easiest way to do this is simply to make it explicit, to welcome confusion into meeting spaces, to ask people to come with developing ideas, to ask, "What did we learn today?" at the end of each meeting. When you hold the idea of these different, growing sensemaking systems in mind, meetings become opportunities to see into another set of perspectives, a clear chance to grow ideas, solutions, and minds. (You can find a step-by-step guide to what I mean here in Exhibit 8.3.)

THE BEGINNING

Development is not a race to the finish line. There's no prize for being the most self-transformational on your death bed or the first in your high school class to become self-authored. Development isn't just about this theory or these forms of mind; it is the journey of our lives, the way we come to see and re-see the world around us.

Paying attention to someone's particular form of mind is not going to change the world. Paying attention to the sensemaking of yourself and others, however, might change the course of your life. Those of us who work in this space find ourselves being more gentle with those around us, less frustrated by the foibles of humanity, more filled with admiration and affection for those who are doing their best. This becomes a virtuous cycle. Our stance opens us to new possibilities in other people. As we do this, it leads other people to become bigger in our company and they become aware of those possibilities themselves. Spending time with people who are being their biggest selves is a delight which pulls us to be at our most complex.

Creating contexts and spaces for people to reach their full potential may sound like specialized work for those of us who happened to be born with an orientation in this direction. Really it's the work we're all called to. All humans have a biological need for connection, for relationship—even for love. Our expression of this need is individual, but our requirement for it is not. Supporting someone to be at their biggest—whether as a leader, as a coach, as a teacher, or as a colleague—brings us into the space where we are at our biggest, too. Our people and our planet require that bigness right now; it is no longer an option for us to be small. Leading systems thinker Peter Senge says the world is at too critical a point to allow for the luxury of hopelessness. I believe it is also at too critical a point to allow for the luxury of smallness. As we create possibilities for growth for ourselves and for others, we increase the whole store of capacity for thinking, collaboration, compassion, and even love on the planet. That seems like a good beginning.

EXHIBIT 8.3   Thinking and creating together:
Cultivating developmental meetings

Here's the bottom line on this. At every regularly held meeting, everyone in the room should learn something. At every regularly held meeting, something new should be created—a new idea, plan, product, solution. At every regularly held meeting, most people should agree that it's not a waste of time. If these things are already true for you—fantastic! If you're not quite there yet, here are some ways you can think about creating more value from your time together.

Once again, the first powerful thing to do is keep developmental ideas in mind as you have a meeting. What would it mean if you really believed that everyone else in the meeting was making sense of things in a different way? How would that change the questions you asked? Meetings are often places where culture is carried and lived out and spread, but people live inside cultures in different ways, as we have seen throughout this book. How will you make space in the meeting for everyone to be as big as possible, to contribute as much as they can?

Prepare

Most meetings go wrong before they've even begun, and we'll have to do some nondevelopmentally related sorting to even make room for meetings that support development and learning. Agenda setting and the before-meeting work are not glamorous business, but they would make the meeting space infinitely more productive and would leave us time to get work done and also grow. This is basic stuff but rarely done: We all collect ideas for a meeting, but we rarely know what kind of ideas they are: Is one idea an informational item for one person to inform the others? Is it a discussion item that some person or group wants to gain advice or perspectives about before making a decision themselves? Is it a matter that this whole collective needs to decide on? Tag every possible agenda item with its designation.

If you're going to make room for learning, informational items should almost always be handled outside of meetings. Generally, when someone comes to the meeting with an informational item, others ask questions in which the asker is at least vaguely interested, others might be totally disinterested, and no one can particularly change (or else it would have one of the other tags). So many senior teams use (waste) their collective time on

(continued)

EXHIBIT 8.3   Thinking and creating together:
                Cultivating developmental meetings (*continued*)

informational agendas because the person who would have to type up the information doesn't have time to do that, and the others don't read memos from one another anyway. Commit as a group to do that prework, write the information down, ask questions off-line. This creates better relationships, and if you're creating a culture of curious questioning, the whole enterprise will be self-reinforcing.

Select

Now that you've gotten the informational items off the agenda, you have to decide which remaining items make it on. A vital question that's rarely asked is: *What group of people would be most useful thinking partners about this issue?* Is it the whole team or a subset? The research on team effectiveness shows that a key to effectiveness is to have a team that forms intentionally and works together for some purpose. But most of the senior teams I work with meet more out of habit than intention. When you're picking the agenda for a meeting, you want to pick things about which everyone in the room might have a useful perspective. You want to pick things from which everyone in the room might potentially learn. You want to pick things about which you might disagree. Now you've got the ingredients for a helpful meeting. Give everything the time it needs (go slow to go fast) and send out any prework that would save time when you're in person together.

Question curiously

Now that you've got an agenda and you've done your prework, it's time to change how you show up with one another in the meeting room itself. This is a time to ask questions rather than make points, to open up to curiosity rather than defend perspectives, and to remember that everyone in room has a different and helpful viewpoint. This means that the goal of the meeting, in part, would be to make some things object for people rather than having the group be subject to their assumptions. Often the assumptions are ones like: We've tried that before. That will never work, because the SVP doesn't approve of those sorts of things. Customers aren't sophisticated enough to want that. And so on. If one of the goals of the meeting is development, naming those things that are hidden is a key ingredient, which means that meetings need to be designed in such a way that there is space and time for people to question assumptions—and that they have the structures and ideas in order to do that.

Two things will help you in this regard: (1) If everyone remembers that the larger goal (e.g., solving an important team or organizational problem) is bigger than any individual person, you'll have people reduce their ego connection to the issue (inasmuch as they can, developmentally); and (2) if people can make—and keep each other honest about—a commitment to ask questions that are really questions and not points they want to assert, the questions won't create a battlefield and won't be as likely to raise defenses. If you've got a space where people can ask curious questions, assumptions get put on the table, and the invisible becomes visible, people will find the meeting a good use of their time, the solution to whatever the problem is will be richer and more significant, and you've increased the chance that the people in the room will grow.

Agree (this is about making sure you're doing the work)

An oddly-missed step in many meetings is to agree on whatever action plan came out of the meeting. This is something many people somehow collectively fear to make explicit. Who agreed to do which things? What exactly is it that person is supposed to do? By when? What are the conditions for the satisfactory completion of that item? Who judges? This step is the low-hanging fruit of meeting productivity. If everyone does this consistently, even if meetings don't become more developmentally supportive, they'll be more productive.

Review learning (this is about making sure you're learning)

Just as groups should review the task assignment, it's really helpful for them to take a few minutes at the end of every meeting to review the learning that the team has done together. Again, this helps make things object and solidifies the learning (as well as creating more of the culture that learning and growth are part of what goes on in your organization). If someone hasn't learned anything, the meeting was at least partially a failure.

REFERENCE MATTER

Appendix A

REPRODUCIBLE HANDOUT

Key Concepts in Adult Development
Jennifer Garvey Berger

Constructive–developmental: This core set of theories is "constructive–developmental," a term that joins together two different schools of thought. *Constructivists* believe that the world isn't out there to be discovered, but that we create our world by our discovery of it. Humans make meaning of their surroundings, and that meaning *is* the surrounding; two people who see the same picture differently may actually, in their seeing of it, be creating two different pictures. *Developmentalists* believe that humans grow and change over time and enter qualitatively different phases as they grow. Cognitive, moral, and social development, however, unlike physical development, isn't a matter of simply waiting for nature to take its course. Development can be helped or hindered (and in some severe cases arrested) by the individual's life experiences. *Constructive–developmentalists* believe that the systems by which people make meaning grow and change over time.

Information: In-form-ation is new knowledge that you add to the current *form* of your mind. New skills or knowledge may be important for keeping up with the newest technology or the latest cutting-edge work in your profession. Information, however, while helpful, is generally by itself not a sufficient kind of growth for adults. Often the thing that needs to change, however, is not *what* we know but *how* we know. If how we know needs to change, we need more than information; we need *trans*formation.

Transformation: Transformation is more than simply adding information into a container (your mind, for example) that already exists. Transformation is about changing the very *form* of the container—making it larger, more complex, more able to deal with complexity and uncertainty. Transformation occurs, according to Harvard Professor Robert Kegan, when you are newly able to step back and reflect on something and make decisions about it. There are many ways that transformation can happen; one of them is the movement of things from "subject" to "object" (see below). Robert Kegan says transformative learning happens when someone changes "not just the way he behaves, not just the way he feels, but the way he knows—not just what he knows but the *way* he knows."[1]

Subject: Things that are subject are by definition experienced as unquestioned, simply a part of the self. They can include many different things—a relational issue, a personality trait, an assumption about the way the world works, behaviors, or emotions. Things that are subject to you can't be seen because they are a part of you. Because they can't be seen, they are taken for granted, taken for true—or not even taken at all. You generally can't name things that are "subject," and you certainly can't reflect upon them—that would require the ability to stand back and take a look at them. You don't *have* something that's subject; something that's subject *has you.* For example, I once thought that all people learn things in basically the same way—the way I learned them. When students came to me with difficulty about an assignment or test, I thought the problem was *theirs;* I was being so clear and they were still not learning. I struggled and struggled to help them learn, but to no avail. I was subject to my own teaching and learning styles. I didn't know different styles existed (because I figured everyone taught and learned like me), so I was powerless to change my style to meet the needs of diverse learners.

Object: Object is the opposite of subject. Again, something that is object can be a relational issue, personality trait, or a belief about the world. While things that are subject *have you,* you *have* things that are object. While all of us necessarily have many parts of our world to which we are subject (if we gave much conscious thought to our assumptions about gravity, we might not have time to go to sleep at night!), one part of development is about moving more and more things from subject to object. The more in your life you take as object, the more complex your worldview because you can see and act upon more things. In the example above, as I struggled to help my students learn, I found out about teaching and learning styles—especially as they relate to personality type. For the first time I could examine something I hadn't even known existed before—my own teaching and learning styles—and I could take action to help my students be more successful. What was once unknown and unnamed—subject—became within my ability to reflect on—as object. The most profound example of a move from subject to object is when the entire meaning-making system moves from that which unquestioningly runs me to that which I can actively take charge of and control. This shift of entire systems from subject to object is what gives form to the five forms of mind.

Forms of mind: There are five forms of mind, ranging from a 2-year-old to a (mostly theoretical) person well into the second half of life.[2] Each form is a qualitative shift in the meaning-making and complexity from the form before it. We do not give up what we've learned in a previous form of mind; we grow new capacities like rings on a tree, including and transcending our previous ways of making sense of the world.[3] Perhaps the most important thing to remember about the forms of mind is that, while they become more complex with time, there is no form of mind that is inherently *better* than any other form (just as a more complex idea isn't necessarily more valuable than a simple one). People can be kind or unkind, just or unjust, moral or immoral at any of these forms of mind, so it is impossible to measure a person's worth by looking at his or her form of mind. What is more important is the *fit* between the mind and the task each person is required to do. Each of the five forms of mind is described briefly below, but the ones to pay closest attention to are the ones where the majority of adults spend most of their lives—the socialized mind and the self-authored mind. To help understand this system, I'm going to offer a fictional small village made up of members from all five forms of mind. I'll give the people in the village roles based on the strengths of their particular mind.

Magical childhood mind (mostly young children): Psychologist Jean Piaget was the first to point out that young children cannot yet hold the idea of "durable objects"—which is the notion that things in the world retain the same qualities over time. When they look out an airplane and see how small people look, they believe the people actually *are* small. A child with this form of mind believes that others in their lives can live in his mind and is mystified when others hold different opinions (about what the best color is, for instance) or can't pick right up on a game in an imaginary world. When water is poured from one container to another, and the quantity of the water looks different, he believes the water actually has grown (or shrunk), and no amount of persuasion will convince him otherwise. He believes he can slip down the drain in the tub because he can't hold himself as different from the water that slips away. Children in this form of mind need to be reminded of the rules over and over, because they can't hold the ideas in their mind for very long; the rule that existed yesterday about drawing on the walls might not seem to apply today. The magical childhood mind is a time of magic and mystery as the world inexplicably changes from second to second. If we imagine a member of our village with this form of mind, we'd see someone who needs constant supervision and is not yet ready to police himself because he simply can't remember the laws from moment to moment (we'd keep him firmly under adult supervision). His job is to learn about the world.

The self-sovereign mind (older children—7 to 10—and adolescents, but also some adults): When children learn that objects stay the same no matter what their own relationship is to the object (when I walk away from the car and it looks smaller, the car isn't actually shrinking), their world becomes less magical and more complex. They discover that they have beliefs and feelings that remain constant over time, as well (I love chocolate but hate mashed potatoes; I'm great at ice skating). This insight lets them know that other people have opinions and beliefs that remain constant, too. Their concrete understandings let them know that a rule yesterday is probably a rule today, too. Their orientation is to figuring out how to get past the rule if it is in their way. While they are aware that others have feelings and desires, true empathy isn't possible for them yet because the distance between their minds and other minds is so great. Mostly other people's interests are important only if they interfere with the interests of the person with a self-sovereign form of mind. When irritating rules are not broken, it's because of a fear of being caught; when friends don't lie to each other even when they're tempted to, it's because of a fear of retaliation. Children—and adults—at this stage are self-centered because theirs is the only perspective they rightfully know how to take. A villager with this form of mind follows the laws because she's afraid of punishment; if the laws don't seem to meet her needs and she can find a way to break them with minimal risk, she will. We can count on her to work in her own best interests, so we'll give her a job that is in her own best interests (like tending a garden for her family) that has clear boundaries and limited scope. We'll also make sure that she is fairly well supervised by others.

The socialized mind (older adolescents and the *majority* of adults): People with this form of mind no longer see others as simply a means to an ends; they have developed the ability to subordinate their desires to the desires of others. Their impulses and wishes, to which they were subject when they had more of a self-sovereign mind, have become objects for their reflection and decision making. They internalize the feelings and emotions of others and are guided by those people or institutions (like an organization or synagogue or a political party) that are most important to them. They are able to think abstractly, be self-reflective about their actions and the actions of others, and are devoted to something that's greater than their own needs. The major limitation of this form of mind is that, when there is a conflict between important others (or between a single important other—like a partner, and an institution—like a political party), people with a socialized mind feel torn in two and cannot find a way to make a decision. There is no sense of what *I* want outside of others' expectations or societal roles. This is generally admirable in teenagers, but, in adults, it can often seem like a personality flaw. As Kegan notes, "When I live in this balance as an adult I am the prime candidate for the assertiveness trainer, who may tell me that I need to learn how to stand up for myself, be more 'selfish,' less pliable, and so on, as if these were mere skills to be added on to whoever else I am. The popular literature will talk about me as lacking self-esteem, or as a pushover because I want other people to like me."[4] Kegan goes on to point out that the very notion of "self-esteem" is inappropriate at this order, because self-esteem implies an *internal* source for feeling good about oneself. Those with a socialized mind don't have an independently constructed self to feel good about; their esteem is reliant on others because they are, in many ways, made up of those people, ideas, or ideals around them. A villager with this form of mind could be a model citizen[5] and may follow the laws out of loyalty to the others in the village (or his religion or his organization or his family). He tries hard not to break the rules because he wouldn't want to feel he had let others down. In our small, homogenous village, someone with a socialized form of mind can hold nearly any position that doesn't require independent leadership. He can be a teacher, have his own business, or be a member of the military. As long as he has someone whom he respects to help him make difficult decisions, he can do nearly anything in this village.

The self-authored mind (some adults): Adults with a self-authored form of mind have achieved all that those with a more-socialized mind have, but now they have created a *self* that exists even outside of its relationship to others. The opinions and desires of others that they internalized and that had great control over them when they were making meaning with more of a socialized form of mind are now object to them. They are now able to examine those various rule systems and opinions and are able to mediate between them. Those with a self-authored form of mind have an internal set of rules and regulations—a self-governing system— which they use to make their decisions or mediate conflicts. Unlike those with the earlier self-sovereign form of mind, those who are more self-authored can empathize with others, and consider the wishes and opinions of others when making decisions. Unlike those with a more-socialized form of mind, though, those who are more self-authored don't feel torn apart by the conflicting opinions of other people, theories, or ideas because they have their own system with which to make decisions. Instead, they feel torn when their own internal values are in competition. These are the people we read about in the literature who "own" their work, who are self-guided, self-motivated, self-evaluative. A villager at this form of mind would make a good mayor because she has her own internal governing system. She could create the rules from her internal system and fight hard to protect those rules. This guidance would help the village run smoothly according to her inner vision of village life. The self-authored mayor may not be an excellent diplomat, however, because when other people don't understand or see the need to follow her rules, she may be so invested in her own way of doing things that she cannot easily see connections between her ideas of what is right and other people's ideas of what is right.

The self-transforming mind (very few adults): Adults who have a self-transforming form of mind have achieved all that those who are more self-authored have, but they have learned the limits of their own inner system—and the limits of having an inner system in general. Instead of viewing others as people with separate and different inner systems, those with a self-transforming mind see across inner systems to look at the similarities that are hidden inside what used to look like differences. For example, they see that the ways that ideas like homosexuality and heterosexuality actually create one another, that there would be no word that described sexual preference if there weren't more than one option. People with this form of mind are less likely to see the world in terms of dichotomies or polarities. They are more likely to believe that what we often think of as black and white are just various shades of gray whose differences are made more visible by the lighter or darker colors around them. A villager with this mind might be an elder whose job it is to mediate conflicts between the many villages. While he generally follows the laws set by the mayor, he sees that the many different villages have a variety of laws that are basically designed to do similar things, and that the differences are much more like similarities than any of the mayors can see. He helps the mayors find a common ground and reminds them that they are all members of a larger community— the community of human beings, perhaps, or of members of our planet.

THE POINT OF IT ALL
Development is not a race to the finish line. There's no prize for being the most self-transformational on your death bed or the first in your high school class to become self-authored. Development isn't just about this theory or these forms of mind; it is the journey of our lives, the way we come to see and re-see the world around us.

Paying attention to someone's particular form of mind is not going to change the world. Paying attention to the sensemaking of yourself and others, however, might change the course of your life. Those of us who work in this space find ourselves being more gentle with those around us, less frustrated by the foibles of humanity, more filled with admiration and affection for those who are doing their best. This becomes a virtuous cycle. Our stance opens us to new possibilities in other people. As we do this, it leads other people to become bigger in our company and they become aware of those possibilities themselves. Spending time with people who are being their biggest selves is a delight that pulls us to be at our most complex. Adult development theories exist to give us a glimpse into what sense the world makes to us and to others in the present and to show us all a path to a different set of possibilities for the future.

Dr. Jennifer Garvey Berger is a coach, leadership developer, researcher, and writer. She works with leaders around the world to see bigger, more inclusive perspectives and to think in more creative and collaborative ways about their challenges. She also offers advanced workshops to coaches in these practices. Jennifer is a partner in the small leadership development consultancy, Cultivating Leadership (www .cultivatingleadership.co.nz). She has a doctorate from Harvard University, where she was mentored by Robert Kegan. This is reprinted with permission from *Changing on the Job: Developing Leaders for a Complex World.*

Appendix B

LIBBY'S ALMOND BREAD

Okay, so it's admittedly quirky to have a recipe in this book that doesn't contribute to anyone's development. In fact, much of the point of this recipe is that it's low in fat and high in protein so as *not* to contribute to our growth!

But there are many important facets to what it means to be human, and complexity is only a tiny piece of what makes life worth living. I can't give you the brilliance of a New Zealand sunset or the scent of the Tasman Sea, but I can share a key fuel I used for the writing of this book. And if you want a developmental lesson, here it is: This is the most forgiving of all recipes. Author it yourself by changing the nuts or the color of the sugar, by adding lemon peel or candied ginger. Make the slices as thin or thick as you like, cook them for longer or shorter than I recommend. One bite of these and you'll know that sometimes it is simplicity, rather than complexity, that makes life most delicious.

INGREDIENTS:

   3 egg whites

   ½ cup sugar

   1 cup all-purpose flour

   1 cup almonds (whole, unblanched)

DIRECTIONS

   Preheat the oven to 180°C (350°F).

   Lightly butter a loaf tin (size and shape are mostly unimportant).

   Beat egg whites until soft peaks form.

   Gradually add the sugar and beat at high speed until the sugar is mostly dissolved and the meringue is silky and firm.

Fold in sifted flour in two batches. Fold in the almonds.

Place in the loaf tin and cook for 30 minutes or until golden on top.

Leave in tin until cold, then cover for as long as you can stand (overnight is great, a full 24 hours even better, but I often can't wait that long).

With a very sharp knife, cut into wafer-thin slices.

Place the slices on a baking tray and cook at 120°C (300°F) for 20–30 minutes. (Check to ensure the cookies are not browning too much after 10 minutes. Sometimes they take longer than 20 minutes. I like them only barely colored but crisp all the way through.)

Allow to cool on a wire rack. These probably keep well, but they don't last very long in my house.

NOTES

CHAPTER 1

1. All case studies are compilations of people I have worked with as a researcher, coach, or consultant. No case is drawn from a single example, and thus all names and identifying features are obscured.

2. E.g., Robert Kegan, *In over our heads: The mental demands of modern life* (Cambridge, MA: Harvard University Press, 1994).

3. E.g., Dalmar Fisher, David Rooke, & Bill Torbert, *Personal and organisational transformations through action inquiry* (Edge/Work Press, 2000).

4. There are many different opinions about what "capacity" means in the adult learning and development world. Is capacity a fixed thing, like a glass, that you can fill up but that has a maximum limit—which, like IQ, might be fixed for each individual? Maybe—lots of smart people believe this. I've never seen any evidence, though, that would lead me to believe in a fixed capacity (and have never heard an argument that leads me to believe that the fixed-capacity view is more helpful). In my mind, capacity grows like an enormous balloon. It is as big as the contents it holds right now, and will get bigger as the contents grow. (I don't have a theory yet that extends the metaphor to a bursting balloon, but I'm working on it.) So capacity in this book is a current limit that can change and grow over time.

5. For example, Erik Erikson, *Adulthood* (New York: W. W. Norton & Co, 1978); Daniel Levinson, *The seasons of a man's life* (New York: Random House, 1978); Daniel Levinson, *The seasons of a woman's life* (New York: Alfred A Knopf, 1996).

6. For example, Michael Basseches, "Dialectical thinking and young adult cognitive development." In R. A. Mines & K. S. Kitchener (Eds.), *Adult cognitive development: Methods and models* (New York: Praeger, 1986, pp. 33–56); Marcia Baxter Magolda, *Knowing and reasoning in college: Gender-related patterns in students' intellectual development* (San Francisco: Jossey-Bass, 1992); Mary F. Belenky, Blythe M. Clinchy, Nancy R. Goldberger, & Jill M. Tarule, *Women's ways of knowing: The development of self, voice, and mind* (New York: Basic Books, 1997); Dalmar Fisher, David Rooke, Bill Torbert, *Personal and organisational transformations through action inquiry* (Edge/Work Press, 2000); Robert Kegan, *The evolving self: Problem and process in human development* (Cambridge, MA: Harvard University Press, 1982); Robert Kegan, *In over our heads: The mental demands of modern life* (Cambridge, MA: Harvard University Press, 1994); Karen S. Kitchener, "The reflective judgment model: Characteristics, evidence, and measurement." In R. A. Mines & K. S. Kitchener (Eds.), *Adult cognitive development: Methods and models* (New York: Praeger, 1986, pp. 76–91); William

G. Perry, *Forms of intellectual and ethical development in the college years* (Cambridge, MA: Bureau of Study Counsel, Harvard University, 1968).

7. Ronald Heifetz, *Leadership without easy answers* (Cambridge, MA: Harvard University Press, 1998).

8. Kegan makes this distinction throughout his work; see, for example *In over our heads*, pp. 163–164.

9. Kegan and Belenky et al. parse adulthood into four large meaning-making worlds; Fisher et al. offer seven; and Perry suggests nine. I follow Kegan's distinctions because I find the smaller number easier to track—and more elegant—but I also sketch a midpoint that extends the number of forms of mind to seven. Readers familiar with Kegan will note that his distinctions actually start with a description of a fully childhood mind, which forms the first of his five life orders. I leave that one out in this book about adults, so if you're counting along, my forms of mind begin with Kegan's Second Order (which I call "self-sovereign") then move to Kegan's Order (which I call "socialized"). His Fourth Order is called "self-authored" by Kegan and lots of other theorists, and his Fifth Order I call "self-transforming." (Kegan often uses these other names, as well.)

10. The data for these figures and the others in this chapter comes from Kegan's *In over our heads* (see especially pp. 185–195). These studies and others suggest that both age and education—among other things—are at least partially correlated with development.

11. For instance, Marcia Baxter Magolda, *Authoring your life: Developing an internal voice to navigate life's challenges* (Stylus, 2009); Susanne Cook-Greuter, "20th century background for Integral Psychology," *AQAL: Journal of integral theory and practice* (Vol. 1, No. 2, pp. 144–184); Fisher et al., *Personal and organisational transformations through action inquiry*; Bill Joiner & Stephen Josephs, *Leadership agility: Five levels of mastery for anticipating and initiating change* (San Francisco: Jossey-Bass, 2006).

CHAPTER 2

1. Robert Kegan, in his course at Harvard, talks about how frustrating this form of mind can be in a criminal and offers an example of someone with this mind answering a judge's question about why he robbed a bank. The defendant answered, "Because that's where the money is."

2. Robert Kegan, *In over our heads: The mental demands of modern life* (Cambridge, MA: Harvard University Press, 1994).

3. A caveat: While it is true that those who are self-authored tend to form opinions through their own sensemaking system, they come to those opinions only after a time of getting to know the particular content area—and often that getting-to-know process is reminiscent of the socialized form of mind as they search for the views and opinions of outside experts. This is "micro development," which is when the small parts of our lives develop on a micro level in the same way and with the same pattern as these larger developmental movements.

4. The issue of emotion is developmentally interesting. Increasing development means an increasing ability to have perspective on your emotions and not get swept away by them. At the same time, though, since emotions are a complex biochemical soup, and since they arise in parts of the brain not associated with logical thinking, they are unlikely to ever be overcome by development—rather, development offers new ways to think about and sit with emotion.

5. I write about this form of mind slightly differently than the others because this form of mind is so hard to get our heads around. The easiest way to understand it (and this does not mean it will ever be easy to understand) is to see the self-transforming mind in the trajectory of growth from the self-authored mind.

6. Notice that there is something in the self-transforming mind that is reminiscent of the socialized mind. While there are interesting similarities, the move to the socialized mind is about giving up your own voice for the voices of others, whereas the self-transforming mind is about opening up your mind so that your voice is joined by—and is an equal partner with—the other voices.

7. Susanne Cook-Greuter finds a similar pattern in her research (personal communication).

8. For an extensive and enjoyable description of the leadership and organizational benefits of these later forms of mind, see Bill Joiner & Stephen Josephs, *Leadership agility: Five levels of mastery for anticipating and initiating change* (San Francisco: Jossey-Bass, 2006).

CHAPTER 3

1. Thanks to Mark Leach for this metaphor.

2. The best source way to deepen your understanding of this measure and its administration is to begin with an excellent guide to its use. See Lisa Lahey, Emily Souvaine, Robert Kegan, Robert Goodman, & Sally Felix, *A guide to the subject-object interview: Its administration and interpretation* (Cambridge MA: The Subject–Object Research Group, Harvard University Graduate School of Education, Laboratory of Human Development, 1988). As of this writing, however, you still have to order the guide from the Harvard Graduate School of Education.

3. The SOI is created specifically to be a research tool and was not intended to be a support for someone's growth—although many people feel supported when they are interviewed. With colleagues, I have created a Growth Edge Interview (GEI), which emerges from the SOI work but goes beyond it to create feedback that is helpful for clients.

4. This is actually a fantastic way to listen, too, and is useful even if you have no interest in someone's form of mind. When you name back to someone the dichotomies she is assuming that exist in the world, you give her new choices to consider and reconsider as opposites.

5. Again, I'm not suggesting that you necessarily *should* hasten your development. I'm aware, though, that those who follow their own development in open and curious ways seem to change before their own eyes.

CHAPTER 4

1. My gratitude and apologies to my friend and Kenning Leadership colleague Neil Stroul, whose clear ideas about hero-in-victory (and the more nuanced hero-in-retreat) have helped me and the hundreds of coaches he's taught through the Georgetown University Leadership Coaching Program. Neil's version of these ideas is more sophisticated and psychologically spacious than this fictional protégée, but Steve and Neil are joined in sharing the role of adoring father.

2. The term "Growth Edge" emerged in conversation with my Kenning Associates colleagues years ago (I think it was Mark Ledden, but in a collaborative group sometimes real ownership gets lost). The Growth Edge Interview Group, a collection of us fascinated by the

ways adult development could be used more explicitly with clients in a coaching context, trialed, practiced, and honed the Growth Edge Process. Group members are Paul Atkins, Carolyn Coughlin, Jane Gray, and Keith Johnston. Paul Atkins and I wrote about what we found as we researched our thinking and the thinking of our participants at the beginning of this process. See the 2009 article by Jennifer G. Berger & Paul Atkins, "Mapping complexity of mind: Using the Subject–Object Interview in coaching," *Coaching: An international journal of theory, research and Practice* (Vol. 2, No. 1, pp. 23–36). Many of the coaching practices and insights in this chapter emerge from that group and what we learned with our early clients as we trialed the process.

3. Interested readers may ask here if it is necessary for a person to pass through each stage on her way to the next. Couldn't someone pole vault over the socialized mind and land in the self-authored? This seems fraught with theoretical peril, but might be possible in practice. However, I should say here that in longitudinal studies, people seem fairly consistent in their progression through each stage (although the rate of their progression is not standard).

4. See Chapter 2 in Kegan's book, *In over our heads: The mental demands of modern life* (Cambridge, MA: Harvard University Press, 1994).

5. It's key for coaches to understand the difference between current *capacity* (e.g., Is this person able to do the thing required, that is, does he have the intelligence or background or current developmental capacity?), current *skill* (e.g., Does he know *how* to do it?), and current *desire*. This is connected to the common skill/will question but adds on to it the developmental capacity question, which may be the first question you'd want to address— even before asking about either skill or will.

6. Joiner and Josephs talk at length about the different capabilities of these post-self-authored leaders in their helpful book, *Leadership agility: Five levels of mastery for anticipating and initiating change* (San Francisco: Jossey-Bass, 2006).

7. For a very helpful exercise to help people uncover not just their regular assumptions but also their Big Assumptions, see Robert Kegan and Lisa Lahey, *Immunity to Change* (Boston: Harvard Business School Press, 2009).

CHAPTER 5

1. More about this at Jennifer G. Berger, *Exploring the connection between teacher education practice and adult development theory* (unpublished doctoral dissertation, Cambridge, MA: Harvard University Graduate School of Education, 2002).

2. For another, not necessarily developmental take on transformational learning, try Jack Mezirow (Ed.), *Learning as transformation: Critical perspectives on a theory in progress* (San Francisco: Jossey-Bass, 2000).

3. I have played with a variety of terms for the title of what this person does. In some settings, he is called a "trainer" and in other settings he's a "teacher." In some cases he is a consultant and in some cases he is in-house (and some in-house people are called "consultants"). I'm going to use the most common "facilitator" to include all of these things, but with the caveat that I think while "trainer" goes too far in one direction (unless we are "training" people to tighten widgets), "facilitator" probably goes too far in the other direction (because we often are teaching particular forms of content and not just facilitating things). I prefer "teacher" as a word I can get my arms around (because to my mind

teachers both offer content and facilitate conversations), but early readers found that too constrained into school settings. So facilitator it is.

4. For example, we might be smaller than normal during those times when we are feeling unusually constrained due to intense stress or anxiety (like during times when layoffs are imminent) and larger than normal when we are feeling unusually expansive due to some new life event or new developmental experience (perhaps a ten-day meditation workshop).

5. This doesn't necessarily mean that this person follows the boss's ideas or the professor's; it might be that this person doesn't care one way or another, or has older attachments to the best way to do things that the boss or the professor doesn't support. You can't tell what someone will believe in or who she'll follow based on her form of mind, just the sensemaking which creates that following or belief.

6. Before you think there's a bad case of blaming-the-students going on here, I'll say that I've watched lots of others teach listening in lots of different ways, and there are still some people who seem somehow "tone deaf" to listening no matter what the individual scaffolding or group support. It seems developmental because it is not just one way for one set of people and a different way for a different set, but something that is seen by most but is completely invisible to others.

7. I could have talked about consolidation at any of the other forms of mind as well, but in the leadership space, as I have previously written, often development toward the self-authored form of mind is an implicit requirement. It is only once we reach the self-authored form of mind that the pressures of organizational life stop pushing us down a developmental path and allow us to make decisions about whether consolidation or growth is best for us. It is also true that the move from self-authored to self-transforming is often taken on purpose and with some measure of forethought. The other developmental moves are less conscious.

8. The huge number of books about joint thinking and collaborative work points to this—as people write about communities of practice, action learning, team work, etc.

9. See, for example, Marvin Weisbord & Sandra Janoff, *Don't just do something, stand there!: Ten principles for leading meetings that matter* (San Francisco: Berrett-Koehler Publishers, 2007).

CHAPTER 6

1. See the classic Peter Senge book *The fifth discipline: The art & practice of the learning organization* (New York: Crown Business, 2006).

2. See, for example, Jean Piaget, *The construction of reality in the child* (New York: Basic Books, 1954).

3. Mihaly Csikszentmihalyi, *Flow: The psychology of optimal experience* (New York: Harper Perennial Modern Classics, 2008).

4. This can be especially important for leaders because of the interaction between the leader's own brain and the others around the leader. While a leader's brain is working hard to hold a single perspective, the others around him are likely shielding him from their perspectives as well. It is a well-documented phenomenon that people will withhold key information from leaders—especially information that others believe the leader might find negative—and this information-withholding gets worse as leaders climb to the top of the organization. This combination means that leaders get increasingly limited and myopic at just the time when they need the most expansive view.

5. 60, the next in the line of even numbers.

6. This one is harder than the multiplication table but in this case, $x = 5$.

7. These examples—in simple ways—come up in stories for very young people (like the old Aesop's fable, "The *Town Mouse and the Country Mouse*") and for grown-ups (like John Gray, *Men are from Mars, women are from Venus: A practical guide for improving communication and getting what you want in your relationships.* New York, NY: HarperCollins, 1993). For more on the difference between the way Americans/Western Europeans think and Asians think, see the very interesting: Richard E. Nisbett, *The geography of thought: How Asians and Westerners think differently . . . and why* (New York: Free Press, 2004).

8. For a helpful tool to expand anyone's ability to cope and manage polarities, see Barry Johnson, *Polarity management: Identifying and managing unsolvable problems* (Amherst, MA: Human Resource Development Press, 1992).

CHAPTER 7

1. Even if the strategy is an emergent one, a leader needs to have some way of thinking about how to work toward some uncertain future.

2. See, for example, Malcolm Gladwell, *Blink: The power of thinking without thinking* (New York: Little, Brown, 2005) or Paul Ormerod, *Why most things fail: Evolution, extinction and economics* (Hoboken, NJ: John Wiley, 2007).

3. Shawn W. Rosenberg, *The not so common sense: Differences in how people judge social and political life* (New Haven, CT: Yale University Press, 2002, p. 20).

4. Note that here there is a different kind of distinction we're trying to make between capacity and skill. These leaders have a more comfortable capacity with this, but they still may need a variety of tools or theories to help them use this *capacity* of theirs.

5. We are not the first ones to notice this as a problem, of course. Robert Kegan's 1994 book (see Note 2 in Chapter 1) is called *In over our heads: The mental demands of modern life* for a reason. Similarly, Walter T. Anderson talked about the need for self-transforming capacities in his book *The future of the self: Inventing the postmodern person* (New York: J. P. Tarcher, 1997). Finally, Joiner and Josephs (2006) take us through increasingly complex sensemaking systems of leaders in their book, *Leadership agility* (arguing that the most complex systems are the most agile—and they focus on the differences of complexity mostly in the post-self-authored space.

6. Susanne Cook-Greuter finds similar patterns in her own research; those with the most complex sensemaking systems are less likely to be found inside organizations (personal communication).

7. Catherine Fitzgerald, "On seeing the forest while among the trees: Integrating business strategy models and concepts into executive coaching practice." In C. Fitzgerald & J. Berger (Eds), *Executive coaching: Practices and perspectives* (Palo Alto, CA: Davies-Black, 2002, p. 251).

8. Robert Kegan & Lisa L. Lahey, *How the way we talk can change the way we work: Seven languages for transformation* (San Francisco: Jossey-Bass, 2002), pp. 121–145.

9. My favorite books about feedback take a much more helpful and sophisticated approach. See Barry Jentz, *Talk sense: Communicating to lead and learn* (Acton, MA: Research for Better Teaching, 2007); Kerry Patterson, Joseph Grenny, Ron McMillan, & A. Switzler, *Crucial conversations: Tools for talking when stakes are high* (New York: McGraw-Hill, 2002);

Douglas Stone, Bruce Patton, & Sheila Heen, *Difficult conversations: How to discuss what matters most* (New York: Viking, 1999).

10. Remembering, of course, that this person—whoever he might be—probably doesn't think of himself as the central problem, but rather sees his interactions as well-intentioned and potentially helpful.

11. For a small example of a method that teaches this kind of feedback, see Chapter 8.

12. And of course, in addition to seeing the system and understanding how this task relates to the problem, there are many other systems to see. You can see the problem forward and backward in time, you can see how this problem bumps up against other problems—and this solution bumps up against (or competes with) other solutions. You can see how the people relate, what supports or reinforces the problem, and what the leverage points might be to make a change.

13. The Leadership Circle 360 indicator and the Leadership Agility 360 are examples of leadership development tools used to evaluate competency in an adult development framework—enabling a more powerful conversation.

CHAPTER 8

1. My favorite book in this area is Jane Gilbert, *Catching the knowledge wave? The knowledge society and the future of education* (Wellington: New Zealand Council for Educational Research Press, 2005).

2. For curiosity's connection to happiness, see Todd Kashdan, *Curious? Discover the missing ingredient to a fulfilling life.* (New York: William Morrow, 2009).

3. While they don't talk specifically about curiosity in their book, Chip and Dan Heath do talk about cultivating "the growth mindset" rather than the "fixed mindset," and they offer examples of the learning that emerges from the simple act of being open to learning—believing that learning is a key part of what work is about, whether you're a principal, a golfer, or a heart surgeon. See Chip Heath & Dan Heath, *Switch: How to change things when change is hard* (New York: Broadway Books, 2010).

4. Whole new fields—like behavioral economics—are springing up to explore the patterns in our irrationality. A great book to explore more is Dan Ariely, *Predictably irrational: The hidden forces that shape our decisions* (New York: HarperCollins, 2008).

5. For a book on how little you can access your own mind, see Timothy D. Wilson, *Strangers to ourselves: Discovering the adaptive unconscious* (Cambridge, MA: Harvard University Press, 2002).

6. I am indebted to Joan Wofford and Barry Jentz for these ideas, and to my partners at Kenning Associates for the way the ideas now live inside me.

7. Readers might resist my dichotomizing these two elements—as though there really are objective facts that are separate from the meaning we give them. Fair enough. I cringe whenever I type the word "fact," too. But for the sake of this particular exercise, knowing the difference between the description of an activity in its most pared-down sense so that most people would agree on it, and the meaning individuals make of that activity, is a helpful, if false, dichotomy.

8. One wonderful book that helps us think about a new way to go about entering a new position is Barry Jentz's *Entry: How to begin a leadership position successfully* (Newton, MA: Leadership and Learning, 2008). This book is available at www.kenningleadership.com

9. Great books that walk you through some of this thinking are all of Barry Jentz, *Talk sense: Communicating to lead and learn* (see Note 9 in Chapter 7); and Robert Kegan & Lisa Lahey, *How the way we talk can change the way we work.*(see Note 8 in Chapter 7), particularly Chapter 7, "From the language of constructive criticism to the language of deconstructive criticism."

APPENDIX A

1. Robert Kegan, *In over our heads: The mental demands of modern life* (Cambridge, MA: Harvard University Press, 1994, p. 17).

2. Two caveats. First of all, while every form of mind sounds like a complete description, most of our lives are spent in the spaces in between each of these minds—on our way to the next place. In fact, we can measure four distinct stages along the continuum of each of the numbered forms of mind (which adds a level of complexity we won't even begin to get to). Secondly, this system actually begins at birth with babies and toddlers at a kind of baby form of mind, which has its own way of constructing the world.

3. Philosopher and theorist Ken Wilber writes extensively about the "transcend-and-include" phenomenon as a key developmental movement.

4. Robert Kegan, *The evolving self: Problem and process in human development* (Cambridge, MA: Harvard University Press, 1982, p. 96).

5. In our small village, there isn't a lot of disagreement about what the rules are and where they come from. In a more diverse society, however, a citizen with this form of mind could easily be a "model" parent and employee or a "model" gang member or a "model" white supremacist; he would be "following the rules" of his particular society, even if that society was very different from the mainstream of the community or nation.

INDEX

Italic page numbers indicate material in tables.